THE
RYE & CAMBER
TRAMWAY

A Centenary History

by LAURIE A COOKSEY

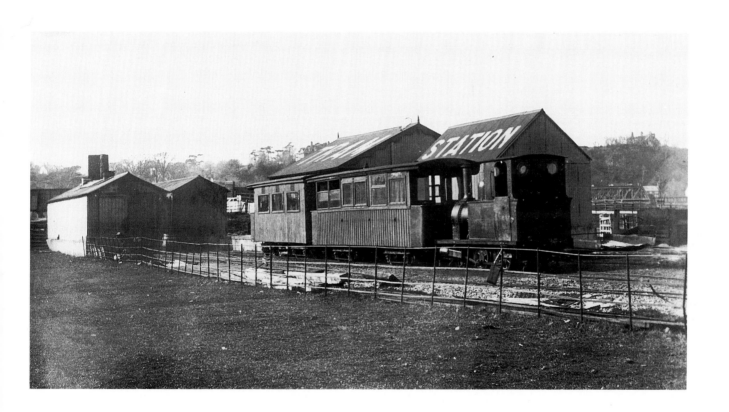

Plateway Press, PO Box 973, Brighton BN2 2TG
ISBN 1 871980 26 7

British Library Cataloguing in Publication Data

Cooksey, Laurie A.
Rye and Camber Tramway: Centenary History

I. Title
388.42094225

ISBN 1-871980-26-7

Printed in Great Britain by Amadeus Press Ltd., Huddersfield.

Typesetting by Highlight Type Bureau Ltd., Bradford.

Book Design by David H Smith.
Cover Artwork by David H Smith.

Front cover illustration: **A portrait of VICTORIA and her train shortly after leaving Camber Sands station, en route for Rye, c.1912.**
(from an oil painting by Eric Bottomley)

Back cover illustration: **CAMBER and VICTORIA in their respective original liveries.** *(from paintings by Paul Jenner)*

Frontispiece: **This is how Rye Station looked on 10 April 1909. Note the prominent TRAM STATION painted on the roof of the buildings, the Monkbretton road bridge in the left background, and the S.E. & C.R.'s bridge to the right.** *(Collection Allan C Baker)*

THE CAMBER TRAM

1. Some person with less wit than face
   Describes Rye as a sleepy place!
   Let them look around and survey take,
   There's proof that it is wide awake
   In Camber Tram.

2. All folk may now, by easy ride,
   Run down to Links or Harbour side,
   Enjoy a pleasant healthful stroll
   Where English Channel's waters roll
   By Camber Tram.

3. How jolly for picnicers out
   To have a spread and roam about
   On grass grown banks, by rippling sea!
   Their blessings sure counter'd will be
   On Camber Tram.

4. And children too, in happy throng,
   Will voices lift in joyful song
   While paddling on the sandy shore,
   And say with glee "We do adore
   The Camber Tram."

5. And workmen will most surely find
   In it a friend to fit their mind,
   'Twill help them on their weary way
   They'll ne'er forget the opening day
   Of Camber Tram.

6. But will it pay? Ah! There's the point.
   Will it shareholders' palms anoint?
   Let all sincerely hope it may,
   'Twill be a boon in every way,
   This Camber Tram.

Rye, August 1895.   E. R. Y.

Published in The South Eastern Advertiser, Saturday 10.8.1895.

CONTENTS

ACKNOWLEDGMENTS

With special thanks (in alphabetical order) to:

Amberley Chalk Pits Museum, Arundel, G. Ashbee, Allan C. Baker, J. Barrowdale, Tim Binding, J. Burke, Claude Auberson, Ann Carrees, R. M. Casserley, R. Clark, N. J. Claydon (The Railway Correspondence & Travel Society), C. Coleman, the staff of the County Records Office, Lewes, G. R. Croughton, Alan Dickinson, Messrs. Dawes, Prentice & Herington (in particular Lisa Bond, Audrey Hatter, Cindy Blackhall and J. P. A. Simpson) J. Evans, Peter Ewart, Andrew Gainsbury, Mrs. E. Gomm, Peter A. Harding, the staff of Hastings Reference Library (in particular Bryon Purdey, Brian Scott, "Paddy" Padgham and Michael Higginson), M. A. Hillebrandt, Mr. Igglesden, Alan A. Jackson, Ian B. Jolly, Frank Jux, Nicholas King (the M & D and East Kent Bus Club), Mrs. Jo Kirkham, M. Lawson Finch, L.C.G.B. (for the Ken Nunn photograph collection), Tom Middlemass, E. J. R. Miller (Hon. Archivist of the Kent & East Sussex Railway), S. C. Nash, the staff of the National Railway Museum, York, Andrew Neale, F. Nelson, Chris O'Donoghue, Mike Pannel, Mrs. J. E. Robbins, Frank Rook, Angus Scouler, John Scott Morgan, Chrissy Sewett, Peter Smith, William Perfitt, Mrs. Lilian Phillips, Mrs. P. Scriven, Phillip Shaw, Peter D. Shearan, H. W. Sheppard, Michael Spellen, Keith Taylorson, John L. Townsend, Denis Vidler, J. G. Vincent (Trustee of the Talyllyn Railway Preservation Society), Frank Wenham, Alan Withers, D. J. Woodcock and A. N. Wright.

Very special thanks must go to Commander John Bradley (secretary of Rye Golf Club) for allowing me access to the Club Minute Books, Eric Bottomley for his superb cover painting, Richard Jones (great-grandson of E. P. S. Jones of Rother Ironworks) for his drawings of CAMBER, VICTORIA and the Bagnall carriage, and Andy Leaney for all the other plans and drawings taken from my higgledy-piggledy (Andy's description) originals.

PREFACE

"The town of Rye, a small isolated spot, may seem at first sight little deserving of being recorded in history....., then we see that this little town is no longer the insignificant spot which at first glance it appeared to be....." So commenced the "History of the Antient Town and Port of Rye" by William Holloway, published in 1847, and the same might be said of the 1$^1/_2$ mile, 3 ft. gauge Rye & Camber Tramway which opened in 1895 to serve the interests of the un-likely combination of a new Golf Course and a fishing community. The Tramway was not built specifically for Rye Golf Club, but without the Club there would have been no tram and similarly, it has been suggested that were it not for the Tramway, the Golf Club would not be the flourishing concern that it is today.

From the earliest years the Golf Club, and other Clubs in Rye, had to pay a subsidy to cover the losses incurred by winter running, yet the Tramway managed to celebrate its 13th birthday in fine style by opening a half mile extension right onto the foreshore of the famous Camber Sands. By the early 1920s, however, the Tramway had outlived its usefulness as far as the Golf Club was concerned, and with the subsidy paid in 1925 being the last, the line operated in the summer months only, catering in the main for holidaymakers and day trippers, until the Second World War caused its premature closure in 1939. The Tramway did enjoy a brief second lease of life in 1943 when it was requisitioned by the Admiralty in connection with some works being carried out at Rye Harbour, but the line was destined never to open again to the public, and the Company was wound up in 1947.

INTRODUCTION

The old town of Rye stands on a sandstone promontory some 50ft. above sea level just under three miles from the eastern boundary of the county of Sussex with Kent, and was one of the "Two Antient Towns" (the other being the neighbouring "new" town of Winchelsea) added to the confederation of the original Cinque Ports of Hastings, New Romney, Hythe, Dover and Sandwich around the year 1336. Following many violent storms in the thirteenth century, during which time the old town of Winchelsea was drowned, the River Rother had been diverted from its previous course of entering the sea at New Romney, to flow into Rye Bay so close to Rye that by 1350 it had begun to undermine the eastern side of the town, and within 25 years East Street and the fortified Baddings Gate had been washed completely away. Over the next three centuries, draining of the surrounding marshes reduced the tidal flow of the combined Rivers Rother, Brede and Tillingham to such an extent that the sea receded almost two miles from the town.

On 13th February 1851, the South Eastern Railway opened its line between Hastings and Ashford, serving Rye en route, and three years later constructed a single track branch from Rye to serve a coal dump supplied by coasters on the west bank of the River Rother close to the village of Rye Harbour, and serving the works of the Rye Chemical Manufacturing Company and a gravel pit on the way. There was talk at the time of the branch being used to connect with a proposed ferry service to France, but the project came to nothing, and the line was destined never to carry passengers.

As early as 1876 the local Highways Board had discussed the suggestion of constructing a bridge across the River Rother just downstream of the single track swing bridge of the S.E.R., together with a direct road to East Guldeford which is situated just over half a mile to the east of Rye as the crow flies, but it was not until 1890 that the necessary land for the bridge and road (2,000ft. x 25ft.) was made available by Rye Town Council.

The sea may have long since deserted the town, and the railway had taken over most of the coastal trade, but Rye could still boast a brewery, several ship-building yards and a large and busy fishing fleet, and by the early 1890s was beginning to attract a new kind of people - weekend visitors. At this time, throughout Britain, the game of golf was becoming a popular pastime with the well-to-do and had already become established in Sandwich and Littlestone in neighbouring Kent. Having been introduced to the game by his son who had played at Cambridge, the Rev. J. Lockington Bates, the rector of Iden (a village two miles to the north of Rye) held a meeting on 6th February 1893 with three Hastings solicitors where they decided "to inspect the Camber sand hills and the land around Camber Castle" midway between Winchelsea and Rye "to determine their relative capabilities for golf links". [1] The considerable area of sand dunes to the east of the River Rother opposite Rye Harbour on the site of what just three centuries before had been the natural sheltered harbour known as "Le Chaumbre", [2] were now covered with esparto grass, and with easy access from Rye soon to be available via the almost completed Rother road bridge, it was resolved that the new club should be formed there. On 24th March 1893, the day was spent arranging the putting greens and marking out the nine hole course, and by 14th April golf was being played there.

At last the long awaited bridge across the Rother was opened with much pomp and ceremony on Tuesday, 25th April 1893. Carried on two sets of piles, the 140 feet long bridge had been built by Messrs. A. E. Munn of Tenterden, Kent, with the ironwork supplied by Messrs. Brettle & Co..

Strangely, nothing more was heard of the new golfing

venture until the same Rev. J. Lockington Bates chaired a meeting at the George Hotel, Rye on 28th November 1893, where the unanimous decision was to form a golf club with "the links situated over the Camber hills".[3] No time was wasted in constructing a new temporary course, and the magazine "Golf", dated 13th December 1893, somewhat prematurely called the "attention of golfers to the new Club just started.... near the picturesque old town of Rye on the eastern border of Sussex. The Camber sand hills have been acquired at a moderate cost by the Committee of the Club... The new golf links are situated close to Rye Harbour, about 20 minutes drive from Rye station... and not many miles from the well-known Littlestone Links, which the Camber sand hills in some way resemble...." The new course had not yet opened (the first competition is recorded as having taken place in February 1894) but the Committee felt so confident about the Club's future that a 21 year lease was negotiated with the Curteis Estate who owned the land, and they began planning a permanent 6,000 yard course at a cost of £350, and this was completed and inspected on 12th April 1894.

Back in March, the Committee had approved the plans of a founder member, Reginald Blomfield (later to become a leading architect of his day) for a club house to be situated on top of the tallest hill, with authority to raise £500 in debentures to pay for its construction. By 30th May, however, they had a change of heart and decided to build a temporary club house, leaving the hill-top site for a permanent building at a later date. Imagine the Rev. Lockington Bates' anger when, on his return from a six week business trip to the United States at the end of July, he found that the walls of the temporary club house were already in place on top of the hill! It should be noted, however, that this "temporary"

2. With hopes of becoming the forerunner of many such establishments in the new resort of Camber-on-Sea, the replacement Royal William Hotel, which had "sprung up mushroom-like" on the site of its weatherboarded namesake opposite the Golf Club House on the Camber road, was opened with an inaugural dinner on 31st October 1894. *(Rye Golf Club)*

club house, altered and extended over the years, is still in service to this day.

Also nearing completion opposite the Club House on the Camber road was the new Royal William Hotel which had been constructed on the site of what had been affectionately known as "The Billy". The original wooden weatherboarded shack had been built around 1807 to provide liquid refreshment for the fishermen of Rye Harbour, but had been destroyed by fire in 1893. Designed by architect Charles Smith and built by George Huggett for Messrs. Chapman Brothers, the new hotel was opened with an inaugural dinner on Wednesday, 31st October 1894, and although in no way comparable to the Ritz or the Hilton with a total of only five rooms to let, it was hoped that it would be the forerunner of many such establishments in the so-called "marine suburb of Rye".

Even though the new road bridge across the River Rother had appreciably shortened the road distance between Rye and Camber, it was still a 20 minute coach drive via East Guldeford and the un-made up and circuitous Camber road, and it was clear that to encourage the continued growth of the Golf Club and the fledgling resort of Camber-on-Sea, a more efficient and speedy means of transport was necessary. Thus the stage was set for the first chapter in the history of the Rye and Camber Tramway.

1. The Royal William, Camber, known affectionately as the "Old Billy", had been built around 1807 to serve the fishermen of Rye Harbour and is seen here shortly before it was destroyed by fire in 1893. The fine model ship over the entrance was carved by the first licensee, William Morris, who had been ship's carpenter on the sloop "The Royal William". *(Rye Golf Club)*

1. "Rye Golf Club - The First 90 Years" - Denis Vidler, 1984.
2. It is from "Le Chaumbre" that the modern name of Camber is derived.
3. The first minute in the Rye Golf Club Minute Book, 28.11.1893.

3. Fishermen pose nonchalantly for the photographer at Rye Harbour c, 1890. Within the next five years the sand hills in the background will form part of Rye Golf Course and Camber station will be constructed on the raised ground to the left of the predecessor of today's shipping mast already occupying the grassy mound on the eastern bank of the River Rother. The steps in the stonework provided access at all states of the tide to the rowing-boat ferry that plied, as required, between there and Rye Harbour village on the opposite side of the river.

(John E. Ray Glass Negative Collection, courtesy of Hastings Library)

4. The Rye Harbour ferryman poses in one of his two rowing boats for the photographer who is standing by the ferry steps close to Golf Links station. In the background the buildings are (from right to left) Charles Tunbridge's cottage, "Squatter's Right" and, partly hidden amongst the rigging, "Gorse Cottage". The simple wooden stages on this eastern side of the Rother were joined together to form the 1,000 ft. Admiralty Jetty in 1943.

(Les Bearman collection)

Chapter One

THE BIRTH OF THE TRAMWAY (1895)

On Friday, 11th January 1895, some influential members of Rye Golf Club, along with some local businessmen, held a meeting where they discussed the idea of constructing a tramway from Rye to serve the new golf links at Camber, and the community of Rye Harbour village on the opposite bank of the River Rother by means of a ferry. All were in favour of the scheme and it was proposed that Rye Town Council should be requested "to grant a lease on a strip of land for as long a term as possible from the south-east corner of the land near the Rother Bridge [1] across the Corporation property to that of the trustees of the late Rev. Thomas Curteis".[2] With the title of "The Rye & Camber Tramway Car Company Ltd.", the proposal came before Rye Town Council at their meeting on Monday, 14th January 1895 when the surveyor (Mr. C. Smith) explained that the tramway would run across the Corporation field as near to the present footpath as possible, and on the railway side (i.e. to the east of the footpath). Councillor John Neve Masters welcomed the scheme, noting that as it was taken up "by such able and business-like men" it would be sure to turn out a success, but there was one thing that he would like to see stipulated for, and that was, if the line was extended to Rye Harbour, that the workmen should have reduced fares allowed them. He added that should the fares be made prohibitive, the tramway would not be a benefit to those chiefly interested in its construction.

Alderman John Symonds Vidler, one of the tramway promoters, asked for an expression of opinion from the whole Council, as he said that they were anxious to get the line open by Easter. Councillor A. E. Hinds, whilst welcoming the scheme, thought at the same time that as it was to be in the hands of a private Company, the Corporation should not put themselves out of pocket, but as Councillor Cuthbert Hayles explained, this was not the intention of the Company either and he confirmed that, no doubt, favourable terms would be granted to the working classes. He went on to say "They (the working classes) will be no worse off than they are at the present time if they choose to walk! We are taking nothing by placing a tramway here, and if it is delayed by a month or two, we could not proceed with it this year." Councillor H. J. Gasson considered that it would be an excellent way to open out the sand banks and sea coast at Camber, but John Neve Masters wondered if the laying of the lines would endanger the re-letting of the land. The surveyor replied that no land would be broken up, except where it was necessary to level. It was suggested by Councillor Longley that the land be let at 6d. per 10 rods (approximately £5 per acre) and that the remaining particulars be left to the Land Committee, with the Company paying all compensation to the tenants. He did not think that the tramway would take up more than one acre of land.

The Town Clerk then read the draft resolution that an application having been made by the proposed Camber Car Company Ltd., and discussed favourably by the Council, it be referred to the Land Committee to report upon the terms of the lease, it being the feeling of the Council that the promoters should pay any compensation due to the tenants and that a nominal rent be charged by the Corporation. Councillor J. L. Deacon proposed that the nominal rent be fixed at £1 and his proposition was carried unanimously.

Having inspected the proposed course of the line, the Land Committee's report was put forward for adoption at a special Council meeting held on Thursday, 24th January 1895. It referred to the proposed Tramway as follows:

"We have viewed the proposed course of the tramway and recommend that an agreement for a lease of a piece of ground next the new bridge 100ft. x 50ft. be entered into with the promoters of the Rye to Camber Tramway Company Limited, when formed, for the erection of a car house and other necessary buildings at £2 per year for 21 years, the lease to contain the usual clauses and to be at the lessees' option to determine the same at the end of the first seven or fourteen years, and that the lease include the right of laying and working an un-fenced tramway at £1 per annum, of a gauge not exceeding 3ft.0in. from the Rother Bridge in a direct

5. John Symonds Vidler (1845-1912) was "one of the initiators, if not the instigator" of the Rye & Camber Tramway.

(Les Bearman collection)

6. Mermaid Street is said to be one of the five most famous streets in the world. George Wratten, the petrol locomotive's driver, lived at no. 40a a few doors above the picturesque Mermaid Inn. (*Les Bearman collection*)

7. The Landgate is the last remaining of three gateways that provided access through the old town walls into Rye. The Prince Albert Memorial Clock, which caused some Tramway passengers a little aggravation in the Spring of 1916, was installed in 1863.

(*Les Bearman collection*)

8. In this view looking east along Rye High Street c.1898, Messrs. R. & J. Bennett & Company's horse omnibus, which operated a daily service between "the antient town" and Tenterden, waits outside the George Hotel. As the leading hotel in Rye, The George was popular for civic dinners, dances, concerts and auctions, whilst the first, and many subsequent Rye & Camber Tramway Company's Annual General Meetings was held here.

(*Les Bearman collection*)

RYE

9. This is the view looking eastwards from the west end of Rye High Street on a summer's afternoon at the turn of the 19th century. The Rye & Camber Tramways Company Ltd. banked with the London & County, whose premises are on the extreme right, whilst the offices of Messrs. Dawes, Son & Prentice, where Cuthbert Hayles worked as a solicitor, were situated a few doors away on the same side of the road behind the photographer.

(Les Bearman collection)

10. In this postcard, postmarked 27.7.1914, from right to left can be seen in the middle distance the Rye & Camber Tram Station, the tree-lined Guldeford Road, the South Eastern & Chatham Railway crossing the river by the 1903 double track bridge before curving away towards Ashford, the zig-zag course of the Rother, and the Royal Military Road that provided part of the original roundabout route to Camber prior to the Monkbretton bridge being opened in 1893. Today, thousands of holidaymakers per year still climb the church tower for what is rightly claimed to be the finest view of Rye.

(Les Bearman collection)

11. Although taken from the western side of the built-up banks of the River Rother, this is a similar, but closer view of Rye that passengers would have seen from the tram as it approached the Broadwater Stream bridge from Camber. Rother Ironworks, with its tall chimney, is visible below and slightly to the right of the parish church.

(Les Bearman collection)

line towards Camber to the last footbridge, but should the Company find it necessary to fence the tramway, further arrangements will have to be entered into."

Whether it was the Tramway Company or Rye Town Council that stipulated that the gauge was not to exceed 3ft.0in. is not clear, but the use of the word "Tramway" in the title is, perhaps, a little easier to explain. The Company's Board of Directors included several gentlemen of the legal profession and they would have been well aware that railways were subject to many onerous requirements, such as the need to fence their lines and maintain level crossings, but by describing their line as a Tramway, the Company might be better able to resist any disagreements that might occur in the future with the Railway Inspectorate.

The course of the line had been altered slightly from that proposed at the Council's previous meeting as it was thought, after a second viewing that, if the tramway was not to be fenced, it would be better sited across the centre of the fields, thus dividing them more equally. Another advantage, as Councillor Masters pointed out, was that the footpath would not now at any point cross the tramway. It was asked if the tramway would be detrimental, and Councillor Henbrey replied that if the question referred to the possible killing of sheep, then he supposed that the Company would be liable for compensation. He did not know if it was in the province of the Council to ask the Company to fence the line, but added that he should personally have liked to see it done.

Meanwhile, negotiations had been taking place with the Curteis Estate Trustees, and it was agreed that the promoters of the Tramway Company should be granted a 21 year lease commencing on 25th March 1895 on "a piece or parcel of land situate near the Rye Harbour Signals Station in the Parish of St. Thomas the Apostle Winchelsea in the County of Sussex containing by admeasurement one hundred feet by fifty feet more or less.... and that piece or parcel of land situate as above of an average width of twelve feet and extending as shown (on the plan) from A to B.... together with liberty to build and maintain upon the demised land... such Car House, Station and buildings as shall be necessary or proper for the use of the Tramway". The yearly rent was to be "Three Pounds by half yearly payments on the twenty fifth day of March and the twenty ninth day of September in every year, the first of such payments to be made on the twenty ninth of September One thousand eight hundred and ninety five". The Company was given the option to determine the lease at the end of the seventh or fourteenth year upon giving the lessors six calender months previous notice in writing, but should the rent at any time be in arrear of forty days, the lessors could "put an end to the demise.... and take possession of the Tramway for their own use and benefit".

At the Rye Trade Association's meeting at the George Hotel on the evening of Monday, 11th March, whilst discussing the proposed tramway, Councillor Cuthbert Hayles advised that they had got so far as obtaining a tender to construct the permanent way which would be provisionally accepted in a day or two, the amount being about £1,200. The whole cost would not be much more than £2,200 which, he hoped, would be taken up. So far £500 in debentures and £1,100 in ordinary shares had been taken up, and although they were very grateful for the encouragement given by so many tradesmen taking a practical interest in the movement, a further £600 was still required. The information that the tramway was so nearly becoming an accomplished fact was warmly applauded.

Confirming what Councillor Hayles had said at the meeting, Mr. Holman Fred Stephens of Cranbrook, Kent, was awarded the contract a few days later to build the line and, wasting no time, Mr. Stephens duly discussed his proposals with the Assistant Secretary of the Board of Trade on Monday, 25th March. Holman Fred Stephens was born in Hammersmith, West London on 31st October 1868, and after attending University College School, he studied engineering under Sir Alexander Kennedy at London University. Even now he was only 26 years of age, yet he had already completed his first project, the construction of the Hawkhurst & Paddock Wood Railway in Kent, on which he had been the resident engineer.

In his letter to the Board of Trade dated 28th March, containing details of their meeting, Mr. Stephens explained that his estimate was based on the permanent way being laid with flat-bottomed steel rails of 24 lbs. per yard at 3ft.0in. gauge, fished points, spiked to sleepers 2ft.9in. centre to centre. There was to be a gradient in the centre of 1 in 100 for about 10 chains, and a curve of 20 chains radius at the Harbour end for about 10 chains in length, with the rest of the line being almost straight following the surface of the land with no cuttings more than 3ft.0in. deep, and no banks more than 3ft.6in. high. The stations would be small corrugated iron shelters with the platform 2ft.0in. above rail level and 6ft.0in. wide, and there were to be three small culverts of 15ft. to 20ft. span built with concrete walls and steel joists as rail bearers. He added "..... the funds are practically subscribed, and the Company are anxious to proceed with the construction forthwith as it will enable work to be found for many men who are at present unemployed" and concluded "I submit that the method of fastening the rails, although not in accordance with the Railway requirements of the Board, will be sufficient in the case of this tramway when the weights are so small and the speed so slow". His accompanying plan was crude in the extreme, being nothing more than a thick red ink line, marked off in furlong intervals, drawn onto the current 6" Ordnance Survey map of the Rye area.

Mr. Stephens' letter was discussed at a meeting of the Railway Department of the Board of Trade the following day when the questions considered were:

(1) Whether the Board of Trade could sanction the use of such a line, apart from any question as to their authority to construct it, and:

(2) Whether the promoters need any statutory authority to construct a line on land in their possession.

The Inspecting Officer, Sir T. Blomefield, said he could see no objection "to the construction of this Tramway or Tramroad, upon such lines as have been adopted in Ireland, supposing that there is power in this Board of Trade to give permission for this to be done". He was, however, unable to recommend that fencing should be dispensed with ("this was never done in Ireland in such cases") and was clearly unhappy with Mr. Stephens' suggestions for fixing the rails and he would insist that there must be fang bolts and clips at the joints. He agreed that signals would not be necessary and that the other arrangements would probably be sufficient provided "tramway stock" was used. The Board eventually came to the conclusion that they did not "seem to have any power to authorise the use of the line", but that they would pass on Sir Blomefield's recommendations to Mr. Stephens.

A directors' meeting was held on the evening of Wednesday, 3rd April, where it was announced that, although there were a few shares still available, sufficient capital had been subscribed to warrant the starting of the Company. Work would be taken in hand with as little delay as possible, and it was hoped that the line would be open for both passengers and merchandise traffic early in the summer. Six days later on 9th April, the Rye and Camber Tramways Company Limited was incorporated (Company Number 43800), the business being registered as "a constructing and working tramway", with its registered office at Bank Chambers, High Street, Rye, Sussex.[3] The word "Car" had been deleted from the original title, but why should such a humble concern use the plural "Tramways" in its title?

Messrs. Mancktelow Brothers, who styled themselves as Builders and Farmers of Pennington's Farm, Horsmonden, Kent, were employed as the contractors to build the Tramway, having previously worked under Holman Stephens on the Cranbrook & Paddock Wood Railway that had opened for traffic to its eventual terminus of Hawkhurst on 4th September 1893. As construction of the Tramway commenced, the Company had a change of heart and, taking Sir T. Blomefield's advice, decided to fence the line, at least for the first half mile from Rye station as far as the Broadwater Stream. This decision was much appreciated by Rye Town Council, and at their meeting on Monday, 13th May the Land Committee recommended that the sum of £50 should be contributed to the cost "providing it was of iron and corresponded in every way with the Corporation's iron fencing dividing the upper portions of the field, and be placed on both sides of the permanent way to the satisfaction of the Borough Surveyor". It was not so much the safety aspect that appealed to the Council! Having already divided the field into two with a fence costing £75 they had increased their rent from £74 to £122 10s.0d. per annum, and with the Tramway further dividing the fields, Councillor H. G.

Henbrey believed that they would bring in an even greater rent because "with smaller pieces of land there would be more competition". There was one small problem in that the position of the tramway would cut off the water supply to the portion of Mr. Bowen's field beside the river, so it was agreed that a main be run across the field before the new fence was erected, at a cost not to exceed £25.

The Tramway fencing was again on the agenda at Rye Town Council's meeting on Friday, 14th June, when a letter from the secretary of the Tramway Company, Mr. H. G. Henbrey, was read out which confirmed that the fence on either side of the line would become the property of the Corporation on the termination of the lease. Alderman John Symonds Vidler argued that a post and wire fence, which could be erected for £90, would be equally suitable and far less un-sightly than the proposed iron fence that would cost £150, and he suggested that Mr. Stephens (the tramway engineer) should be allowed to address the Council on the matter. Councillor G. Henbrey, Chairman of the Land Committee, pointed out that when that Committee had met, the members were unanimously in favour of an iron fence, and he believed that that proposed to be erected by the Tramways Company would meet all requirements. It was to be practically the same as other fences on Corporation property, except for a thickness of one eighth of an inch in the top bar, but the uprights were a little stouter. He failed to see what good purpose would be served by Mr. Stephens speaking upon an alternative plan which was not before the Council. After yet more discussion it was "almost unanimously" decided to approve of the style of fencing as described in Mr. H. G. Henbrey's letter.

Although there were some delays to begin with, construction of the Tramway eventually proceeded rapidly. A slight amendment to the original plan resulted in the proposed gradient of 1 in 100 for 10 chains across Northpoint Beach being eased to 1 in 160 for a length of approximately 16 chains. Rye Town Council accepted Mr. Sharpey's tender of £34 19s.0d. to lay in a new 1½" water main from the Fishmarket to the East Guldeford side of Monkbretton Bridge, thence across Mr. Bowen's field to a tank to be provided for watering cattle, and this work was completed by 8th July, allowing the much-discussed iron fence to be erected. It was also arranged that the Tramway Company would be supplied by the same meter at the rate of one shilling per 100 gallons, the Council's estimated income being around £10 per year.

Because the line had been constructed without Parliamentary Powers, an official Board of Trade inspection was not legally necessary, but even so, the Company wrote to the Assistant Secretary of the Railway Department of the Board of Trade on 29th June as follows:

"Sir,

Rye & Camber Tramways Co. Ltd.

The directors desire me to say they are anxious to

open above on Saturday, 13th July and they would be glad if you could inspect it on 11th, 12th or 13th."

In his reply dated 5th July (reference R16126) Sir Francis J. S. Hopwood asked whether the tramway was to be used for goods traffic only, to which Mr. Henbrey replied the following day

".... the tramway is being used for luggage etc., and the Directors desire to open it for passenger traffic on Saturday next 13th. inst.."

Just how this "luggage etc." was being carried with no motive power available is not explained! The Board of Trade's file dated 8th. July noted

"This is a tramway about 1¹/₂ long (sic) which has been constructed without any statutory authority. It is, I understand, intended to connect the town of Rye with some golf links in the neighbourhood, and it is constructed on private property, no public roads or footpaths being crossed.

"It is intended to use an oil motor, [4] or failing that steam. One motor only to be used and the speed to be restricted to 10 m.p.h.. It is not proposed to fence the line. The Company submit the line for inspection and desire to open it for passenger traffic on the 13th inst..

"There is no obligation on the Board of Trade to inspect the line, and I am not aware of any precisely similar case. But we have on several occasions inspected tramways or other works by request where we have been under no statutory obligation to do so, and I think we may inspect in this case.

"An inspection would probably result in a recommendation that the line should be fenced."

Contradicting what had been suggested above, three days later on 11th July, Sir Cosmo Monkhouse, on behalf of the Board of Trade wrote (reference R16397):

"Sir,
With reference to your letters of the 29th ult. and 6th inst. applying for an inspection of the Rye & Camber Tway (sic) I am, etc. to state that as at present advised they do not consider that the duty of inspecting the line devolves upon them under provision of the Tramway Act...."

Putting the ball back into the Tramway Company's court, he concluded his letter by suggesting that if there was any statutory reason that rendered an inspection necessary, the Tramway Company should furnish the Board of Trade with such details!

The locomotive and carriage, which had been ordered from Messrs. W. G. Bagnall of Castle Engine Works, Stafford on 28th May, must have been giving some cause for concern as on Friday morning, 12th July, a reporter for the South Eastern Advertiser wrote (for publication the next day):

"It is proposed to open the Rye & Camber Tramway today (Saturday). The engine and car were expected during the early part of the week, but up to the time of writing they had not arrived, so we are unable to give you a description of them. The arrangements for the opening ceremony must greatly depend on circumstances, and we hope that the Rye public will not be behind in lending a liberal hand in the launching of a project which will be one of the attractive facilities of the town."

The rolling stock did, in fact, arrive at the S.E.R's station at noon that day, and Mr. E. P. S. Jones of Rother Ironworks, Rye, took charge of transporting the locomotive (appropriately named CAMBER) and carriage to the Tramway Station, "the Herculean task being accomplished in a marvellously short space of time considering the circumstances and by no means small difficulties which had beset him". [5] Regrettably, no reference as to how the rolling stock was moved through the town has been found. Then, just before midnight, with everything having been thoroughly checked over, and the section of main line back in place after being detached and diverted to receive the rolling stock, "a few adventurous spirits had a trial trip on the engine and a trolley attached, steaming safely out into the darkness and back again". [6] They did not travel far, and the actual testing was wisely left until the morning.

1. Rother Bridge refers to the new "Monkbretton" road bridge.
2. The Curteis family had possessed property in Kent and elsewhere from as early as the 13th and 14th centuries.
3. Letter from Companies House Archive Records dated 4.2.1993.
4. See Chapter Eleven, "Motive Power".
5. Sussex Express & County Herald, Saturday, 20.7.1895.
6. Sussex Express & County Herald, Saturday, 20.7.1895.

Chapter Two
THE GRAND OPENING (1895)

Saturday, 13th July 1895 dawned bright and sunny, fitting weather for such an auspicious occasion. Steam had been raised on the engine at an early hour, and several short runs were made during the morning, but it was not until noon that the first trip was undertaken along the whole length of the line, with Mr. H. F. Stephens' assistant, the young W. H. Austen acting as driver. [1] The locomotive CAMBER is reported to have "worked admirably, to everybody's satisfaction" [2] and covered the return journey of just over a mile and a half in eight minutes.

By early afternoon a large number of townspeople had gathered on the short platform and around the station at Rye, either hoping for a first trip on the Tramway, or who were just interested in witnessing the successful start of the new undertaking. The proceedings were pleasingly brief. At 1.45 p.m. the official declaration was made by the Mayoress of Rye, Mrs. F. Bellingham, when she said (with no claim for originality) "I have much pleasure in declaring the Rye and Camber Tramway open". Then, amidst much cheering from the crowd of well-wishers and a fusillade of fog signals, the little train "gaily decorated in honour of the occasion" set off "at a rapid pace" for Camber with the first section of the company on board. With accommodation for only 32 pasengers, several journeys had to be made to convey all of the honoured guests to the southern terminus, whence they made their way the short distance across the golf links past the Club House to the Royal William Hotel. After grace had been said by the vicar of Rye, Rev. A. J. W. Crosse, they all sat down to an excellent luncheon provided by the hotel's host, Mr. J. Terry.

Once the Chairman of the Tramway Company, Cuthbert Hayles, had proposed the loyal toast to the Queen, there followed the usual speeches that accompany such occasions. The Mayor of Winchelsea, Mr. G. M. Freeman, proposed the health of the Mayor and the Mayoress of Rye in a humorous speech in which he pointed out that had it not been for the tremendous exertions, both oratorical and physical, of the Mayoress in opening the Tramway, they would not have been down there that day. She had given them invaluable assistance in their first start. He would remind them that where they were gathered was, in fact, under his jurisdiction as the Mayor of Winchelsea. [3] and that he felt a very great responsibility in respect of his brother mayor. When he was elected he had to take "an awful oath" in which one of his duties was to see home all persons who were out late, or otherwise misconducted themselves, and he now quite trembled at the thought of the grave responsibility which would rest upon him now if the Mayor of Rye did anything wrong whilst within his jurisdiction! Joking apart, he felt a sincere pleasure in proposing the toast and thanking Mr. and Mrs. Bellingham for "their hearty co-operation in connection with the Tramway and all other matters of public interest".

Receiving a warm reception, the Mayor of Rye replied that he and his wife had had the greatest of pleasure in taking part in the proceedings of the day and added that, although some people at times had accused him of giving scant support to the Tramway, he could honestly say that no two persons in Rye wished the Tramway Company better success than did the Mayoress and himself. He went on to thank all those friends who had worked so hard since noon the previous day, moving and

12. Opening Day, Saturday, 13th July 1895 at about 12 noon, and before the crowds of well-wishers arrive, CAMBER and her carriage are ready to make a trial trip along the Tramway. The young man acting as driver standing beside the locomotive on the ballast is Mr. H. F. Stephens' "man" William H. Austen. This is the only known photograph of CAMBER heading chimney first from Rye; the reason for her being turned round so soon after the opening remains a mystery. Messrs. Bagnall were to use this picture to advertise their products in several of their earlier catalogues.
(Colonel Stephens Railway Museum & Archives, Tenterden)

making ready the rolling stock, and he hoped that it would not be thought invidious of him to mention especially Mr. E. P. S. Jones "who had gone through an immense amount of work in an exceedingly short space of time".

Colonel Brookfield was the next to speak and he was accorded a hearty reception. He pointed out that he had not come to address a mass meeting of the employees of the Rye and Camber Tramway Company, but was there as "a very humble shareholder" to wish success to the undertaking which was another factor in the march of improvement and success of the Ancient Town and of Camber. He was there at the invitation of Mr. John (Symonds) Vidler who, though his name had not been mentioned, must be remembered as one of the initiators, if not the instigator, of the Tramway. Though there were "unkind prophets" who hinted that the Tramway wouldn't pay, he said it was a maxim in all railway undertakings that no matter how humble they might be, the traffic always exceeded expectations (?!)

Although not wishing to trouble the assembled guests with a historical account of tramways, he thought that he might mention that at the Battle of Prestonpans, near Edinburgh, in 1745, John Cope took up a position behind a tramway, and jokingly added that perhaps they might use the Camber Tramway in the same manner against their foes on the other side of the English Channel. In his opinion, an important item in the success of an undertaking was the appreciation of outlay in the first place, and that quite modest undertaking (the Tramway) was characteristic of the modesty of the people of Rye! Once the laughter had died down he continued by advising that their old friend, the South Eastern Railway, whom they must begin to look upon as a rival (more laughter) had a solicitor to represent them when their Bill was before Parliament and his bill, which filled 10,000 folios, came to about £240,000, so it was comforting to know that the solicitor to the Rye and Camber Tramway was engaged on their side (more laughter and applause) and that he had to mention in connection with the toast that honoured member of the legal profession, Mr. Cuthbert Hayles, their chairman.

As a matter of interest, the cost of laying the Tramway with 24 lb. per yard rails, the engine shed, two stations and the iron fencing, had amounted to £1,520, and the locomotive CAMBER and the rolling stock were purchased for £404 7s.6d. and £288 respectively. [4]

Colonel Brookfield then spoke of the only other railway that he had personal knowledge of, that ran between Blaenau Festiniog and Portmadoc in North Wales, which was a narrow gauge line of 2ft.0in., but on which "a terrific speed could be obtained". He wondered if the directors of the Tramway looked forward to anything so promising as 30 per cent which was paid by that railway, and that if there was one man who could get that for them, it was Mr. Cuthbert Hayles. Hoping that they all might live to see the day when the Rye and Camber line, short as it was, would be only a little link in the great chain of revised prosperity which

they could foresee for the town of Rye, he thought that more would use "that vehicle of communication" than was generally expected, and he believed at heart that it would not be a failure, though it might be over sanguine to say that it would be a great success. He concluded by suggesting that with the excellent golf links becoming famous, and with closer communication with the main railway system and the town of Rye, it was likely that many classes, whom they did not think of at present, would certainly avail themselves of the neighbourhood and of the Rye and Camber Railway (sic) to which he proposed "Success", coupling with the toast the name of their chairman, Mr. Cuthbert Hayles.

The Colonel resumed his seat to loud applause, after which the toast was drunk with much acclamation. Cuthbert Hayles replied that he had much to thank the Colonel for, but even in their wildest dreams they did not think of realising 30 per cent, at least, not in their life time. What success they did achieve depended much on those present and their friends and relatives. They proposed to encourage golfers and visitors to the seaside by issuing guinea season tickets, and he then gave details of the timetable and ordinary fares, adding that they had now established the quickest present means of transit between Rye and Camber. He took occasion to compliment Mr. E. P. S. Jones on his achievement in setting the rolling stock on the line in so remarkably short time, and Mr. Stephens, the engineer, who had made a thoroughly good job of the permanent way for which Messrs. Mancktelow Brothers were the contractors. After thanking Colonel Brookfield for the compliment paid to him, he then proposed a toast "to the healths of the Engineers and the Contractors", regretting that Messrs. Jones and Stephens were still hard at work on the line and not with them.

Mr. T. Mancktelow briefly responded, wishing the Tramway every success, followed by the chairman proposing a toast to "The Press". Mr. W. Carless proposed "The Ladies" and amid much laughter, coupled with it the name of Doctor E. W. Skinner whose marriage had taken place that week. Doctor Skinner modestly replied and the formalities came to an end.

As the guests left the Royal William Hotel they separated to enjoy either a game of golf, or to take a leisurely walk over the links and the sands in the summer sunshine before making the return journey to Rye on the tram. From the incorporation of the Company to running the first tram had taken less than 14 weeks - no mean achievement. Each director and shareholder ought now to be able to look forward to what would hopefully be a successful and profitable future.

1. William Henry Austen (1878-1956) had first been engaged by Holman Stephens as a "chainman" on the Cranbrook & Paddock Wood Railway at the age of 12 years, and he was later to become Stephens' assistant.
2. South Eastern Advertiser, Saturday, 20.7.1895.
3. The drowned town of "old" Winchelsea is believed to be buried under the sands at Camber.
4. From a letter sent by John Symonds Vidler to the Board of Trade on 17.4.1896.

Chapter Three

EARLY YEARS (1895-1899)

The public service began the following day and, being Sunday, ran during the afternoon and evening only, when large numbers of people took the opportunity of taking their first trip on the new tramway. Trains left Rye, and on succeeding Sundays, at 2.00 p.m., 2.30 p.m., and then hourly from 3.00 p.m. until 8.00 p.m., returning from Camber at 2.15 p.m. and 2.45 p.m., and then every hour between 3.30 p.m. and 8.30 p.m., eight minutes being allowed for the single journey. On weekdays eleven return trains were advertised as leaving Rye at 8.20 a.m., 9.50 a.m., 11.20 a.m., 1.15 p.m. and hourly between 2.00 p.m. and 8.00 p.m., returning from Camber at 8.40 a.m., 10.45 a.m., 12.30 p.m., 1.40 p.m., and then at half past the hour from 2.30 p.m. until 8.30 p.m.. It would appear that "owing to some inconvenience" that this timetable was not adhered to very strictly "owing to more suitable times being fixed upon". [1] Intending passengers who arrived at Rye station on Friday mornings would have been disappointed, as this time was set aside to allow the engine to be cleaned out!

Full details of the opening ceremony of the Tramway appeared in the Sussex Express & County Herald on Saturday, 20th July under the heading "A Happy Inauguration", the report concluding

"The tramway and the engine and car are very satisfactory in all respects as, indeed, are the stations and all the accessories, and the journeys made on the opening day were safe and pleasant, and the whole of the arrangements met with the utmost appreciation of the many who made the trip.... We have already expressed our opinion as to the great boon the tramway is bound to be to Rye and Camber, and need only say now that we believe the Rye and Camber Tramway Company will also derive a satisfactory financial benefit from their enterprise, and we look to a near extension being required, at any rate in car accommodation, the present number now catered for per journey being 32".

Reading between the lines, it would apear that there were still some Tramway Company shares available when, in a separate paragraph in the same edition, the newspaper advised

"We are glad to state that the new tramway has been patronised extremely well during the few days it has been open, and everything points to the probability of it proving a really paying concern and that, as Colonel Brookfield pointed out on Saturday, the anticipated traffic will be exceeded. Such being the case, the directors are seriously considering whether or not, after the next few days, any further shares shall be issued to the general public, who will, therefore, have to act promptly if they wish to participate to any greater extent in the undertaking."

Also that day, the following description of the Tramway was published in the South Eastern Advertiser:

".... As to a description of the line, very little is necessary in this direction, seeing that most of our readers have been amongst those who have patronised the Tramway during the week, and have, therefore, had an opportunity of seeing for themselves. The line commences close to the new Rother Bridge, where a station, with waiting-room, has been built, and where a shed for the protection of the rolling stock is in the course of erection. The line, which is of three-feet gauge, first runs across two fields belonging to Rye Corporation, which charges a nominal rent for the privilege, and thence across a bank dividing the Broadwater. A few yards further the only bridge in the course of the line is crossed, passing over a channel which drains the property beyond, and then most of the remaining part of the journey is across the immense beach field. On the way is passed a large new lodging-house in course of erection, which is intended to accommodate the numerous visitors to the sands and the Golf Links. At this point the sand banks of Camber and the shipping of Rye Harbour appear into prominent view, and the locality which the Tramway is intended to open out and popularise presents itself before the spectator. The line runs along a bank a few hundred yards further, when the terminus is reached some yards to the east of the Rother, opposite Rye Harbour, where there is a waiting room similar to that at the other end. The passengers here alight, and the engine, after being detached, is run on a side line and attached to the other end of the car ready for the return journey.

"In any mention we make of the Tramway we cannot omit to call attention to the evident signs that its utility is being felt immediately. The number of visitors who have taken the tram to the sands during the week has been very encouraging indeed, the average takings per day being about £3, and one of the great encouragements to visit the sands of Camber is the fact that Councillor I. Longley, of Rye, has anticipated that visitors when down there will need refreshments, and has provided accordingly. At a very convenient spot, in the vicinity of the most favoured part of the sands, he has constructed a refreshment building, where a light repast will be provided at a very small charge, and even large parties catered for on arrangements being made".

Owing to the limited accommodation at the Royal William Hotel, it had been impossible to invite everyone to the opening ceremony on 13th July, so "in a kindly and jocular spirit" a number of tradesmen from Rye arranged an informal opening ceremony of their own. This second opening was held on Tuesday evening, 30th July, when "a good party journeyed over the line and partook of dinner at The Royal William Hotel, Mr. C. Hayles, chairman of the Tramway Company presiding, and by the last tram the party returned, thoroughly satisfied that they had in their truly official manner "opened" the tramway, and that it would, after their sanction, proceed onward with its well deserved success". [2]

Holman Stephens wrote excitedly to his father on 2nd August ".....as I told you in my last note, we opened the Rye job some weeks since, and they have been taking £20 a week ever since - the working expenses are under £8 per week and the capital is only £2,000 or thereabouts...."

On Saturday, 3rd August the South Eastern Advertiser proudly wrote:

"Since the commencement of the Rye & Camber Tramway great interest has been taken in the venture and the traffic, as prophecied by Colonel Brookfield M.P. at the opening lunch, has exceeded all expectations. It is beginning to be looked upon, not in the light of a private venture, but as one of the public accomplishments of the locality, and its utility is now beyond question."

The Tramway soon settled into its daily routine of transporting golfers to the links, day trippers to the sands, and fishermen and residents to and from Rye Harbour village. After all of the initial excitement, contrary to what Holman Stephens had advised his father in his recent letter, the second week's takings dropped to £12 13s.0d., but had increased to £16 a week later, and £12 5s.0d. was taken on the August Bank Holiday alone. Unfortunately this, the Tramway's first Bank Holiday Monday, brought with it a new and quite unexpected problem! The morning was bright enough and gave promise of a fine day, and with the chief attraction being the sands at Camber, hundreds of holidaymakers travelled down on the new Tramway. The traffic began to gain large proportions round about 11 o'clock, and from this time onwards every journey found "fully a hundred passengers" in the carriage and the two small wagons that had been pressed into service. Not surprisingly, this un-precedented rush caused a few delays, mainly in keeping up a good head of steam on CAMBER, along with having to take on water.

At about 3.00 p.m. a storm was seen advancing from the south-west, and by 4 o'clock a steady downpour had commenced which lasted, with little intermission for the next five hours, successfully putting a stop to all outdoor enjoyment. With no prospects of the weather clearing up "crowds of visitors betook themselves to the terminus for the return journey. The capacious waiting rooms and platform were packed with people, and each successive tramful which left had no appearance of making an impression towards reducing the number. Happily Councillor I. Longley's refreshment tent, which he had removed close at hand, served a most useful purpose, and the beleagured passengers were able to obtain warm refreshment, which greatly counteracted the inconvenience experienced by waiting. Towards 7 o'clock the crowd had considerably reduced, and shortly afterwards the tramway had accomplished its difficult task of re-conveying the passengers back to Rye." Concluding its report on "The Bank Holiday in Rye" the South Eastern Advertiser dated 10th August advised "The tramway undoubtedly, according to its capabilities, did its work well, but the occasion had shown that at least another car is necessary to cope with the enormously increased traffic at such times, and the directorate will do well to provide adequately against this for next year".

Thieves gained entry the following evening into the Tramway station at Rye by breaking a window in the door, thus enabling them to unfasten the catch. The intruders had, no doubt, been attracted by the large receipts the tramway had taken during the week, but, unfortunately for them, none of the takings had been left in the office overnight. Chagrined at their failure to find cash, the thieves vented their disappointment by scattering the tram tickets and workmen's tools that had been left there. [3]

During the evening of Friday, 9th August, the first General Statutory Meeting of the Rye and Camber Tramways Company was held at the George Hotel Assembly Room, Rye, being presided over by Cuthbert Hayles, who explained that the first meeting had been delayed for as long as possible in order that the shareholders could see the line open and in working order before they met. He then gave details of the receipts from the first three weeks of operation and, to much applause, told them that for the present week they had already taken £28. Besides this, some forty season tickets had been issued, though not all at a guinea, and arrangements were being made to let fishermen travel at a reduced rate on weekdays only. He could see no reason why expenditure should exceed £250 per year, and thought that it would be less, and even if receipts were only half the present rate over twelve months, he could see no reason to regret their investment.

As previously mentioned, The South Eastern Advertiser, referring to the recent Bank Holiday traffic, had said that another car was necessary, but as Mr. Hayles explained, cars were not bought for a £5 note, and the shareholders could easily reckon up for themselves how many bank holidays it would want to buy another car! Shareholders numbered 80, and although all of the shares had been taken up, there were still several persons wishing to buy some, so it could be safely said that all was satisfactory, and it was hoped that it would long remain so. The only business to attend to was to appoint auditors, and Mr. J. Adams and Mr. G. W. Strick were both duly elected.

Three days later, on Monday, 12th August, it was agreed at the meeting of Rye Town Council to let an additional piece of ground to the Tramway Company "extending about 12ft. or 15ft. from the iron fence, the harbour end of the station, and thence to the wall at the corner of the New Bridge", the rent to be increased to £6

13. **Judging by the clean condition of the ballast, this fine view of CAMBER at the station of the same name, was probably taken in the summer of 1896, soon after the arrival of the Rother Ironworks carriage which is coupled next to the engine. The driver, Albert Edward "Jokey" Rhodes, looks down proudly from the cab, and the conductor is possibly Charles Thatcher whose career with the Tramway ended abruptly when he fell from the moving tram whilst he collected fares on 8th October 1898.** *(Courtesy of T. Middlemass)*

in consideration. Access to the station had so far been for foot passengers only, but now the Council gave permission for "the space between the wall and the bridge and the small gate to be filled up so that a road entrance with a large gate could be made".

At their monthly meeting, also held at the George Hotel on Tuesday evening, 3rd September, the Rye & District Trade Association held a discussion on "The Development of Camber-on-Sea" where it was suggested that with its sands being looked upon as "the finest in England", Camber should stand an equally good chance with other health resorts springing up along the south coast, especially now that there was the new bridge across the river AND the Tramway. Attractions that should be provided include pleasure trips to sea and musical entertainments of a more refined character than the usual beach performances at seaside places. Mr. E. P. S. Jones suggested that an embankment be built to enclose an area of still water for bathing and boating, but all present were well aware that nothing would get done until there was more house and hotel accommodation, and seats or shelters were urgently needed. One member thought that the Tramway Company could "put up a few shelters and bathing places" and so help their traffic, but the President explained that the Tramway

Company, under its articles of association, only had powers to run a tram, but that it might be possible for them to get the powers extended. Several members urged that the Tramway Company was the proper body to move in the erection of shelters etc., and it was decided that the Company be asked to provide two shelters. [4]

The first mention of extending the Tramway came in an amusing speech by the Rev. A. J. W. Crosse (vicar of Rye) at the Trade Association's Dinner on Thursday, 3rd October, when in his toast "Success to the Trade Association" he suggested "that the dear little tram might go on, at any rate, as far as Dungeness". The President replied that the idea of taking the tram as far as Mr. Battam's [5] during the present year had been formally received by the Company, and also by the golfers, and that accommodation would be increased. He added that, as far as the development of Camber-on-Sea and the construction of the new Tramway were concerned, the Association had always been at the back of the Tramway Company, and though circumstances were at times disheartening, every member of that Association who could afford it, took shares and showed practical appreciation. He did warn that in the development of Camber there was a danger of being too enthusiastic,

18

and with the area coming within the parish of Winchelsea, they did not want their rates raised for the purpose of improvements, even though there was still much to be done to make Camber more attractive and comfortable.

Regarding the extension of the Tramway, Cuthbert Hayles advised the guests that the Company had already had the matter under consideration, but that they had not arrived at any decision. T. G. Sharpe had his doubts as to the practicability of making the extension owing to the continual shifting of the sands, and commented that a bathing machine out there had recently been washed 150 yards away!

That the Tramway was seen to be doing well had already tempted thieves to break into the station at Rye, and the following Saturday there was another attempted burglary at the Tramway offices. As before, none of the takings had been left, and the thief's object was again frustrated. [6]

On Thursday and Friday, 19th and 20th December, the Company took the unusual, (but no doubt necessary) action of closing the Tramway "to allow a thorough inspection and overhauling of the capital little

engine which has been in constant use since the opening". [7]

Holman F. Stephens was justly proud of "his" tramway, and on 23rd January 1896, he wrote from Tonbridge in Kent to Sir J. S. Hopwood at the Board of Trade:
"Dear Sir,

"I enclose two photos of the Rye Tramway referred to in our recent conversation. Will you be kind enough not to consider these photos, in any way, "deposited" with the Board of Trade, but, knowing the interest that you take in the matter of "economical transport" it occurred to me that you would be interested in the enclosed pictures.
Yours faithfully,
H. F. Stephens."

The photographs featured CAMBER and the Bagnall carriage at Rye station prior to running the inaugural tram on 13th July, and a later general view of the station.

On the morning of Friday, 21st February 1896 the first Annual Meeting of the shareholders of the Rye and Camber Tramways Company Ltd. took place at the Cinque Ports Arms Hotel in Rye, being presided over by Cuthbert Hayles who, the previous autumn, had received

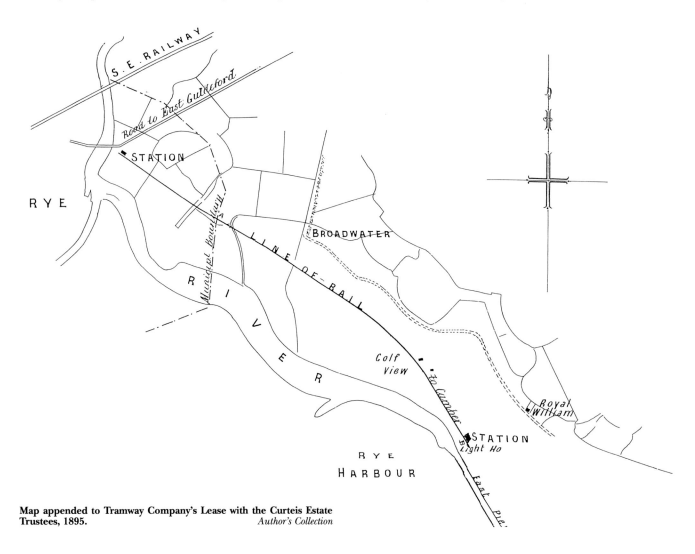

Map appended to Tramway Company's Lease with the Curteis Estate Trustees, 1895.   *Author's Collection*

the honour of being elected as the Mayor of Rye. The Directors' Report described the Tramway as having been an unqualified success since opening, and that "daily takings alone" up until 31st December had amounted to £269 10s.5d.. The net profit for the six months was £83 3s.2d., out of which the directors recommended a dividend of $7^1/_2$ per cent per annum from the dates of payment for the respective shares, with the remaining balance of £39 19s.11d. to be carried forward to a reserve fund. The tram had run some 7,000 miles at an average of less than 7d. per tram mile.

As originally printed, the second part of the Directors' Report had stated incorrectly that the dividend would be paid at the rate of 15 per cent, and it had had to be amended in ink to the correct $7^1/_2$ per cent owing to what Mr. Hayles described as "a slight mistake in the figures", and this aroused a good deal of amusement! As to the proposal of extending the line along the sand banks, the directors thought that, as the line had only been open for six months, and that for the most part the best part of the year, it would not be wise to go in for any extension until at least they had the opportunity of what the year's working would bring forth. Apart from the financial question of raising additional capital, they would have to cope with "a kind of different soil" through which the line would be carried.

The directors were pleased to announce that a further car was to be built which, they hoped, would take the public more comfortably, and it was very possible that they would have another engine, the chairman explaining that although the present engine was "an uncommonly good one", it had been running much longer than any train engine without being thoroughly overhauled. He believed that railway companies once a month, or every six weeks, had their engines into docks and saw that everything was right, while their own engine had been running since the commencement of traffic without allowing any time for thoroughly inspecting it. If they had a second engine it might take the place of the present one and run on Friday mornings also when there were more people to carry than usual. He then optimistically added "We might also run on two lines some day!"

Although the Tramway had proved to be a great boon to the town and the neighbourhood, Walter Dawes said that he would be very sorry to see the directors subsequently crippled through paying too much interest and moved an amendment that only 5 per cent dividend be paid, but with only six in favour, the chairman's motion of a $7^1/_2$ per cent dividend was carried. Joseph Adams then suggested that as it was usual in all business concerns to vote a sum to the directors, that £2 be voted to each director for his past year's services, more especially after the excellent results that they had achieved. Messrs. A. E. Hinds and W. E. Colebrooke appealed to Mr. Adams to defer the motion until the next meeting, but he urged that with the shareholders not being called together for another year, and because

during the past ten months the directors "had done far more work than any of their successors would be called upon to perform" he would not withdraw his motion! However, the motion failed to find a seconder, and the proceedings of the First Annual General Meeting terminated rather abruptly!

Immediately after the meeting Holman Stephens forwarded a copy of the balance sheet to Sir J. S. Hopwood with the accompanying letter:

"21st February 1896.

"My dear Sir,

"I enclose the balance sheet of the Tramway I spoke to you of privately some time since: you will see that these small undertakings can be worked at a profit.

"In my last letter to you I fancy I omitted to mention that I have been engaged both in Locomotive and Civil Engineers' department of Railway work, this in case you may be able to advise me of any berth vacant in Light Rlys.

"Please excuse me bothering you.
Yours faithfully,
H. F. Stephens"

Having received Mr. Stephens' letter, the Board of Trade's file, No. R.2313, dated 24th February carried the following interesting comments regarding the Rye & Camber Tramway:

Sir T. Blomefield:	A promising Light Railway but the profit comes mostly from carrying people to the Golf Links. It is "un-authorised"
Sir C. Boyle:	A very wholesome object.
L. W. Dudly:	The accounts of this Co. are bewildering in their magnitude!

The March 1896 edition of "The Railway World" contained a long and detailed description of the new Tramway and reported that

".... the traffic has so far exceeded the original expectations that another second class bogie car, capable of seating 25 passengers, is now in course of construction. Arrangements are also being entered into for the supply of a second locomotive to cope with the large summer traffic, the splendid sands and beach at Camber being in great request as a holiday resort for the surrounding population".

The article concluded

".... From these facts it will be seen that we have in Sussex, without the aid of Parliament, local authorities or other public bodies, an un-pretentious, but eminently practical example of the way in which light railways - if regarded strictly as such - may serve the interests of semi-rural districts. In this case, a few capable businessmen, without flourish of trumpets, have put into practise what has been talked of all over the country and while obtaining, we trust, a fair return for their enterprise, have conferred far greater benefits on the district". [8]

A notice appeared in the Sussex Express & County Herald on Saturday, 28th March, advising that "commencing with Good Friday next, there will be a full service of steam trams on every day instead of traffic being delayed to 2.00 p.m. on Fridays", so that from that date there were only Sunday mornings available for the cleaning out and routine maintenance of the hard-working little locomotive CAMBER.

During the afternoon of Tuesday, 31st March, the new carriage was delivered to Rye Tram station and with everything proving satisfactory on its trial trip to Camber and back, it was immediately put into service. Carried on bogies supplied by Messrs. W. G. Bagnall of Stafford (similar to those on the original carriage that had arrived eight months previously) the vehicle had been constructed by E. P. S. Jones of the nearby Rother Ironworks, and was a new venture for that Company. Its arrival was most opportune as Easter fell that very next weekend. With so many townspeople visiting the golf links and the sands at Camber, the Tramway carried no fewer than 700 passengers on Good Friday, and over 1,500 on Easter Monday, with a total of 2,700 tickets being issued between Friday and Monday inclusive, these figures not taking into account those who had travelled to and fro on previously purchased season tickets. [9]

A new summer timetable came into effect on Saturday 2nd May, and then in the evening of Thursday, 14th May, the tram enjoyed a change in routine when it was used as "an armoured train" by the "E" Company of the First Cinque Ports Rifle Volunteers as part of their tactical practises. The idea was that a hostile force had landed at Dungeness and was marching along the coast with the intention of taking Rye Harbour, the Tramway and the town of Rye. The invading force duly took the Tramway and advanced sections towards the town, supported by the tramway engine and wagons manned with volunteers. Needless to say, the defending force were greatly surprised when the invaders opened fire from the train but, after a while, with their sections being hard pressed, the invaders were compelled to retire, with the defenders ultimately forcing them to take up a position on the top of the sand hills. After the manoeuvre the men were provided with refreshments at the Royal William Hotel and then, headed by their band, they marched back to Rye where they arrived soon after 10.00 p.m. having passed what was described as a most profitable and instructive evening. [10]

Whitsuntide in Rye proved to be a great success, and it was reported that the Tramway Company had a record day, the number of passengers carried being close on 2,000. [11] Throughout the summer the Tramway receipts remained very satisfactory, peaking at £73 7s.9d. during August, but expenses were already beginning to rise out of proportion to them, partly because the Company now had to provide its own staff to maintain the permanent way whereas, for the first 5½ months this work had been carried out by Messrs Mancktelow Brothers, the contractor. A further sum had to be spent on the construction of a second corrugated iron shed across the end of the line at Rye to house the Rother Ironworks carriage and some more robust open wagons that had recently been acquired to carry sand. CAMBER had so far given excellent service, but could not go on for ever without a proper overhaul so, with finances unable to entertain the purchase of another new engine, the directors inspected several second-hand locomotives, but were unable to find one "in a satisfactory condition at a suitable price".

After the excitement of the busy August Bank Holiday weekend when "the tram did a roaring business in carrying passengers to Camber Sands", [12] ticket sales for September fell to £39 14s.10d. and from 1st October, with just golfers and fishermen in the main to cater for, a suitably reduced timetable came into effect with, once again, no service on Fridays until after lunch.

There was a return to the George Hotel, Rye for the Tramway Company's second Annual General Meeting which took place on Friday, 5th March 1897. The directors regretted that the amount of profit had not been so large as they had anticipated, taking into account the success of the first 5½ months. Their report continued

".... In the winter months a considerable loss is entailed, and unless additional support be given during that season, the directors will have to consider the necessity of stopping the traffic during those months."

To illustrate the problem, each month's takings were shown in the accounts as follows:

January:	£16 8s. 9d.	February:	£15 1s. 7d.
March:	£18 17s. 9d.	April:	£52 14s.11d.
May:	£55 8s. 3d.	June:	£86 15s. 2d.
July:	£59 8s. 3d.	August:	£73 7s. 9d.
September:	£89 14s. 10d.	October:	£36 6s. 8d.
November:	£19 0s. 10d.	December:	£18 19s.11d.

Even so, 44,887 tickets had been issued over the year, giving a net profit of £37 1s.11d., after writing off £19 8s.10d. from the formation expenses. A dividend of 2½ per cent per annum was recommended, which would leave a balance of £3 6s.6d. to be carried forward to a reserve fund. Cuthbert Hayles, in moving the adoption of the Report, thought that if several more season tickets were taken up, [13] they still might be able to carry on the traffic during the winter, or else (referring to the golfers!) they could increase the price for those who did travel at that time of year "when the tram was run a great deal for the convenience of certain gentlemen". He did not think that many went to Camber Sands for pleasure in the winter, other than to play golf, or that their business pursuits compelled them to go there. Seconding the adoption of the Report, Councillor John Neve Masters said that the Tramway had proved a great accommodation to the people who came to the town, and if golfers were deprived of the service, he believed that the town would feel the loss, and he would rather take 2½ per cent dividend than to see the trams taken off. He did not think that any of the shareholders

14. Shortly after the opening, the whole of the Tramway's rolling stock is posed for the camera just outside Camber station where the embankment has yet to have faggoting added as a protection against high tides. How flimsy the two open wagons look and see how their buffing bars do not quite line up with either the engine or carriage.
(Colonel Stephens Railway Museum & Archives, Tenterden)

15. Having just arrived from Camber, VICTORIA poses at Rye soon after delivery in1897. Note weighing machine inside the waiting room to the left.
(Plateway Press)

originally expected to get more than $2^1/_2$ per cent, and if this had been paid instead of $7^1/_2$ per cent the previous year, no one would have been disappointed.

Mr. T. G. Sharpe next proposed a vote of thanks to the chairman and remarked that they should fully look in the face what running the tram during the winter months for the benefit of outsiders really meant. They were only able to declare a dividend of $2^1/_2$ per cent, had not allowed one half-penny for depreciation, and had barely sufficient sums wherewith to purchase a second-hand locomotive. He thought that unless the Company were better remunerated by the people using the golf links, he should vote for the winter trams to be discontinued as they were run for the whole town, and not simply for golfers. Mr. T. Bushby pointed out that the Tramway was not started with the intention of making large dividends, but for the advancement of the town, and there was no necessity for the pessimism displayed by some of the speakers. Taking the two years together, the shareholders had been paid at the rate of 5 per cent, with a summer and winter service, and there were other sources of revenue open to it. Mr. G. Henbrey suggested that as the S.E.R. issued cheap tickets during the summer, so might their own Tram Company, leaving those who required the winter service to pay adequately for it. He believed that, were the winter service abandoned, it would be very prejudicial to the Company. Cuthbert Hayles confirmed that he did not want the tram closed during the winter, but that greater support would have to be forthcoming.

It could hardly come as a surprise that a suitable second-hand 3ft.0in. gauge locomotive could not be found, so the directors agreed to purchase a new engine by the issue of additional debentures and shares. The shares were offered to the shareholders pro rata to their holding, but as none of them responded, the directors had to take them up themselves, and a locomotive, a little larger and more powerful than CAMBER, was ordered from Messrs. W. G. Bagnall of Stafford on 8th April 1897. Named VICTORIA, the new engine arrived at Rye early in June and entered service straight away, so releasing CAMBER for her long overdue major overhaul. The original little locomotive had run continuously for one year and ten months, and because there had been no time to maintain her properly during that period it should not have come as too great a shock to find that a considerable sum of money had to be spent on her. By the end of the month she was again "in very good condition" and the Company could boast of two excellent engines to run their services. On 3rd July, it was announced that there was to be "an acceptable alteration to the Tram Timetable, whereby it will be seen that the Tram will now run on Friday mornings also, at the same times as other weekdays", [14] and the unusual arrangement of no service on a Friday until after lunch became a thing of the past.

The August Bank Holiday was "blessed by the most brilliant weather", and it was reported that the resources of the Tramway were "taxed to the utmost" in carrying the vast number of visitors and relatives of residents who visited the sands at Camber that day. [15] To the onlooker the Company must have been seen to be doing very well, which indeed it was during the all too short summer season, but as already seen, the winter was a different matter. In an effort to offset the predictable losses of those months, the directors announced that they were to increase the fares slightly from 1st November. They felt sure that the public would much prefer meeting the slight increase rather than experience the entire cessation of winter traffic. [16]

At the Rye Trade Association's 5th Annual Dinner at The George Hotel Assembly Room on Tuesday, 7th December, the President, Alderman John Symonds Vidler, described the local Tramway as "a very great success", quoting that in 1896 it had carried no less than 50,000 people [17] which, in his opinion, conclusively proved that it was wanted. He admitted "Whether also it would be a paying concern was a different question. Those who put money into it thought less of a possible dividend than they did of the benefit of the town". He thought that if it was not for the Tramway they might not get any visitors at all and confirmed again that the members of their Association liberally supported the Company, and the Corporation did all they could to further it, giving the land practically free, which showed that they recognised the advantage that it would be to the Borough.

Brave speeches or not, even with the slight fare increase, the end of the year figures showed a slight drop in passenger totals (43,662), with takings about £10 less than those of 1896. Cuthbert Hayles at the poorly attended 3rd Annual Meeting of the Tramway Company on Monday, 28th March 1898 opined

"I do not think it is a matter very much to complain of if you bear in mind that, although there are a great many people in Rye, they are not, if I may say so, monied people who came there and took furnished houses for the season, and liked to indulge in the luxury of going to the seaside. Our visitors have been principally artists, and our "ancient town" abounds in such attractions which keep them so busily employed, that many of them do not find time to go frequently to the seaside."

A profit of just £18 had been made over the year, and with this being written off against construction expenses, it was regretted that no dividend was to be declared. Mr. Hayles said that he did not know that anybody need look again for a large dividend - at all events, not until Camber became a fashionable seaside resort and, in the meantime, if they paid a fair rate of interest on the money invested in the Company, he believed that all would be satisfied. The main reason for no dividend being paid, he surmised, was because repairs and stores had amounted to £179, compared with only £85 of the previous year.

Councillor Frank Jarrett thought that, with a comparatively new plant, the expenditure on repairs seemed rather heavy, to which Mr. T. G. Sharpe replied that it could only be accounted for in one way. He said

16. This is a copy of one of the two photographs (the other was the scene on Opening Day) that Holman Stephens sent to the Board of Trade on 23rd January 1896, showing Rye station in almost original condition with its neat lattice fence on either side of the station building. Although pictured within a few months of the opening, the ticket office has already gained a side window, but the locomotive shed has only one smoke ventilator on the roof to the rear. Note the single nameboard, the water tank to the right of the building that collected rain water from the station roof, and the red warning circle on the engine shed doors. *(Colonel Stephens Railway Museum & Archives, Tenterden)*

17. An early picture of Camber station. As at Rye, rain water was collected from the station roof, the top of the tank being just visible above the gentlemen's convenience to the right. With the waiting room door open, a part of the bench seating that was fixed to three of the four walls can be seen. *(Colonel Stephens Railway Museum & Archives, Tenterden)*

"It is useless shutting our eyes to the fact that the first engine we bought was not up to the work, and it had to be kept going much harder than it was capable of running." This was hardly a fair comment considering the sterling work that CAMBER had performed for almost two years without proper maintenance, but he then added that, from what he had heard from experts, the engine had done "a wonderful lot of work", but it had also landed them in considerable expense when it was gained some relief by the new engine. Expenses were inevitable in connection with machinery, and perhaps they had been running the trams a little too cheaply, and he wondered whether the directors would have to consider that such fares be charged "as would return some reasonable amount to the shareholders".

Once again, Councillor F. H. Chapman noted that nothing had been written off for depreciation, bearing in mind that the total cost of engines, cars and rolling stock amounted to about £1,200, and that in the course of time renewals would be required. He considered the Company was, therefore, in a worse position than not being able to pay a dividend. The chairman replied that there was a reserve fund of £44 and added sarcastically "We might have written off £500, or any other amount, but it would not alter the Company's position!" Doctor E. W. Skinner and Mr. T. G. Sharpe were both unanimously re-elected as directors, and the latter said that it must not be assumed, because there is no dividend, the affairs of the Company were not receiving the closest attention of the directors, who had done their very best. They had bought their experience, and he trusted that in a year or two they would not only meet Mr. Chapman's views with regard to writing off a fair amount for depreciation, but that they would be able to pay a small dividend to the shareholders. He confirmed that he was in no wise discouraged at the position of the Company, and the chairman in closing the meeting agreed, saying

"It is quite true that the directors have given a great deal of time and attention to the affairs of the Company and, I believe, will continue to do so. Although there is no dividend, the matter somewhat appeals to the directorate, who are mostly the largest shareholders, and would like to have a dividend the same as the others connected with the Company."

For almost forty years, sand from the sand hills and shingle dredged from the River Rother had been used to manufacture concrete blocks at a site on the western outskirts of Rye Harbour village, from whence they were transported by sea to form the outer arms of the Admiralty Pier being built at Dover. Seeing an opening for increasing its business, in May 1898, the Rye & Camber Tramways Company applied to the Rye Harbour Commissioners for permission to "lay a tramway for the carriage of sand between their rails and the stonework [18] at Rye Harbour". Discussing the application at the Rye Harbour Commissioners' meeting on Tuesday, 17th May, it was thought that if they could get a cheaper way of conveying it from the sand hills, the sand trade might greatly develop. The chairman, Mr. Kingsnorth Reeve, thought that his colleagues were "a little before their wicket" and that if the tramway was laid, a stage would have to be built, but not a word was said about that in the application. Alderman John Symonds Vidler thought that if the Commissioners did their duty in clearing away the mud, there would be no necessity for a stage, but Mr. T. Smith suggested that that would cost more than a stage. Ultimately, on the proposal of Mr. J. Adams, the Commissioners agreed to sanction the Tramway's application, so far as they were empowered to do, the details being left in the hands of the executive committee.

On Tuesday, 5th July, the executive committee duly reported to the Harbour Commissioners Annual Meeting that "persuant to the resolution of the last quarterly meeting, a new stage had been constructed on the town side of the Harbour ferry steps, and four barge loads of mud (have been) taken away". The Harbour Master was instructed to keep the stage, as far as was practical, for crafts loading with sand from the siding of the Rye & Camber Tramway and it was stated that the stage was constantly in use in this respect. The siding referred to was the extension of the main running line eastwards beyond the station into the sand hills, but sand still had to be transhipped the 60 yards between the Tramway and the River, probably by wheelbarrow.

As in previous years, August proved to be the most profitable month with £90 being taken, and no less than 1,535 passengers (exclusive of season ticket holders) were carried to "our always popular marine suburb, Camber-on-Sea" on the Bank Holiday Monday alone. The sands at Camber were becoming increasingly popular as a venue for Sunday School outings and the like, and on Monday, 15th August 1898, the inmates of Rye Workhouse were given a special treat when all those who were able to go, were taken to Camber for the day. Messrs. Wright & Pankhurst (a local hansom cab operator) kindly took the old people to and from the tram station in waggonettes free of charge and special trams, slotted in between the advertised services, were provided to take the inmates to Camber and back. [19]

Although both Rye and Camber stations had ticket offices, that at Camber appears never to have been used, whilst that at Rye was out of use at a very early date, and it was customary for the conductor to issue tickets on the tram. He would make his way along the train whilst it was in motion via the full-length foot-boards that were fitted to the platform side of each of the carriages specifically for that purpose. This method of fare collection had worked successfully for over three years until on Thursday, 8th October the conductor, Charles Thatcher, lost his footing and fell from the moving tram. The unfortunate man was taken to his home where he lay for some time unconscious, but he eventually made a slow, successful recovery. It is not recorded whether he resumed his duties as conductor on the tram. [20]

On Tuesday afternoon, 20th March 1899, the 4th Annual Meeting of the Rye & Camber Tramways

Company Ltd. was held at the George Hotel in Rye. In presenting their report the directors congratulated the shareholders on the increased traffic of the past year, which had resulted in a net profit of £86 9s.8d. from which, after writing off £19 8s.10d. from the construction account, and for the first time allowing for depreciation of the permanent way and rolling stock, left an available balance of £27 0s.10d.. Of this sum the directors recommended that £10 10s.10d. be added to the reserve fund, and that the balance be carried forward to the next year. Receipts had totalled £684 9s.9d., with passenger fares accounting for £508 17s.1d., and 49,870 passengers had been carried, exclusive of season ticket holders.

Cuthbert Hayles said that it was his privilege to move the adoption of the report which was a little more satisfactory than the report presented at the previous year's annual meeting. The Company's takings had increased by something like a hundred pounds, while he was pleased to add that the expenses were not quite so heavy as they had been on previous occasions. To illustrate this, he might say that under the item of repairs the expenses had been reduced by nearly £60, which he considered was highly pleasing. He then drew attention to a new item on the Balance Sheet, namely £45 13s.10d. in respect of Passenger Duty for the years 1897 and 1898 and advised

"We do not feel justified in paying this without every demur possible but ultimately, the Government have the whole wealth of the nation at their beck and, supposing the Company had resisted their claim and won in the first instance, they would probably have appealed and gone right to the House of Lords until they had carried their point. Even should the Company have eventually won, we would have found that the law costs would have absorbed a very large portion of the capital and we must, in any event, have made a very bad bargain. Having tried by the persuasion of friends, and in other ways, to gain exemption, but without success, we ultimately paid so that the amount for duty for the two years comes in the lst year's accounts, in addition to the law costs amounting to £12 10s.9d.. With the exception of two guineas this sum represents the costs of the plaintiff, or in other words, the Government, our solicitor, Walter Dawes, having given us the benefit of his services for nothing" (applause).

Partly because of the added expense of Passenger Duty, the Company did not propose to pay a dividend that year. Mr. Hayles continued:

"Ours is a leasehold property and is, therefore, getting a little less valuable, and though even railway lines wear out, locomotives wear out a little more rapidly. We thought it advisable to write off as much as we could, but much too little, from the cost of those materials. The shareholders could, however, go home and say that they have got a very nice thing which is a very great convenience to the town and which, no doubt, added to its popularity. I take it that this is your dividend and perhaps, after all, you could not have found a better

investment. I might tell you that during the past two months the receipts are higher than in 1898, and I hope, with favourable weather, the increase will continue. I make no promises, but trust the next balance sheet will be a more favourable one."

Walter Dawes seconded the adoption of the Directors' Report saying that they should "interest themselves zealously" in the concern whether it paid a dividend or not. Some of them seemed under the impression that no sooner had they invested their money than they would receive in return a dividend. He was very pleased to find that the Company had had such a record year and he thought, considering the diminutive nature of their line, that they had every cause for congratulation. Referring to August's record takings of £90, he contended that this was a lot of money for the public to spend on such a small railway, and it proved that the Tramway provided a great want. Mr. Dawes' comment that he did not believe that the Rye Golf Club would have been in its present flourishing condition had it not been for the Rye and Camber Tramway was deservedly greeted with much applause.

Joseph Adams confirmed that he also supported the adoption of the Report, but could not quite agree with Walter Dawes as to the shareholders not looking for any immediate dividend. If the undertaking was carried on simply in the public interest, then the Company should be taken over and run by the local authorities in order that all the inhabitants of the town should bear their fair proportion of the burden; but those who had a number of shares in the Company did look for some small return for the money they had invested. The chairman hoped that they did not understand him to say that the Company would never pay a dividend. Drawing attention once more to the Balance Sheet, he said that although they had expended about £2,740 on their rolling stock, up to last year not one penny had been written off for depreciation. Even the £40 set apart for this purpose was, in his opinion, much too little, they ought to have fully that much every year. If the Company took £100 or £200 more than formerly, he would be very disappointed if they did not pay a dividend. He neither believed in working for nothing, or in having money invested without any return for it. The motion was then put, and it was carried nem. con..

Mr. J. L. Deacon asked whether the Company had fixed fares for passengers as he understood that, at present, fares varied according to the social position of the passenger, and he thought that such matters should be looked into. [21] Several observations had been made to him in respect of the different charges demanded from passengers, and one gentleman, a new-comer to the town, had informed him that he should never use the Tramway again as he had to pay as much to go to Camber by rail as he would have done had he travelled by carriage. The chairman surprisingly said that he failed to understand what Mr. Deacon meant by "different charges".

In explanation, Mr. Deacon explained that

sometimes 2d., 4d., and 6d. was demanded of a passenger. Workmen were privileged to travel for 2d., but it was not only workmen who took advantage of the 2d. fares. Mr. R. Milsom advised that it was left to the discretion of the ticket collector as to whether a passenger could pay first or second class fares. Joseph Adams mentioned that he knew of a Captain who, travelling from Camber in his working clothes, was only called upon to pay 2d., but when the same Captain travelled in his best attire, he had to pay the First Class fare!

Mr. Deacon said he wanted to see some better system adopted, and that the Company should make some definite charges and not simply trust to the conductor as to how much a passenger should pay. He moved that the directors be asked to consider the question of fares, but the motion failed to find a seconder. Mr. Hayles added that all complaints of this nature should be reported to the directors, who would investigate each case on its merits. He agreed that the selection of *bona fide* working men, who were allowed special privileges, was a somewhat invidious task, but with regard to the increased fares charged, they had proved advantageous as their increased receipts proved!

Changing the subject, John Symonds Vidler told the meeting that a project had been discussed for adding a new car to the rolling stock, suitable for the summer months, but his colleagues were not at present inclined to go for it. Personally, he favoured the idea as the cost would amount to only £160, and he believed that the additional income arising from the car would be more than £20 per annum, while it would also add to the comfort of pasengers. Councillor W. Colebrooke agreed, and thought that if they had the summer car their balance sheet would be in a much more satisfactory condition next year. The Company undoubtedly required additional rolling stock, for at times they could not comfortably accommodate all of their passengers. Joseph Adams thought that Mr. Vidler's idea was "a capital one", but that the Company could not afford to carry it into practise at present. Walter Dawes suggested that the car should not be an open one as it would be extremely dangerous. Fortunately the Company had not had an accident on its line yet, [22] but he thought that this record would soon be broken if they ran an open car. Mr. Adams was afraid that it would not pay the Company to run a third car with their small engines, and Mr. W. Selmes asked whether the existing cars could be converted to summer cars. "I think not!" replied the chairman, and with there being no proposition, the question was dropped. In bringing the meeting to a close, Joseph Adams proposed a vote of thanks to the directors for their services to the Company during the past year, giving a special mention to F. A. Inderwick, Q.C., who had worked so hard for the Company in respect of the Government's demand for Passenger Duty.

1. South Eastern Advertiser, Saturday, 20.7.1895.
2. South Eastern Advertiser, Saturday, 3.8.1895.
3. South Eastern Advertiser, Saturday, 10.8.1895.
4. No further action was taken by the Tramway Company in this respect.
5. Mr. John Battam was connected with the Keddle net fishing trade, and he owned and farmed land at Broomhill to the east of Camber.
6. South Eastern Advertiser, Saturday, 2.11.1895.
7. South Eastern Advertiser, Saturday, 14.12.1895.
8. Much of "The Railway World" article of March 1896, was to be repeated in several editions of Messrs. Bagnall's future catalogues.
9. Sussex Express & County Herald, Saturday, 11.4.1896.
10. Sussex Express & County Herald, Saturday, 16.5.1896.
11. South Eastern Adveretiser, Saturday, 30.5.1896.
12. South Eastern Advertiser, Saturday, 8.8.1896.
13. Season Tickets to the value of £57 15s.0d. had been sold during 1896.
14. Sussex Express & County Herald, Saturday, 3.7.1897.
15. Sussex Express & County Herald, Saturday, 7.8.1897.
16. Sussex Express & County Herald, Saturday, 30.10.1897.
17. 44,897 tickets had been issued, suggesting the balance of more than 5,000 journeys by season ticket holders is a slight exaggeration.
18. Quayside
19. South Eastern Advertiser, Saturday, 27.8.1898.
20. South Eastern Advertiser, Saturday, 10.10.1898.
21. Passengers were charged according to their dress, rather than the compartment in which they travelled. See Chapter Thirteen.
22. Walter Dawes could only have been referring to accidents involving passengers.

H. G. Henbrey Secretary
1895

[signature]
1895

[signature]
1908

[signature] Secretary
1908

[signature]
1929

[signature]
1929

1937
[signature]
Secretary.

Chapter Four

A TRANSFER OF OWNERSHIP? (1899-1901)

Throughout the summer of 1899 there had been growing dis-satisfaction at the way in which the Tramway was being run, in particular, condemnation of the way in which passengers were being charged fares according to their assumed "class", which had resulted in a series of un-complimentary letters being published in the local press. [1] Another rumour was that the directors, in an attempt to pay a dividend to their shareholders, intended to close the Tramway between the months of November and March inclusive. Worried that the Tramway might close altogether, several businessmen in the neighbourhood approached John Symonds Vidler (a director of the Tramway Company) stating that, in their opinion, if the undertaking was in the hands of Rye Council, the concern might be placed on a sounder basis. Mr. Symonds Vidler was also the President of the Rye Trade Association, and at their meeting at the George Hotel on Monday, 6th November 1899, he moved the resolution

"...that a committee be appointed to consider the advisability of approaching the Tramway directors with a view of acquiring possession of the Company, if thought desirable, and to memorialise the Town Council to take over the work of the same as from December 31st 1899".

He confirmed that the directors of the Company had intimated to him that they had no objection to bringing this question before the Association, and he believed that they would be willing to consider any favourable scheme that the Trade Association might suggest to them. [2] John Symonds Vidler explained:

"Very good profits are realised during the summer months but afterwards the tram is run only for the benefit of the golfers, the fishermen and the ticket holders. The Tramway Company last year produced a very good balance, although they could not pay a dividend, and this year they will probably be in a similar position. It is thought by some that if the Tramway was in the hands of the Council it could be made to pay. There are two ways in which this could be done. One would be for the Corporation to purchase the concern outright, and to lease it, and to guarantee the pay of it, say at the same amount of interest as they pay in Corporation Bonds, namely 3 per cent. Last year the Company carried some 45,000 passengers, exclusive of season ticket holders, and I think it is essential for us, as businessmen, to see that the Tramway is always kept going as a going concern.

"At the present time the concern is perfectly solvent, has a decent bank balance, and the Tramway is in good working order. But suppose for a moment that this state of affairs does not continue, and that they find themselves in financial difficulties, the concern might then be disposed of to a syndicate of businessmen, whose main object would be to make it a financial success, and with that object in view, would probably run the tram during the summer months because of the good profit to be secured then, and abandon it during the winter.

"I must point out that the tram was principally started by influential golfers who thought more of "pro bono publico" than of the concern proving a good investment. It would be most detrimental to the town if the tram does not run during the five winter months I have referred to. As various criticisms have been made with respect to the manner in which the business is conducted, perhaps in the hands of the Council some means might be devised whereby the interest of the town might be served, and financial success achieved at the same time. Of course, this suggestion, when made, will meet with opposition, but I would take that opportunity to remind them of the extraordinary opposition which was brought to bear against the proposal of building the new Rother Bridge, an opposition in which not only the town shared, but the members of the Town Council. They who at first opposed the matter eventually came round and supported the scheme, which had been a turning point in the commercial history of the town, and added to its prosperity. I therefore move that a Committee be appointed to go thoroughly into the matter, with a view to bringing about the desired result."

Mr. R. Milsom seconded the motion, saying that if the resolution was to be accepted, then the Council would be in the unenviable position of a go-between connecting the directors with the Corporation. He could quite see that it would be most injurous to suspend the running of the tram during the winter, but was of the opinion that the members of the Golf Club should, in those months, pay a higher fare. He could see that there were a number of difficulties in the way, such as whether the majority of the Corporation would be in favour of the purchase, and with regard to the fact that a large portion of the Tramway lay outside the Borough Boundary.

Mr. J. Molyneux Jenkins regretted that there was not a greater attendance of members, for the subject was the most important one they had had for their consideration since the Association had been inaugurated. He was, in the first instance, dead against the proposal, but had to confess that his opposition had somewhat lessened after the lucid and very fair way in which the Chairman had stated the matter. The difficulty with regard to the boundary referred to by Mr. Milsom had also occurred to him, and he doubted whether the Local Government Board would sanction the purchase under such conditions. He thought that the tone of Mr. Vidler's remarks was not very complimentary to the present directorate, and there he was thoroughly at one with him. Mr. Molyneux Jenkins' comment that he believed that if the Council would adopt "anything like up-to-date principles", they could make the Tramway pay, was greeted with applause, and he was sure that the various anomalies could easily be removed. He opinined that the distinction in fares was much too anomalous. Two sisters that he knew, travelling in the same car were charged 4d. and 6d. respectively. and on this account he had many times walked to Camber, not because he begrudged the 6d., but because he did not like the classification idea. He agreed that it would certainly be exceedingly detrimental to the town if the tram did not run in the five winter months, but he could not help thinking that the Golf Club expected a little more from the Company than was their due. It might also be said that the tram was run almost exclusively for the benefit of the golfers and a few fishermen during those five months, and he certainly thought that during that period a higher rate should be charged. It was proposed that they should ask the Corporation for a guarantee of £90 per annum at 3 per cent, but he very much doubted whether they would get any Local Government Board Inspector to recommend the taking over of a non-paying concern and suggested that a sliding scale might be implemented whereby the debenture holders and shareholders might take more or less according to the results.

The President replied that he would not deny that the tram was intended primarily for the benefit of the Golf Club and that he had to state that influential members of the Club came forward and made themselves personally responsible for considerable amounts. At one time they stood to lose no less that £800. Both Messrs. Milsom and Jenkins seemed to think that he had referred to the Tramway as a non-paying concern, but he did not mean to do so. Taking into consideration the amount of wear and tear, they did not think it expedient last year to declare a dividend, and the same course might be adopted at the next annual meeting. Some considerable complaint had been made about the fares charged. He was willing to bear the blame of being the mover of the resolution which had been much criticised by them. In his own opinion, "the golfer and better class passenger" should pay more than the working classes and that was why he had been a supporter of the charging of 6d. and 4d.. The deciding as to who belonged to the working classes and who didn't was a most invidious task, but he considered the principle on which the practise had been based was a right one, and had proved advantageous, although it had not always been judiciously enforced. At the same time, he considered that the Company had done their best. If the Corporation, as some people thought, could place the Tramway on a better footing, he did not think the directors would consider their position was being usurped, but would be ready to listen to any reasonable proposals, and it was with this object in view that he had moved that a Committee of the Association should be

appointed to go thoroughly into the matter. As to the objection regarding a portion of the tramline being outside the Borough, he was assured by a gentleman learned in the law that the obstacle was not insurmountable.

The directors may have not had any objection to the Trade Association discussing the affairs of their Company, but the Mayor, Cuthbert Hayles, and chairman of the Tramway Company, after quietly listening to all that had been said, was not in the least impressed and firmly stated in typical fashion

"As far as I am concerned, I might say that it has nothing whatever to do with the Trade Association whether the directors properly manage the business of the Tramway Company or not. This is a matter which can be gone into by the shareholders at the next annual meeting which will take place about February or March. I am quite prepared to argue the question with them, and possibly to make room for a better man to occupy the position that I do. I am certainly not going to discuss the matter before the Trade Association at this meeting!"

Mr. Molyneux Jenkins said that he would just like to state that his criticism arose entirely out of their President's opening remarks. If the Association recommended the scheme to them, he contended that they had the right to consider whether they had a scheme which could be made to pay or not. The President added that the promoters of the Tramway Company had sent out a very quiet prospectus. They had estimated their receipts at £250 per year, and they had come to six or seven hundreds. The tram had been running for some years, and he knew that the Company was still in a sound financial position. It was for the managers to decide whether they would incur the risk of the tram, as it had done heretofore, running all the year round, or stop for five out of twelve months. After Mr. Molyneux Jenkins' suggestion that perhaps the Golf Club, rather than lose the tramway service, might be willing to subsidise the Company, Mr. Truelove supported the chairman's motion, and the matter was referred to the General Committee.

The South Eastern Advertiser dated 11th November 1899, had this to say in its regular feature headed "Rye Comments":

"The future of the Camber Tramway was again under consideration on Monday, this time by the Trade Association. It is not financially a very flourishing undertaking, but its abandonment, or even its alienation into the hands of an outside Syndicate, would be a very serious loss to the town at large, and to the golf playing community in particular. It is to be hoped, therefore, that the Committee will succeed in finding some means for its preservation. There is undoubtedly room for criticism of the methods by which it is at present operated. The system of collecting fares is probably unique, and is certainly wonderful, but it is rather too hard a task to impose on the discretion of any tram conductor to ask him to estimate the extent of a man's bank balance by the cut of his clothes, and the greater or less remoteness of the last time he shaved. It is quite possible now for a man to ride out to Camber for 4d. as a member of the "lower classes" and be charged 6d. on his return for looking like a gentleman - a state of things which is disturbing to the equilibrium of the social fabric. It is not in these days generally supposed that clothes make the man, but such is certainly the case on the Camber Tramway. The only drawback is that many highly respectable people who could well afford to pay 6d. do not dress up to their character, while, on the other hand, the "working classes" do not always go about in smock frocks or corduroy trousers; and how is the poor conductor to know?

"However, the tramway, besides being a great curiosity in its way, is also a great convenience and the proposal of Captain Vidler who, I believe, though connected with the existing Company, acts entirely on his own responsibility is, at any rate, worthy the consideration the Trade Association's Committee was instructed to give it. Whether it would be advisable for the Council to take over the tramway as Captain Vidler suggests, is a question which can only be answered by going very thoroughly into the matter, and this is a course which a small Committee is much better qualified to take than any public assembly. The present owners have undoubtedly done what lay in their power for the good of the town, but should they be succeeded by an alien Syndicate, the concern is likely to be run with a single eye to profit-making and general disregard of local interests."

One would have thought that Rye was served well enough by the South Eastern Railway's line for passengers wishing to travel along the Sussex and Kent coasts, but a new Company was being promoted under the title of "The Cinque Ports Light Railway" which was to run from Hastings, through Rye, to Ramsgate. Using electric traction, the gauge was to be 3ft.6in. to allow through running over the Corporation Tramways at Dover, and to join up with the Isle of Thanet Electric Tramway and Lighting Company's route then under construction between Ramsgate and Margate. It was proposed to erect a generating station at Rye which would supply the whole of the current between Hastings and Dover.

Mr. Mark Parker, the resident engineer of the Light Railway, was present at Rye Council's meeting on Friday morning, 8th December, to explain the plans of the scheme. He advised that there would be two classes of car and the maximum fare would be 1d. per mile first class, with probably a fare of 1/2d. per mile second class, and the service would run at least half hourly. Between Hastings and Ramsgate the road would be direct with no changing, with the speed "from 25 m.p.h.", but limited to around 8 m.p.h. in towns. After some discussion as to the route that the railway might take through the town, the Mayor's resolution that the plans for this and The East Sussex Light Railway that intended connecting Rye with Northiam on the Kent & East Sussex Railway, should

be considered by a Committee, was carried unanimously.

Despite the Trade Association's suggestion that Rye Corporation should take over the running of the Rye & Camber Tramway from 31st December 1899, the Company entered the 20th century with the original management still in control. There may have been criticism in the way in which the directors had handled some of their Company's affairs in the past, but with none of them having had any previous experience on how to run a tramway, they were having to learn their lesson the hard way - by experience. In all fairness they had always tried to do what they considered to be the best in the interests of the Tramway and the town.

At the Town Council's quarterly meeting held at Rye Town Hall on Friday morning, 9th February 1900, the Railway Committee, after stating that, in their opinion, as both the East Sussex Light Railway and the Cinque Ports Light Railway were likely to be of benefit to the town, no opposition would be offered subject to certain conditions being met. In respect of the latter line they reported as follows:

".... As regards to the approach to the town from the east, we believe that the route suggested from Rye to Lydd is ill-judged. It would lay through an uninhabited district, and over the best and most expensive land in the Marsh, while were the railway to follow the line of the sea coast to Rye Harbour and thence to Rye, not only would the cost be proportionally less, but the want of proper access to the sea from Rye and Lydd would be met. Unless, therefore, the promoters will consent to alter the route as last suggested ..... we recommend that the scheme should be opposed...."

The Mayor, Councillor Frank Jarrett, after explaining the report at some length, proposed its adoption, and this was formally seconded by Councillor W. T. Smith. So, from being of possible benefit to the Tramway, the Cinque Ports Light Railway was fast becoming a serious threat. Councillor Cuthbert Hayles argued that he did not know that the Committee (of which he was a member) had said that there was no proper access to the sea coast from Rye, and sarcastically added that he was sorry that there was no proper access to the sea! The Mayor said that he was under the impression that the report had been submitted to Councillor Hayles for approval, but Cuthbert Hayles answered "It has not as to that part." "I might say", continued the Mayor, "we are deeply indebted to Mr. Hayles and several gentlemen for having proper access to Camber by the tram, but we look forward to going further than that. If we can get access to the whole of the sea coast around to Lydd, so much the better; and I believe it will prove a very great benefit to the town generally." The Town Clerk stated that if Councillor Hayles looked at the report he would find that it had not been altered since he had it, and Councillor Hayles said that he did not suggest that it had, and neither did he think that the Committee went so far as to say that! Cuthbert Hayles' protest was, however, in vain, and the report was carried unanimously.

Only 12 members attended the 7th annual Meeting of the Rye & District Trade Association at the Cinque Ports Hotel on Monday evening, 19th March 1900, where the Committee reported that with regard to their previous proposal that the Town Council should acquire the Rye & Camber Tramway, no definite action had yet been taken, although it was hoped that some useful purpose had been accomplished by initiating the discussion. This was the last that was to be heard of the proposed take-over, and no further moves in that direction were made.

A rumour had reached the Association that the Tram Company had threatened once again not to operate a service during the winter, and after some discussion it was agreed that they should take the initiative and canvass the Golf Club, the proprietors of the Dormy Club, the George Hotel, the Mermaid Inn "and other business concerns which, no doubt, reaped the benefit from the winter traffic" in an effort to raise the £50 subsidy that the president, John Symonds Vidler, thought was necessary to assure continuous running. The rumour was confirmed as fact the following afternoon at the Annual Meeting of the Rye & Camber Tramways Company, held at the George Hotel, when the Directors'

18. CAMBER has pushed both carriages back along the platform to clear the points in preparation for running round her train at the original Camber terminus c. 1901. Her nearside rear spectacle plate appears to be cracked, and why are all three windows of the Rother Ironworks carriage boarded up?

(John Scott-Morgan collection)

19. Soon after her name had disappeared from her side tanks, VICTORIA and her train stand at Rye station. To keep away some of the discomfort of blown sand a metal sheet blocks off the lower portion of the cab opening with a canvas sheet above.

(Colonel Stephens Railway Museum & Archives, Tenterden)

Report was published as follows:

"The Directors beg to present their report for the past year, during which the traffic has been steadily maintained, and the sale of sand increased, but they have to express their regret that, owing to the abnormally large amount expended on repairs, the net profit, including £27 0s.10d. brought forward from the previous year, amounts to but £17 15s.8d. (which sum they propose to write off the construction expense account) thus showing a loss on the year's working.

"The Directors have resolved that, unless a substantial guarantee of subsidy in aid of expenses of running the tram during the winter months be forthcoming, they will, in justice to those who have invested in the Company, be compelled to cease running in future from October to April, though such a step would, no doubt cause serious inconvenience to many people.

By order of the Board, H. G. Henbrey, Secretary."

Receipts for the year had totalled £737 7s.10d., and of this sum fares amounted to £468 2s.11d., the lowest being £17 15s.9d. taken in December, peaking at £89 5s.4d. in August. The chairman, in moving the adoption of the report and balance sheet said the report was short and not very satisfactory. The traffic, taking ordinary fares and season tickets, still kept about where it was last year, and if it had not been for the very large amount spent on repairs, which had amounted to £173 10s.9d., they would have been in a much more satisfactory position, and might have made a dividend. It was a very exposed line, and they were obliged to have engines of small dimensions, because of the funds. The wear and tear was, therefore, considerable. He did not propose to hold out any hopes of a dividend. The repairs during the past year had exceeded the previous year by something like £120, so that they would agree with him that when the report stated they were abnormal, it was only the truth, and he did not suppose that they would be £173 next year. If they were they might as well sell the old engines for what they were worth, and buy some new ones.

The time had come when they, as Directors, felt that they ought to look after the shareholders. It was all very well to run the tram for the benefit of the town, but the people who got the most benefit from it had not supported them. The bulk of the money had been found by a few people, and he did not see why they should keep on finding the money. They had only a leasehold interest and the debentures were running out and he did not know whether they would get them renewed or not. They, therefore, told them in the report that unless someone was prepared to reimburse the Company for the cost of running the tram in the winter they, as Directors, were not prepared to do so. They would run it in the summer time when it did pay, and the people would have to put up with the inconvenience in the winter. It might come as a shock to some people, but it could not be helped. There were towns in this and other countries where they only carried on business during the profitable season, and they must do the same.

Joseph Adams seconded the adoption of the report and remarked that they did not want a big dividend; what they wanted was to put the affair on a sound basis. Mr. R. Milsom said he noticed that the takings, including season tickets, were £25 less than they were the previous year, yet the passenger duty was more at £30 2s.0d., but Cuthbert Hayles advised that if the takings for parcels were added, they were about £5 less than in the previous year. Alderman John Neve Masters asked if any calculation as to what would be saved by not running four months of the year had been made, to which the chairman replied "We would save half wages and half coal." Alderman Masters disagreed. "Not in four months! We may find ourselves no better off by not running!" The chairman corrected him, stating that the Tramway would be closed for five months probably, and there would be the saving of wages and coal. Alderman Masters said they would take £120 less and asked what would be knocked off, and Mr. Hayles repeated again "Half wages, coal, stores and repairs."

Councillor Frank Jarrett added:

"I feel in the interests of the town that it would be a great disadvantage to them if the tram ceased running. If I can be of any assistance myself in trying to raise the subsidy, if it was absolutely necessary, I would be glad to do so. We have now a good connection of golfers who come to Rye, and the tram is most essential to them in the winter months - during which most of the golfers come - I am convinced it would be to the detriment of the town. I myself am prepared to subscribe to the subsidy, and I think many other gentlemen in the town would do the same. I am very anxious that it should not cease running, and sincerely hope that it will not do so. If the Golf Club was approached they might pay some portion of it. You do not say what amount is required, but I know you will not be exacting. I think the shareholders are satisfied with what the directors have done. There are several gentlemen in the town who reap a great benefit from the tram, and do not contribute a penny towards it. If they can get at those men, it will be a good thing. I will be glad to do anything to raise a fund."

Along with the announcement that "on Good Friday the trams will run as on Sunday" the South Eastern Advertiser on Saturday, 14th April 1900 advised:

"The directors of the (Tramway) Company have at last adopted what seems to us a sensible arrangement as to fares. They are now charging First, Second and Third Class Fares and this should do away with all the un-pleasantness, and secure the genial support of the public."

Councillor Frank Jarrett wasted little time in contacting the various establishments asking them for a contribution towards the defecit that would be incurred by the running of the tram during the winter. At the Golf Club's meeting on 5th May 1900, the Chairman stated that he had seen the Mayor on the subject, and in the event of a substantial sum being subscribed by the town towards the £50 asked for, the Golf Club *might* be willing to pay something by way of a guarantee against the loss by the shareholders. The committee, after discussion, resolved to postpone action until a further letter had been received from the Mayor. [3] All through the summer Councillor Jarrett worked on raising the subsidy, and gained promises to the account of just under £30, but he had to admit that there were still many who benefited by the tram and the presence of golfers who did not contribute. As late as 6th October, with rumours that the Tramway service might still be suspended, the South Eastern Advertiser on sale that day asked

> "Is it true that the directors have decided to stop the running of the trams during the ensuing winter months? Surely that would be suicide in the interest of all concerned as the best season for golfers at the Camber Links is now coming on, and we do not want to see them driven away from the town for want of means by which to reach the links. Other places are bidding hard for them, and Ryers must not be surprised if, through a short-sighted policy, the Club should be considerably reduced. We have not heard the result on the Mayor's canvass of the tradespeople. Perhaps that may show some light on the subject."

Unbeknown to them, the newspaper's question was answered that very afternoon when, in response to the Mayor's second letter to them, the Golf Club agreed that they should make up the amount of the subsidy to £50, on the undertaking that the Tramway Company would run a number of trams specifically for the Golf Club. [4] In the nick of time the Tram was kept running, for the forthcoming winter, at least!

"Fairly satisfactory" was the directors' description of 1900, and although there had been a slight decrease in passenger traffic receipts, over 40,000 passengers had been carried in addition to season ticket holders, but this fell well short of the 44,887 passengers carried in 1896, their first full year. The accounts showed a net profit of £41, and the directors recommended the declaration of a dividend of 1.25 per cent, the first in four years, and that £21 2s.0d. (being £19 8s.10d. for the past year and £1 13s.2d. balance from the year 1899) be written off against the construction expense account, with the balance to be carried forward. To achieve this profit, expenses had been greatly reduced, but against these the price of coal had increased dramatically from £73 in 1899 to £148 - more than double! Even at these exorbitant prices, much of the coal had been of very poor quality, but this had been a problem for other railway companies as well. Fares over the year amounted to £425 1s.3d., the highest monthly sum again being August at £80 0s.7d. and the lowest £15 5s.0d. in February. Revenue from season tickets added a further £90 15s.6d..

After four years at the George Hotel, the venue for the Annual General Meeting, which took place on the morning of Monday, 4th March 1901, was changed back to the Cinque Ports Arms Hotel in Rye. The Chairman, commenting that it was the first time in four years that

they had had a dividend, said that it was so very small that he did not know that they could congratulate themselves upon it! He advised that the Company was a little bit to the good of last year and that the repairs had been much reduced. The engines and cars were in as good condition as could be expected after a lot of running, and it was their policy to keep them in such a state as to be able to carry the number of passengers required. Although they had a dividend this year, they would want a guarantee next winter. There was no doubt that they could not run at a profit in the winter without, and in the interests of the shareholders, there was no reason why they should run at a loss.

The Mayor, speaking as to the subsidy, said that he had had great pleasure in collecting the £30, and was much obliged to the gentlemen who had rallied round him. He was glad to have been instrumental in raising the guarantee and felt there was a good field for anyone with energy who followed him. It had not altogether been a pleasant task to undertake, but he did it purely and simply in the interests of the town. He hoped that someone would come forward to do the same again, and he would give them all the information in his possession. He was glad to see the balance sheet so satisfactory, and that it might have even shown a good balance had it not been for the increased expenditure on coal.

Alderman Masters said that he had been in conversation with Mr. Holman Fred Stephens and believed that his election to the Board of Directors would be "a decided acquisition". Since completing the Rye & Camber Tramway, Mr. Stephens had gone on to build the Hundred of Manhood and Selsey Tramway in West Sussex, the Rother Valley Railway, which ran from Robertsbridge to Tenterden, and was currently working on the Sheppey Light Railway that would connect Queensborough with Leysdown. Mr. John Symonds Vidler proposed Mr. Stephens "as he had experience in the plant and would be able to help us in many ways", and Alderman Masters seconded, moving that the Mayor, Councillor Frank Jarrett, filled the other vacancy. Walter Dawes seconded the Mayor and both gentlemen were elected as directors, Councillor Jarrett promising to attend as many meetings as possible, bearing in mind that in his position, he had many calls upon his time.

The following Saturday, 9th March, the South Eastern Advertiser wrote in its regular "Rye Comments" feature:

> "As our readers are probably aware, the directors of the Rye & Camber Tramway had not for several years been enabled to present their shareholders with a dividend. Now, happily, they find themselves in a position to do so. I should be glad to see the concern on a firmer basis in regard to the winter traffic. It was only by the energy and public spirit of the Mayor and other gentlemen, who raised a guarantee of £50, that the cars were kept running during the bad, cold weather season. The heartfelt thanks of all are, in my opinion, due to his Worship for averting what would have been little short of a disaster to the town. The trams, as everyone is aware, run to the Golf Links and

20. VICTORIA makes a fine smoke screen with the aid of a strong south-westerly wind as she curves with her train away from the Golf Course beside "Golf View" in this image enhanced postcard from around the turn of the century. Beyond the house the line falls at 1 in 160 for 16 chains onto the lower level of Northpoint Beach. Along with the brake handle on the dash of the First Class balcony of the Bagnall carriage, it is just possible to make out the full length footboard and brass handrail fitted above the windows of each carriage to enable the conductor to collect fares from passengers en route.

(Lens of Sutton)

Rye & Camber Tram, passing Golf View, Sussex.

21. Postcard by Whiteman's of Rye entitled "Camber and Rye Harbour" with the original Camber station in the centre. The view was taken before the extension to Camber Sands was constructed in 1908, and prominent in the foreground is the 1898 extension of the line beyond the station into the sand hills. On the far left is the harbourmaster's house with, beyond it across the River Rother, the village of Rye Harbour, whilst in the centre (above the station roof) is Rye Chemical Works, and to the right, amidst the ships' rigging, the town of Rye rises on its hill. The South Eastern Railway's siding looks busy with 3 rakes of loaded wagons awaiting collection, and the shipping mast beside Camber station displays two "balls" advising shipping that the river is 9ft. deep. *(L. Bearman collection)*

CAMBER AND RYE HARBOUR

22. An excellent view of VICTORIA (contrary to the name crudely added to the locomotive's side by the publisher of the postcard) at Camber c. 1902. With the wooden panelling and the adjacent central pair of windows removed in hot weather, a canvas screen would be attached to the three lugs on the cant rail, and tied to the horizontal rail fitted to this side of the Bagnall carriage to keep the discomfort of blown sand off of the passengers; the other side would remain open. The previously fixed widow on either side of the Rother Ironworks carriage furthest from the balcony was re-built during the winter of 1901/2 complete with an adjustable leather strap as used on mainline coaching stock at the time, and is shown in its open position. Faggoting, to help protect the embankment from high tides, is now in position.

(Laurie Band collection, courtesy of Rye Museum)

CAMBER

RYE AND CAMBER, TRAM

the Harbour and if they failed it would mean a considerable loss to the borough. I am sorry to say that the Committee will require a fresh guarantee for next winter, but I trust that, after the fine example shown by the Mayor, the directors will experience no difficulty in finding gentlemen with public spirit enough to make a slight sacrifice in the interests of old Rye."

On the morning of Tuesday, 11th March, the Tramway's engineer, Holman Stephens was in Rye to put his case for the construction of the standard gauge East Sussex Light Railway to the Light Railway Commissioners at Rye Town Hall. Mr. Stephens was to be the engineer of the proposed new line and other familiar names present included Councillor Cuthbert Hayles, speaking on behalf of the promoters (Messrs. Selmes and Neve) and Walter Dawes, who was the representative of Rye Town Council. After listening to all of the evidence for and against the scheme, the Commissioners confirmed that they were impressed with the fact that there were three lines [5] in comparatively small districts, each in different hands, but that they would like to see the management joined. Cuthbert Hayles told them that during the last few days a letter had been addressed to the Commissioners on behalf of the Rye & Camber Tramways Company, who were quite willing to be joined in the Order if possible. Closing the enquiry after almost $2^{1}/_{2}$ hours, the Commissioners confirmed that they were of the opinion that the proposed line would be of benefit to the district, and that they were prepared to recommend that the Light Railway Order be granted.

It must have come as a great relief to the Tramway Company that the ambitious Cinque Ports Light Railway was to get no further than the planning stages, but although the East Sussex Light Railway received its Light Railway Order, it was to struggle in vain for 13 years to become a reality, before the First World War finally brought an end to the dream of connecting Northiam and Rye direct by rail.

The removal of sand from the sand hills may have been a profitable sideline for the struggling Tramway, but it was beginning to cause increased aggravation to the Golf Club, so much so that on 16th March, their secretary wrote to them advising that "they would be held responsible for sand blown over the course at the 4th hole, and that they would be called upon to pay any expense incurred in turfing etc., as such blown sand was caused by excavation made by the Tramway Company." [6] Whether or not any notice was taken of the letter is not recorded, but of more importance, the Golf Club's share of the subsidy for winter running remained outstanding, and it was not until 13th April that their cheque for £20 was drawn in favour of the Rye & Camber Tramway. [7]

In April it had been announced in the local press that a third class car had again commenced running at 2d. single fare and 4d. return, with children under the age of 12 enjoying the return journey for the single fare, suggesting that the Bagnall carriage had maintained the service alone throughout the winter. The summer season was hardly under way when the Sussex Express & County Herald dated 24th May 1901, reported under the heading "BAD FOR THE COO":

"Stephenson's celebrated saying, in the early days of steam engines, was verified on Monday on the Rye & Camber Tramway, when a yearling heifer belonging to Mr. E. Ney collided with the engine and received injuries so serious that its decease had to be hastened. Whether or no (sic) the directors at the next annual meeting will recommend the addition of a "cow-catcher" to the rolling stock remains to be seen".

There is no mention as to which of the two locomotives was involved, but could this accident have been the cause of the dent in CAMBER's left hand cylinder casing?

Holman Stephens was deservedly proud of his work and had always been keen that his parents should visit and travel on his railways. On 19th August he wrote to them ".... If you and mam (sic) care to do so when you get back, I shall be delighted to take you over the Chichester, the Rye, the Rother and Sheppey lines...." but then added modestly ".... I am afraid, however, you will be disappointed as they are not great works at all!"

After a poor start during the first few months of the year, passenger traffic picked up well on the Tramway during the summer, and brought in a record £103 during August, despite a wet and miserable Bank Holiday weekend, an amount never approached in any month of the Company's history. In the autumn, with receipts beginning to fall in the now all too familiar pattern, the secretary, H. G. Henbrey, wrote to the Golf Club stating that the Directors had decided to close the tram during the winter months unless a subsidy of at least £25 was forthcoming. The letter was discussed at the Golf Club's meeting on 19th October, but after one of the Tramway's Directors, F. A. Inderwick, Q.C., had explained the position of the Company, it was proposed that a sum not exceeding £10 should be forwarded. [8]

Although the supply of sand and shingle between Rye Harbour and Dover had been transferred from sea to rail some two years earlier, sand traffic still formed an important part of the Tramway's income, and in December the Company applied for a small extra triangle of land adjoining their station at Rye on which to construct a siding from where they could sell sand to local builders. At Rye Town Council's meeting on Wednesday, 11th December, they agreed to lease "about 15 rods" at the rate of 10/- per year, the lease to end at the same time as the rest of the land already leased.

1. South Eastern Advertiser, Saturdays 12.8.1899, 19.8.1899 and 26.8.1899. See also Chapter 13, "Timetables, Fares and Tickets".
2. It should be noted that of the 14 members present, at least 9 of them were either directors or shareholders of the Tramway Company.
3. Rye Golf Club Minute Book 5.5.1900.
4. Rye Golf Club Minute Book 6.10.1900.
5. The Rye & Camber Tramway, The Rother Valley Railway and the proposed East Sussex Light Railway of which Holman Stephens was (or would have been) the engineer.
6. Rye Golf Club Minute Book 16.3.1901.
7. Rye Golf Club Board of Management Minute Book 13.4.1901.
8. Rye Golf Club Minute Book 19.10.1901.

Chapter Five

GROWING PAINS (1902-1908)

At the Annual General Meeting held at the Cinque Ports Arms Hotel on the afternoon of Tuesday, 27th February 1902, the Directors' Report was read as follows:

"In presenting their report the Directors are pleased to be able to state that the passenger traffic has been more than maintained, the receipts from that source showing an increase on 1900 of £4 11s.0d.. The net profit, after writing off £19 8s.10d. off the construction expense account, amounts to £62 4s.11d., and the Directors recommend the payment of a dividend of 2 per cent, free of income tax, the addition of £5 10s.10d. to the reserve fund, and that the balance be carried forward. The advisability of extending the line about 750 yards, so as to reach the usual summer bathing place has been considered by the Directors, and a proposition will be made to the meeting favouring the extension, providing the necessary funds can be raised."

The chairman, Cuthbert Hayles, explained that, whereas profits had been increased, expenses remained very high with the little engines needing constant repair and labour. Repairs had totalled £117 5s.3d. compared with £56 the year before, but as Joseph Adams noted, "a car had been done up and re-decorated" and this had been included in the figures. Wages for the past year had totalled £242, but Councillor Kingsnorth Reeve thought that this was a very heavy amount, "pretty well equal to five men on". The chairman confirmed that the figure included everyone except the secretary, and that four men were constantly engaged, and their own men employed in moving sand were also to be included. The engine driver received 38 shillings per week and, being a fitter, did a certain amount of repair work as well. Mr. G. W. Strick asked if they did not think the repairs ought to be smaller if they had a fitter, and Mr. Hayles agreed, but he did not know how to make them so. Councillor Kingsnorth Reeve enquired if anything special had been done in the way of repairs and the chairman, to much amusement, said he believed that the engine (sic) had been turned inside out. "It must be outside in now!" Councillor Kingsnorth Reeve wittily suggested!

A lengthy discussion then ensued following Councillor F. H. Chapman's comment that they ought not to pay a dividend out of the £35 subsidy which had been given to keep the trams running. The Mayor replied

"As one who partly instituted the subsidy to the Company, I would like to explain that the town received a notice from the Tram Company to say that unless able to pay a profit to their shareholders, they would discontinue running the tram in the winter. The Company was losing so much money by running in the winter which prevented their paying a dividend, and they appealed to gentlemen staying in the town, and to the town, to try and raise a subsidy to induce the Company to run the trams in the winter, as they knew it was beneficial to the town. It was quite understood this amount of money was to go to the Tram Company to enable them to run their trams, and make them pay in the winter. What the Tram Company was going to do with regard to a dividend I do not think was mentioned. The Company only make a profit in the summer, and the subsidy was to induce them to run in the winter when, with the fares and the small subsidy, it about paid. Any profit they make is secured in the summer."

Cuthbert Hayles agreed that that was the position as far as he understood it, but Mr. Chapman said that his recollection did not tally with that of the Mayor. He did not understand that the subsidy was in order to pay a dividend to the shareholders. "Neither is it!" exclaimed Joseph Adams. Mr. Chapman admitted that it was broad as it was long as they were practically paying dividend out of subsidy. Joseph Adams stated that they would not have run the trams in the winter at a loss, and that it was simply a matter for the townspeople apart from the directors and shareholders. The chairman pointed out that the books were always open to the inspection of the shareholders, and from them was the place to get information, rather than by questions at the annual meeting. He found it curious that a shareholder should object to receiving a dividend. It had been decided and supported by a general meeting that they would not run the tram in the winter unless there was a subsidy, and the subsidy helped to pay the loss, not to pay a dividend. Mr. Adams concluded that it was a pure and simple question; if the townspeople wanted trams run in the winter, they had a right to call upon them to pay for it.

As briefly mentioned in the Directors' Report, there was a far more important subject to discuss than how the subsidy should be spent, and that was the proposal that the line be extended 800 yards at an estimated cost of between £400 and £450, provided the necessary funds could be raised by the issue of ordinary shares or debentures. The chairman told the meeting that they had already received an intimation that if the tram stopped where it did, their sand trade (from which a very considerable profit was derived) would come to a standstill. Referring to the earlier complaint from Rye Golf Club, he admitted that the sand drifted in other people's way, but with the extension they would open up a fresh field. Apart from that, many of the people who came down in the summer and swelled their receipts bringing children with them, found the tram did not take them anything like far enough to the usual bathing place. They had to walk some distance over the sand,

and they might think that they might as well walk the whole way. There were also people who rode bicycles in this world (laughter) and if they took the line further along, those people would be more inclined to come by the tram than at present. From his own house in Camber he could cycle to Rye in less time than he could walk to the terminus and come by the tram. If the tram went half a mile further along, he thought that people would derive a benefit from it, and it would be an incentive to excursion traffic. When people heard that it was extended, they would naturally come to see what had been done.

It would not go quite as far as the Coastguard station, but would go about 880 yards from the present station. Everything depended on the money, and unless the funds could be raised the further line would not be constructed. The estimated cost had worked out at £449, but that included a considerable sum for contingencies and some works that he did not think would be constructed, in the nature of a shelter. He believed they would simply have a platform, at all events, however, not so elaborate a shelter as provided in the estimate. He thought that £400, or a little over, would cover the entire cost.

Asked what prospect there was of increased revenue, Cuthbert Hayles said that they proposed to charge 3d. instead of 2d., so that revenue might be increased by some £30 to £40 during the summer. Mr. Kingsnorth Reeve then asked if there was any question regarding the passenger duty if they extended and did not charge an extra fare. The chairman explained that if this was the case, they would certainly save a certain amount of passenger duty, but Mr. Milsom warned that they would not get sand at increased revenue, but as maintained revenue. Joseph Adams was dubious of success, and thought there would be great difficulty experienced with sand in the machinery. Mr. G. Henbrey thought that if they extended for the sand trade only, it would be a very poor outlook, and that they would be greatly deceived in the expected increase of revenue from fares. Mr. Chapman asked if John Symonds Vidler (who had sent apologies for absence as he was unavoidably detained in London on business) was in favour of the extension, to which the chairman answered in the affirmative. Mr. Adams said he was surprised at the number of people Mr. Vidler had quoted as complaining of the distance of the present terminus from the bathing place, but he himself would not vote for or against, merely pointing out the great difficulty he thought would be experienced.

Mr. C. Ashton Selmes, whose opinion was next invited, confirmed that he had viewed the site of the extension the previous Sunday with the secretary at the request of Mr. Vidler, who was the prime mover in the project. He explained that the proposed extension would skirt the western corner of Mr. Longley's building, and with as wide a curve as they could get, go along the lower part of the sand hills, where the best footing could be got. However, whatever they did to make the line, they would have a great deal more sand than was

pleasant and conducive to the good working of machinery. He candidly thought that the line could be very inexpensively laid by their own men, but whether it would compensate for the extra wear and tear to the rolling stock he was not prepared to say. Unfortunately, on being put to the vote, only the chairman and the Mayor voted in favour of the scheme, with Messrs. G. Henbrey, Kingsnorth Reeve and Strick against, the rest remaining neutral.

Cuthbert Hayles warned "You'll hear more of it later on!"

Mr. Chapman: "What, when it has been lost?"

Mr. Hayles: "If the directors decide to go on, you will receive a circular. I do not say what will be upon it. So far as this meeting is concerned, the proposal is lost." [1]

Rather than being put off by the lack of support from the shareholders, the directors tried to raise the necessary capital themselves, but they were unable to obtain sufficient offers, and were forced to abandon the idea, at least for the time being.

Throughout the summer traffic remained steady, but income from season tickets dropped considerably. In September, H. G. Henbrey wrote a letter to the Golf Club stating "The directors intend to discontinue the running of trams in the five winter months unless a sufficient subsidy is forthcoming", and once again the Club resolved to guarantee a sum not exceeding £10. [2]

Mr. Henbrey was soon to move away from Rye to Tunbridge Wells, and the news of his departure was received "with very much regret" at the Tramway Company's Annual General Meeting held on the afternoon of Tuesday, 24th February 1903. Cuthbert Hayles said he had proved most able and energetic, and he very much doubted if his successor would give as much time to the work as he had done. The Directors' Report showed that the profit and loss account, after writing £19 18s.10d. off the construction expense account, had a balance of £59 18s.4d. and they recommended, for the second year running, a dividend of 2 per cent. Mr. Hayles said he appreciated that the dividend was not large, but it was better than nothing, and he did not know how it could be increased unless they could find a way to lessen the cost of repairs. Confirming that the directors still considered the extension desirable, he thought a half mile additional length of line would prove a considerable source of revenue and (contrary to what had been suggested at the A.G.M. the year before) that they would do away with a large portion of passenger duty by carrying passengers the increased distance by the same fare. He knew he was expressing the opinion of his co-directors, and if the general meeting endorsed the view and supported it by taking shares, the work would be done. Councillor Kingsnorth Reeve argued that the proposed extension had been thrashed out at the last meeting, and the figures then given did not show much profit on sand. They could only pay 2 per cent, and with no extra charge for fares, they would have to depend entirely on the profits of the sand business to pay any dividend on the

23. CAMBER and her train at Rye station in the early 1900s with conductor Frederick Sheppard and the driver is possibly Arthur Withers. Only one lamp is provided on the roof of the Bagnall carriage, which must have left the interior of the second class compartment very gloomy although, on this occasion, the "wooden windows" are only fitted to the western side. One of the fixed windows of the First Class compartment appears to be missing, but in readiness for inclement weather, one of the lugs that carries the rail to hold the canvas screen has been moved to that end of the vehicle, leaving a hole marking its original position. The Company's row-boat permanent way trolley stands centre stage in front of the Rother Ironworks carriage beside the run-round loop. *(Blanche Rhodes collection, courtesy of Peter A. Harding).*

24. CAMBER shrieks a warning whistle as she reverses onto the run-round loop to run round her train at Rye soon after her major overhaul of 1907. A grimy canvas sheet has been fitted over the cab opening in an attempt to keep out some of the draught. The brake handle on the balcony and the oil lamp on the roof of the Rother Ironworks carriage are prominent, and it will be seen that, as on the Bagnall carriage, the door to the saloon opens towards the platform. Note the backward "S" in "Station" on this postcard, the original of which is postmarked 18th July 1910.

(R. Clark collection)

extra capital which would have to be raised for the extension. He was still against it, as was Mr. T. G. Sharpe who, once again, stressed that the blowing of sand into the engine on the extension would greatly increase the cost of repairs.

Alderman John Neve Masters advised that the sand and parcels traffic formed an important part of their business, and quoted figures for the past $7^1/_2$ years showing that out of an average income of £600 per year, repairs averaged £120 annually. Walter Dawes added that he, like others, was glad to receive a dividend, but he questioned whether it was wise to declare it with no reserve fund for depreciation, to which the chairman replied that the matter had been considered by the directors. Cuthbert Hayles welcomed Mr. E. H. Hunnisett to the Board, where it was felt his experience "on a rather larger line than theirs" would benefit the Company. [3] Mr. Hunnisett had been asked to accept the office consequent upon the change in the secretaryship, and on account of the time that he had on his hands, and he had agreed to act as the Managing Director of the Company. The appointment would give him a closer insight into the work, and he would give them the benefit of his experience elsewhere. He declined to accept any remuneration for his services, neither would he hear of any bonus.

Two nominations were received for the vacant post of secretary. Alderman John Neve Masters proposed Mr. G. W. Strick in complimentary terms, and Mr. T. G. Sharpe proposed Mr. W. Jeffery. Mr. Hayles said that as Mr. Dawes had seconded his Clerk, he had better follow suit and second his! Both contenders received 7 votes each, and after much joking among those present, the chairman gave his vote in favour of Mr. Jeffery, but with more than the five necessary rising to demand a poll, it was arranged that this should take place at the Cinque Ports Arms Hotel between 11 a.m. and 12.30 p.m. that Friday, 27th February. Mr. T. G. Sharpe and Mr. G. W. Strick were re-elected as auditors, it being understood that if Mr. Strick was successful in his secretarial candidature, he would resign his auditorship which, in fact he had to do, as he received 120 votes compared with 58 in favour of Mr. Jeffery.

All was not well regarding the removal of sand at the southern terminus, and the secretary of Rye Golf Club was instructed to ask the Tramway to plant bents [4] on the ground adjoining the Camber section to counteract the damage being caused [5] and a month later he was further asked to ensure that "no sand was removed by the Tramway Company from any place not authorised or arranged upon with the Landlord's Trustees". [6]

At the beginning of July the new Tramway Company secretary, G. W. Strick, wrote what had now become an annual letter to the Golf Club stating that the tram would not be run during the forthcoming winter months unless a subsidy of £50 was granted! It would appear that the Mayor of Rye, Doctor E. W. Skinner, had informed the Golf Club that in the event of their finding £20 towards the sum, he would guarantee to find the remainder and, after some discussion, it was unanimously decided to accept the Mayor's kind offer. [7] Meanwhile, the Golf Club had written a letter to the Tramway Company asking what reduction could be made on fares for those men who worked on the Golf Course and lived in Rye, pointing out that the usual subsidy granted by the Club should be taken into consideration when fixing their reduction. [8] It seems doubtful that the request was met because, after discussing the Tramway Company's reply, (the contents of the letter being un-recorded) it was resolved "to take no further steps in the matter at present". [9]

On Saturday, 12th September 1903 the following report appeared in the Sussex Express & County Herald:

THE RYE & CAMBER TRAMWAY

"It will be with feelings of great regret that Rye people will hear of the decision of the directors of the Rye & Camber Tramway Company not to run their cars over the line from October through the winter months until April next unless they receive a subsidy from the townspeople. Since its opening some six years ago the tramway has been a great boon to those townspeople who desire to reach the Harbour and Camber, and more especially to those who are devoted to the "Royal and ancient" game of golf, and though the tramway has not been so well patronised in the winter as in the summer, still that is when it has been of the greatest service to those desiring to travel from Rye to Camber or vice versa, for in the summer the journey is a pleasant walk, whereas in the winter the conditions are considerably altered. It is stated that in the past years the Golf Club to some extent subsidised the Company, but their support has been growing less, and it is stated that the directors do not see any prospect of making any profit by continuing the service during the winter months. According to Mr. G. W. Strick, the Secretary of the Company, it is estimated that the cost of continuing the service from October to April will be £166, whilst the receipts are only estimated at £115, and whereas if the service were discontinued from October a very fair dividend could be paid to the shareholders; if the service was continued through the winter it is anticipated that the dividend would be sadly curtailed. Under these cirumstances one can hardly be surprised at the decision of the directors, though they may regret the circumstances which lead to that decision. Of course it will be a great inconvenience to the public, and will also be awkward for the employes (sic) of the Company, but a way may be found out of the difficulty, and it may be found possible to subsidise the Company. We confess we cannot see quite what body could undertake to do this, with the exception of the Golf Club, who are undoubtedly the parties most benefited by the tram service, but £50 is a large sum to raise. The Company, we understand, are, however, only desirous of running the trams without loss and are prepared, should the receipts show an improvement upon the figures estimated, to return any profit made to the body

25. Other than the Golf Course, coastguard cottages, the lifeboat station and a few cottages, there was little else at Camber in the early 1900s.
(Laurie Band collection, courtesy of Rye Museum)

giving the subsidy. This is a fair offer, but we have very little hope of seeing it accepted."

So why was it, that after arrangements had supposedly been made back in July between the Mayor of Rye and the Golf Club to pay the required subsidy of £50, that the Tramway Company had decided that they would have to close their line that winter? Was there a clue in the remark regarding the Golf Club that "there support has been growing less" and they had opted out of paying their share? At the same time, it seems unlikely that the Mayor had had a change of heart when one reads the follow-up report in the Sussex Express & County Herald dated Saturday, 10th December:

"Some weeks ago we announced the decision of the directors of the Rye & Camber Tramway not to run their steam cars throughout the winter months unless they received a subsidy of £50 to enable them to recoup themselves for the loss which would be thus involved. Since then the matter has been put before the various clubs in the town, with the result that at a meeting of the directors on Saturday the secretary was able to state that the Golf, Mermaid and Dormy Clubs had guaranteed to pay two-thirds of the amount required, whilst the Mayor (Doctor Skinner) had guaranteed the other third. Accordingly the trams will continue to run as hitherto, and the Mayor's generous action will earn the gratitude of the townspeople, who will thus be enabled to easily reach the sea throughout the winter, whilst it will be an equal boon to the residents of the Harbour. The

Mayor's action is not, however, without precedent, for in 1900 the then Mayor (Ald. F. Jarrett) benefited the town in similar manner."

Just two days after the above report was published, Rye Golf Club forwarded a cheque value £10 to the Tram Company. [10] There is nothing to confirm that this was, in fact, their contribution towards the subsidy, but it does seem more than likely, and thanks to the generous offers of those other establishments in the town, the Golf Club would appear to have halved the amount that they had originally offered to pay to keep the trams running!

Despite a particularly wet summer and autumn, 1903 turned out to be a surprisingly successful year, resulting in a net profit of £154 1s.2d.. 44,888 tickets had been issued, with takings for August alone approaching £90, but many of the passengers carried during the summer months were holidaymakers rather than locals.

There was growing dissatisfaction with the unpunctuality of the tram service, in particular the 3.35 p.m. departure from Camber which rarely left on time. The delay was possibly caused by adding trucks loaded with sand onto the rear of the train within the five minutes turn round time advertised. The Golf Club found it necessary to complain and also requested that the 4.50 p.m. tram be run at 5.00 p.m. instead. [11] Seemingly always willing to oblige, the Tramway Company acceded to the Golf Club's request, and commencing with the March 1904 timetable, weekday departures from Camber had been amended to 3.40 p.m.

and 5.00 p.m..

Not all late running could be attributed to the Tramway Company. The 10.00 a.m. Sunday service from Rye was run mainly for those golfers wishing to spend a full day on the links, but with some club members in no hurry to commence their game, they were inclined to dawdle down the hill from the Dormy Club [12] where they had spent the night. On many occasions, much to the delight of those already on the tram, the engine driver would sound his whistle in advance of the advertised departure time as if the train was about to start, in an attempt to hurry the stragglers along! Such tactics, however, would have no effect on Captain R. Dacre Vincent, who had been appointed honorary secretary of the Golf Club on 10th September 1898. Many a time a tram with a full complement of golfers would be kept patiently waiting at Camber station as he walked un-hurried across the 15th and 13th fairways from the Club House, knowing full well "that no tram would be guilty of the blasphemy of leaving him behind". [13]

Proposing the adoption of the Directors' Report at the Annual General Meeting on Friday, 10th February 1904, the chairman made allusion to the increased prosperity of the Company, stating that this was the first occasion that they had paid a dividend of 3 per cent since the first year of the Company's existence. Mr. Hunnisett's experience of railway work had stood them in good stead, as from him a good deal of assistance in the management of the line had been forthcoming. Cuthbert hayles advised that £25 was to be added to the reserve fund, and then drew attention to the fact that the liability of the Company on debentures had been reduced by £50, and that it was hoped that in the course of the next few years, they might be able to discharge the whole of their liability.

The subject of extending the line was once more brought up, this time by Mr. John Neve Masters, who spoke strongly in favour of the scheme, and John Symonds Vidler took the opportunity to suggest that such an extension would be "one of the finest things ever done for Rye"! In his opinion, it would make the town into a watering place, a designation they could hardly give it at the present time!

Under its regular column "Rye Comments", the South Eastern Advertiser wrote in typical flowery style the following day:

"Poor though the past summer proved to many people, the uncertain weather uniting with other causes to unsettle trade, upsetting calculations and decreasing the amount of business done, it was a highly satisfactory twelve months for the Company possessing the proprietary interests in the miniature railway at Rye. For the Rye & Camber Tramways Company the past year was a very popular one. For the first time since the initial year of the Company's existence the Directors have recommended a dividend of three per cent, free of income tax. A worse summer for such a venture as the tramway could hardly be experienced (so far as the weather goes) than that of last year and the Company's

receipts are almost entirely dependent on the weather. There are, of course, people who use the line regularly wet or fine, but the majority of passengers are "fair weather friends", and when it is wet and dismal a trip to Camber has no charm for these. It is the more encouraging, therefore, that the receipts during the past summer were so good.

"It is a pity that the line is not further extended. The Directors are quite agreed that an extension is the proper thing. They have, once again, virtually reiterated that opinion through the medium of the Chairman of the Company (Mr. Hayles), but it really seems that if the project ever is to be accomplished they will have to make a bold bid for it without further parley. The way is beset by financial thorns doubtless, but thorns in one's path have to be cleared away. Some say that our difficulties confront us in order that we may surmount them, and if the tram line is to be carried along the coast to bring the Camber sands within easy distance, a determined attack will have to be made upon the obstacles which block the way. Harvest can never be reaped till after seed time, and the Directors will never see their exchequer swelled by a greatly increased number of passengers until they have made it thoroughly worth while to patronise the line. Were passengers deposited in the near vicinity of the Coastguard Station, or at some other spot in the neighbourhood, and the present fatiguing walk rendered un-necessary, it is probable that the line would be used by a far larger number of people during the summer months. Bleak and altogether forsaken though Camber be in the winter, there is no denying that it is a charming place in the "kinder season", but even then the visitor does not care to go too often, under present conditions, for at the best of times, it is an altogether tiring venture."

Another meeting of the Rye & Camber Tramways Company was arranged to take place at the Cinque Ports Arms Hotel on Friday, 4th March, when further consideration was given to extending the line onto the sands at Camber. The subject was again introduced by John Neve Masters who thought that the extension would not only prove serviceable to people in Rye, but those living in the villages in the vicinity would find the additional facility for a visit to the sands especially advantageous. Mr. R. H. Hunnisett, the Managing Director, advised that if they wished to continue their sand traffic, which realised £25 per year, they must extend the line, but he did not think it was necessary to build a station, and that a platform was all that was needed. Mr. Kingsnorth Reeve suggested that they might not be allowed to touch the sand banks, and Walter Dawes was of the opinion that the Level Commissioners would not allow sand to be taken from the sea defences, but it was pointed out that as the sea only came up to the proposed route on very infrequent occasions, the sand banks could hardly be called sea defences. Further questions were asked as to whether the sand would not drift over the line, and from where might sufficient mud be obtained to build the line as it was useless to lay it over the sand. Eventually it was decided that the matter should be adjourned and discussed again when the necessary information was to hand. The other business to attend to was to find a successor for the office of secretary recently vacated by Mr. Strick who had been promoted to a new appointment with Hampshire County Council, and Mr. W. Jeffery was unanimously elected to the position which, had it not been for the shareholders' poll going against him, he would have held the previous year.

"Considerable sensation was caused in Rye on Monday morning when it became known that a man had been found dead in a stream between Rye and Camber" reported the South Eastern Advertiser on Saturday, 5th November 1904. The unfortunate man was Mr. Henry Ball, aged 49, who had, at times, been employed on the Camber Golf Links. At the inquest conducted on Monday evening, 31st October, it was suggested that Mr. Ball had followed the tram line from Rye on his way home to Broomhill Farm, Camber, late the previous evening, and fell through the opening between the rails where the Tramway crossed the Broadwater Stream. The bridge was unfairly described as "a death trap", although pedestrians had no right to be there. A post mortem examination of the body, concluded that death was primarily due to drowning and that the deceased was probably unconscious when he entered the water. The Jury returned a verdict to the effect that death was accidentally due to drowning, but wished to draw attention to the fact that the arms of the "cradle bridge", which was used by pedestrians on the footpath that paralleled the Tramway between there and Rye, and might otherwise have been used by the deceased, were too short as they did not extend to the bank.

The issue of cheap tickets was again raised by the Golf Club, and in November the Tramway Company wrote to them proposing that for the payment of £7, the Golf Club caddies should be allowed to travel for 1d. and for a further £6, the privilege should be extended to workmen on the links. It was decided to pay the £7, their cheque being forwarded on 10th December 1904 [14], but to leave the latter offer for further consideration. [15]

Whereas 1903 had been described as highly successful, 1904 broke all records, with no less than 60,685 passengers being carried, exclusive of season ticket holders. The profit and loss account for the year end showed a balance of £253 2s.8d., and the directors had paid off another £50 debenture out of this sum. There was a tinge of sadness, however, at the Annual General Meeting on Tuesday afternoon, 14th February 1905, when the chairman referred to the great loss that they had sustained by the death of Mr. F. A. Inderwick, K.C., who had been a director since the formation of the undertaking, and whose advice on so many important questions had been of incalculable advantage to them.

Watching the progress (or rather the lack of it!) of the proposed extension of the Tramway along the foreshore, the Golf Club, with their own ideas of expansion, decided to set aside the sum of £70 "for the purpose of experiment of re-claiming ground" to the south-east of their 4th green [16] and agreement was made with the Curteis Estate Trustees to take a 21 year lease on the land at £1 per annum. [17]

Unfortunately, the increased prosperity of the Tramway Company attracted the petty criminal who, being un-successful in attempting to steal the daily takings in the past, had now turned to the easier, though not nearly so profitable, penny-in-the-slot machines that adorned the platform at Rye. Every evening, after the rolling stock had been put away, the machines would be moved into what should have been the safety of the sheds, but here, out of the public view, they would still be regularly rifled. Bringing the matter to the attention of their readers on Saturday, 15th July, the South Eastern Advertiser wrote

".... The mischievous boy with his metal discs was long a source of annoyance to the owners, but a pettifogging thief, who for the sake of a few coppers will damage the mechanism of the machine, is surely the most contemptible. The only remedy is, of course, to remove the machines, but such a procedure would probably be regarded as an imposition by those members of the community who are accustomed to utilise them."

Work on the Golf Club's reclamation of part of the foreshore hit a major setback in early October when "an abnormally high tide" breached the partly completed sea wall, (was this a timely warning to those who were in favour of extending the Tramway?) but having proceeded thus far with the project, it was agreed that the work should continue. This was not the Golf Club's only problem, and the question of "present and prospective" damage of the sand blowing at the 4th hole caused by the removal of sand, was discussed by the Club on 25th January 1906, which resulted in the Green Committee being asked to meet representatives of the Tramway Company "to endeavour to come to some arrangement satisfactory to both sides". [18] At the ensuing meeting, Cuthbert Hayles admitted that the Tramway Company was well aware that the removal of sand could be regulated and restricted by the Golf Club, but the Green Committee agreed that a little more sand should be taken from the rail head, and that the remaining bank north-east of the rail (sic) should be removed. Mr. Hayles confirmed that the Tramway Company would put in supports in an effort to prevent the sand from blowing. [19]

It can be reasonably assumed that the hand rails of the "cradle bridge" that crossed the Broadwater Stream had been lengthened as recommended towards the end of 1904, yet only fifteen months after Henry Ball had drowned in the stream, its cold, murky waters claimed another victim. On the morning of Friday, 2nd February 1906, Mr. John Longley, a local farmer, was out "lookering" [20] his sheep when, as he passed through the Broadwater on his horse, he saw something black a few yards to his left. Upon investigation he found, to his horror, that the object was a man lying face upwards in the water with his coat floating on the surface. It was just 10 o'clock, and seeing that the first tram of the day was leaving Rye station, he waved it down and informed Mr. Hunnisett, the Tramway Company's Managing Director, who happened to be on board, of what he had found, and then hurried into Rye to inform the police. With the aid of a hurdle the driver of the tram, Mr. Albert Edward "Jokey" Rhodes, along with his father, Mr. Alfred Rhodes (employed on the Tramway as a platelayer) managed to pull the deceased ashore and laid him on the bank.

At the inquest at Rye Town Hall the following day, Mr. William Jeffery identified the deceased as being his son, also named William. Amongst the few belongings found on Mr. Jeffery was his watch which had stoped at 2.23, but it was revealed that as soon as P.C. Arthur Osborn had emptied the water from it at the scene of the tragedy, it immediately started working again! The body had been found some 40 yards from the Tramway bridge, but if Mr. Jeffery had fallen from the rails, it was considered possible that he could have been carried to where he finally came to rest. On the left bank of the stream a short distance away there were some footsteps leading into the water, but it could not be ascertained if the marks had been made by the deceased. With no marks on the body to suggest that a blow had been delivered by another person, the Jury, after retiring for ten minutes, arrived at the verdict "found drowned".

The funeral took place on Wednesday afternoon at the cemetery, Rye Foreign, and the South Eastern Advertiser dated Saturday, 10th February wrote

"There were many manifestations of regret, for the deceased was a most popular personage in the Ancient Town. The principal business houses in the town and many private residences displayed signs of mourning, and as the courtege wended its way from the deceased's residence at "Ingleside", Ferry-road, to the Cemetery, many other indications were apparent that a highly esteemed man had departed this life."

A large number of wreathes were received, among them a personal one from Mr. Cuthbert Hayles ("Sincere sympathy") and one ("With heartfelt sympathy") from the Tramway Company employees. All the facts suggest that the unfortunate Mr. William Jeffery was none other than Mr. Cuthbert Hayles' clerk, and the Tramway Company's secretary. Local newspapers do not confirm or deny this, but Mr. Charles A. Gafford had taken over the post of Company secretary by August that same year!

The Annual General Meeting of the Rye & Camber Tramways Company took place on Tuesday, 10th April 1906. It was announced that the profit and loss account showed a balance of £246 5s.10d. and the directors recommended that a 4 per cent dividend should be paid for the second year running and that the balance, after deducting their remuneration of £20, should be carried forward to the general account. There had been a drop in income of around £45, partly due to one or two wet Bank Holidays, but it had to be remembered that the receipts for 1904 included a £25 subsidy (half of that

arranged in 1903) so the falling off was really only £20. Actual fares were less by £9, but Sunday traffic returns had been reduced by some £45, and sales of sand had not been so good. Mr. Hayles pointed out that only three months of the year were devoted to increased fares [21] and that it was satisfactory to note that season ticket holders were increasing, but whether as much could be made out of them as ordinary passengers he did not know! Frank Jarrett thought that expenses had been somewhat heavy, but he was advised that both engines had been repaired and various other improvements had been carried out.

Rye gained some unexpected publicity in an excellent article published in the "St. James's Gazette" dated Thursday, 31st May 1906. The writer was obviously impressed with, and took more than just a casual interest in the old town and advised that

".... Rye is not the prey of the tourist. If I can persuade some wanderers to turn their steps that way, they can be made happy without any dangerous overcrowding of Rye".

He continued:

"The golfer, of course, knows Rye already, for its course is good, lying between the sea and the marshes, with sand dune bunkers and brackish ditches and a green that can only be found on a seaside course."

Regarding Camber and the Tram he wrote:

"You must go to Camber also, Camber being, so to speak, Rye-on-Sea, where the golf links are, and the keddle-nets for mackerel and a long stretch of sands, and the vessels of the fishing fleet where you may lie in the sun and look at the sea, or bathe very peaceably if the tide be not too low, and the difficulty of undressing in decent obscurity can be overcome by means of a tent, or an umbrella, or a sheltering sand dune. To get to Camber you take the curious little tram train, which is not the least attraction of the expedition, and the like of which may be met in many parts of Switzerland, and in some parts of Wales. In it you are rattled along down to the sea with all the pomp and ceremony of a grown-up railway journey, and thereby you are saved a dreary two mile walk across the "Salts", reclaimed from the sea. On the timetable of the "railway" Camber is manfully extolled as the Mecca of all true pilgrims. It is, one learns, famed for the golf, its keddle-net fishery, its deep sea fishing, its utter peace and quiet, with "no sound save the ocean" and as being, to crown it all, "far from the madding crowd".... It is a queer, quaint little place, and there lies the open sea, while the journey to Camber would be made worth while, if for nothing else, but the new aspect of Rye from that side where the town rises most formidably, with Ypres Castle, its oldest fortress, where not a hundred years ago was mounted a battery of fairly modern guns crowning the heights...."

On the Whitsuntide Bank Holiday Monday the tram conveyed no fewer than 1,000 passengers to Camber, but weatherwise the summer of 1906 was disappointing. However, the August Bank Holiday weekend was hot and sunny and, according to the 11th August edition of the

South Eastern Advertiser, general trade in the Ancient Town was the most remunerative for many years. The report continued:

".... Probably the one enterprise in the Antient Town which raked in the shekels more than any other - to a far greater extent indeed - was the Rye & Camber Tramways Company Ltd.. It was, of course, only fitting that it should be so, considering the fact that the summer has not been altogether too rosy, but the returns of Monday should swell the balance-sheet to an extent calculated to draw smiles from the sometimes placid faces of the Directors and shareholders. It was pleasant to watch the countenance of Mr. R. H. Hunnisett who, though naturally somewhat bewildered by the extraordinary traffic, realised how pleasurably the returns would be received by his co-Directors. The Secretary of the Company, Mr. Gafford, had a very trying time, and although in his case the anticipation of an inflated balance-sheet would make very little difference to himself, he entered into the stress of the occasion with a zeal which should be appreciated by all connected with the Company. The number of passengers carried throughout the day was greatly in excess of any previous occasion, and the whole of the Company's officials are to be congratulated upon the methodical manner in which they carried out their very arduous duties...."

The advertised timetable had to be abandoned and the trams ran to and fro incessantly throughout the day. Such were the numbers travelling that the accommodation of the cars was totally inadequate, and the two trucks normally used for the sand traffic had to be pressed into service with makeshift wooden plank seats fitted. Later it was officially announced that records had well and truly been broken with over 2,000 passengers having been conveyed to and from Camber.

The unexpected but welcome boost in receipts over the August Bank Holiday was not enough to off-set the mediocre results of the rest of the year, and the Directors' Report published at the Annual General Meeting on Monday evening, 25th March 1907, showed that the profit for 1906 was slightly down on 1905, mainly due to a further falling off of Sunday takings. Income from passenger fares (including dogs and parcels) amounted to £581 6s.9d., with season tickets accounting for a further £59 19s.5d., but even though the balance sheet was described as only "of a satisfactory nature", a dividend of 4 per cent was once again declared.

In 1907, after the Golf Club refused the offer to purchase the large house known as "Golf View" situated beside the Tramway just to the west of the land leased by the Club from the Curteis Estate Trustees, the property was bought privately by Golf Club Trustee and Tramway Company director, John Symonds Vidler, for around £500. It was used as his family's summer home and became popular with "so called reading parties of Oxford undergraduates" who would spend their vacations there [22], and trams would regularly stop by request to pick up and set down passengers.

Traffic on the Tramway was maintained throughout the year and receipts from passenger fares, again including dogs and parcels, had increased over 1906 by just under £10, but this was counterbalanced by an almost equal fall in season ticket sales. Towards the end of the year, however, a most important step was taken when work at last started on the long awaited and much discussed extension of the Tramway onto the foreshore. On behalf of the Tramway Company, Charles Gafford applied for a new lease of 21 years on surrender of the current lease on the station site at Rye and the first half mile of track bed towards Camber, and the application was agreed by Rye Town Council at their meeting on the afternoon of Wednesday, 11th March 1908.

A new 21 year lease was also negotiated with the Curteis Estate Trustes, but at the increased rental of ten guineas per year which gave the Company the right "to erect a further Station and buildings at the points marked C and D on the plan or either of them". Six calendar months from the commencement of the lease on 25th March 1908 were allowed "to lay down and finish fit for traffic the said extension of the Tramway between points B and C on the plan, and afterwards during the said term maintain and keep in good repair and working order the said extension and any further extension of the said Tramway that may be made between the points C and D, such extended portion to be constructed in manner similar to the existing portions". Also included in the new lease was the reclaimed land behind the new embankment "containing twenty one acres, two rods, ten perches more or less" and the Tramway Company was responsible "to take all necessary steps to prevent the said piece or parcel of land.... or any part thereof from becoming or remaining flooded with water", no easy task with the close proximity of the sea! There was some doubt as to whether the foreshore actually belonged to the Crown, and to cover the Curteis Estate Trustees in this eventuality it was agreed that the Tramway Company would "indemnify and keep indemnified the Lessors against all claims and demands, actions or proceedings by the Crown or by the Board of Trade or other similar authority or body over or in connection with any part of the said demised premises and against all costs, damages and expenses in connection therewith".

Holman Stephens' engineer attended only occasionally and the building of the extension was, in the main, superintended by the Tramway's own honorary director, Mr. R. H. Hunnisett. To save the Company contractors' expenses, the labour was provided by local men under the supervision of Mr. Charles Tunbridge, who was well known in respect of his excellent engineering work in connection with Rye Harbour.

At the Tramway Company's Annual General Meeting held on Thursday morning, 26th March 1908, the Directors' Report showed that the net profit for 1907 amounted to only £25 9s.4d., but as Cuthbert Hayles explained, this was due to the large amount (£156 10s.11d. more than in 1906) being spent on repairs. The increased expenditure was mainly caused by "the renewal practically of the engine CAMBER" and the cost

44

of coal had also increased by £8 2s.9d. to £87 18s.0d.. Even though the actual profit, by charging all the repairs to the year, was very small, there was a balance of undistributed profit, and it was proposed by the chairman and seconded by Mr. W. Peacock that the now customary dividend of 4 per cent be paid to the shareholders, and this was carried unanimously.

Cuthbert Hayles was pleased to announce that the extension of the line towards the sea and Dungeness [23] had been proceeded with and the embankment was now practically complete, while the rails and sleepers were in the process of arrival. John Symonds Vidler referred to the fact that it would be necessary for the Company to raise another £200 in debenture bonds and he asked those present to assist him in taking them up, adding that they were now in a very much better position than before as they had a 21 year lease for the whole line. Apart from the first few yards, the entire formation was built on an un-fenced embankment 3ft.0in. high, constructed of mud with beach on it to keep the sand down, with faggoting added as an extra protection against the sea. The terminus, consisting of nothing but a simple, sleeper-built platform, devoid of any shelter, was situated a little more than quarter of a mile short of the coastguard cottages, and contrary to Cuthbert Hayles' comments at the A.G.M. in 1902, little thought

was given to any custom originating from that end of the line, as not even a footpath was provided to connect with the road. It should be remembered, however, that at that time, Camber was only an agricultural and coastguard settlement of around 20 buildings and it was more popular as a venue for wild duck shooting than as a holiday resort. [24] The Tramway continued some 100 yards beyond the run-round loop (to the authorised point marked D on the plan) into the low sandhills on the sea shore so that sand could be shovelled directly into the Company's wagons.

The works progressed rapidly so that by the end of June the extension was completed and the South Eastern Advertiser dated Saturday, 11th July 1908 reported:

"Next Tuesday will mark a red-letter day in the history of the Camber Tramway Company, for on that day the extension to the sands will be opened for the first time to the public. The name of the new station will be Camber Sands, whilst the station at the original terminus will be called Golf Links. The extension is half a mile in length, and the line now reaches right to the seaside where the tide ebbs and flows. Previously, we might add, the tram only reached to Camber-on-Mud, but now it goes to Camber-on-Sea. The terminus is within a short distance of Camber Coast Guard Station".

After giving details of the new fares to be charged, the

Map appended to Tramway Company's lease with the Curteis Estate Trustees, 1908.

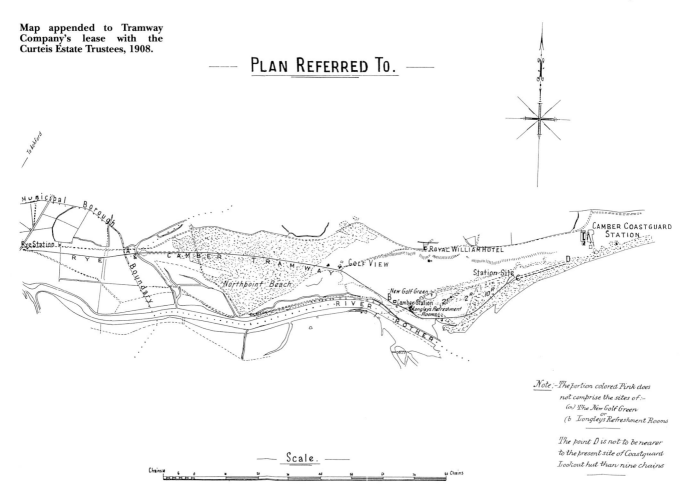

---- PLAN REFERRED TO. ----

Scale.

Note:- The portion colored Pink does not comprise the sites of :-
(a) The New Golf Green
or
(b Longleys Refreshment Rooms

The point D is not to be nearer to the present site of Coastguard Lookout hut than nine chains

description continued:

"The embankment on which the tram will run has reclaimed something like twenty-three acres of land. This piece should prove a considerable asset, as land of this description is extremely valuable for the cultivation of bulbs, celery, asparagus, etc.. It is a picturesque sight to see the tram running along the embankment, especially at high tide, with the water close up to the banks, and as it rounds the curve. Complaints have often been made that the sea is such a long way from Rye to what it was a century ago, but we can surely say now that with the enterprise of the Tramway Company, Rye is much nearer the sea than it was a week since.

"The directors have invited the shareholders to be present at the official opening of the extension late on Monday afternoon, but ..... the line will not be open to the general public until Tuesday morning. Bathing has ever been one of the chief attractions at Camber, and with the facilities now at hand enabling one to get to this fascinating spot, large numbers should enjoy this ever popular summer sport. People living around Rye in the country will now have far more opportunities for enjoying this health-giving recreation. Thanks in a great measure to this new undertaking of the Tramway Company, all who have the welfare of the town at heart will wish this innovation a great success."

With the advertised evening timetable abandoned and a total disregard of superstition, the special tram left Rye station at 5.00 p.m. on the Company's 13th birthday, Monday, 13th July 1908, with close on 50 specially invited passengers on board comprising directors, shareholders, and members of Rye Corporation. The original locomotive CAMBER, suitably bedecked with flags for the occasion, performed the opening ceremony by breaking a red silken cord that had been erected on two posts and stretched across the rails where the extension joined the old line just beyond the original southern terminus. On arrival at Camber Sands station, which was also gaily decorated with flags, the honoured guests left the train for some ten minutes, after which they journeyed back to Golf Links station to partake of an excellent tea provided by Messrs. Longley of Rye in The Retreat close by.

During the course of a short speech, Cuthbert Hayles said he considered that the public would materially benefit as a result of the extension as they would now be taken right onto the foreshore and Mr. Walter Dawes, proposing a vote of thanks to the chairman and the directors, thought that the extension would be one of the greatest benefits to the golfers and the Company. John Symonds Vidler referred to the enhanced value of the land which had been reclaimed as a result of the construction of the embankment and Alderman Masters then proposed a vote of thanks to the debenture holders saying:

"I should like to take this opportunity of thanking Mr. Clark and the other gentlemen who took up the debentures for having done so, for without the money, the work could not have been carried out. Mr. Clark consented to take some debentures when he was asked, and finding there were still more, agreed to take a further lot. There was no difficulty whatever in getting the debentures taken up, which shows the confidence that people have in the undertaking. Some have thought that the tram is not a success, but the first year we paid a dividend of $7^1/2$ per cent, and.... during the last years 4 per cent has been paid, and previous to that 3 per cent. Putting the whole thirteen years together, the dividend has averaged two and three-quarters per cent, and considering the tram was started with a view of benefiting the town, and not as a lucrative investment, I think it must be looked upon as a success, seeing that the shareholders have received a fair investment for their money." [25]

After more than six years from when it had first been seriously discussed, the extension had, at last, become a reality. Only time would tell if the Company had made the right decision in extending their line, and it was now up to the people of Rye to support the Tramway with their patronage, and make it the success that it deserved to be.

1. Curiously, as early as 24th September 1896, Holman Stephens, in one of his regular letters to his parents, advised "... I have the order to extend the Rye line by $1^1/2$ miles..." There are no other references to this early scheme that would certainly have taken the Tramway to the better part of the sands.
2. Rye Golf Club Board of Management Minute Book 13.9.1902.
3. Research has, to date, failed to ascertain on which larger railway R. H. Hunnisett had gained his experience.
4. Stiff-stemmed, reedy or rush-like grass.
5. Rye Golf Club Minute Book 14.2.1903.
6. Rye Golf Club Minute Book 21.3.1903.
7. Rye Golf Club Board of Management Minute Book 1.7.1903.
8. Rye Golf Club Minute Book 11.7.1903.
9. Rye Golf Club Minute Book 12.9.1903.
10. Rye Golf Club Minute Book 12.12.1903.
11. Rye Golf Club Minute Book 13.2.1904.
12. The Dormy House Club, situated close to the Landgate at Hilder's Cliff, Rye, had been formed in 1897 to provide a residential club in Rye for the use of male Golf Club members.
13. Bernard Darwin from "Rye Golf Club - The First 90 Years" - Denis Vidler, 1984.
14. Rye Golf Club Board of Management Minute Book 10.2.1904.
15. Rye Golf Club Board of Management Minute Book 12.11.1904.
16. Rye Golf Club Minute Book 13.5.1905.
17. Rye Golf Club Minute Book 6.10.1905.
18. Rye Golf Club Minute Book 25.1.1906.
19. Rye Golf Club Minute Book 10.2.1906.
20. Checking over.
21. "Increased fares" refers to the extra income of the summer months, rather than passengers being charged extra for travelling at that time.
22. "Rye Golf Club - The First 90 Years" - Denis Vidler, 1984.
23. This is the one and only "official" mention of extending the Tramway beyond Camber.
24. "Sussex County Magazine", May 1952.
25. Sussex Express & County Herald, Saturday 18.7.1908 and The South Eastern Advertiser, Saturday 18.7.1908.

26. Photographed from the Hilly Fields north of Rye shortly prior to leaving Camber for the Isle of Sheppey, Angus Ogilvie flies his Wright bi-plane over the town on 5th May 1911. *(Les Bearman collection)*

27. Monday, 13th July 1908, and in the early evening the Tramway celebrates its 13th birthday in grand style by opening its half mile extension to Camber Sands. The flag-bedecked CAMBER has just run round her train in readiness to take the specially invited guests back to Golf Links station for a celebratory tea at The Retreat close by. Flags also adorn the rear of the crude sleeper-built platform and the fence alongside the run-round loop. Public services to Camber Sands commenced the following day. *(Richard Jones collection)*

Chapter Six

GOOD TIMES, BAD TIMES (1908-1916)

The first public tram left Rye at 9.30 a.m. on Tuesday, 14th July 1908, but being a short-working to Golf Links only, anyone wishing to make a first trip along the extension to Camber Sands had to wait for the 10.00 a.m. departure. Of the 12 trams advertised in the new timetable, only 7 ran through to Camber Sands on weekdays, with an extra short-working to Golf Links on Saturdays at 8.00 p.m.. From 1st November all trams terminated at Golf Links, for there were not many who would wish to travel to the "bleak and altogether forsaken" sands at Camber during the long, cold winter months. One newspaper [1] later commented that in the few months that the new line had been open receipts

".... were nearly sufficient to pay the normal percentage on the cost of the extension. Nothing perhaps better shows how much this great improvement is appreciated, not only by the townspeople of Rye, but especially by the visitors to our charming neighbourhood, and to the salubrious and magnificent sands at Camber. The shareholders may congratulate themselves that they have not only made the Rye and Camber Tramways more convenient to those who want to go to the sands, but in supplying a public want have enhanced the value of their Company's property."

It is a little surprising to learn that, other than the Directorate, only two shareholders attended the Rye & Camber Tramways Company Annual General Meeting on Tuesday morning, 23rd March 1909. Cuthbert Hayles modestly reported that "a considerable number of passengers have availed themselves of the facilities thus offered" and announced that there was a sum of £189 6s.7d. available profit, out of which the directors recommended that a dividend of 4 per cent be paid, along with the directors' usual £20 remuneration, and that the balance be carried forward. As there were so few present, Mr. Hayles said that he would not say very much, but that there had been a good deal of traffic over the extension during the time of the year that it was open. It would be opened again in April and if they had a decent summer, they hoped to take a large number of people down for the benefit of the sands. All the time they could pay a dividend of 4 per cent they could shake hands with each other and congratulate themselves. Total receipts for 1908 amounted to £700 12s.1d. of which the principal items were £589 7s.11d. for passenger fares and £55 18s.3d. for season tickets. Repairs had been kept down to £111 1s.10d., but with the extra mileage, coal expenditure had risen to £94 10s.2d..

The hoped for "decent summer" did not materialise, so the Tramway Company must have welcomed the unusual new attraction that came to Camber in June when Messrs. Alexander Ogilvie and Seawright began flying their Wright bi-plane from the sands. It is believed that Mr. Wilbur Wright visited Alexander Ogilvie at his home at Norton Cottage, Camber whilst over here from the United States. "John Bull's" aero expert prophecied later that month:

"When the Channel is finally conquered (by air) as likely or not it will be found that the landing on the English coast will be made somewhere in the neighbourhood of Rye or Winchelsea. This idea may have weighed with Messrs. Ogilvie and Seawright in their choice of a spot for experimenting with their new Wright machines. They have leased as a flying ground a large acreage at Camber, near the latter place, and are building an aero shed near the sands which stretch out away uninterrupted for miles and are ideal for experimenting on."

A week later, the South Eastern Advertiser dated 26th June suggested

"As the science of aviation progresses, Rye is likely to develop into a town of great importance. Originally a port for those who went down to the sea in ships, it will undoubtedly develop into a port for those who go up in the air in planes. Rye is bounded on one side by marshy, flat, practically uninterrupted country, absolutely ideal for ariel experiments of all descriptions.... For man-kites and such like contrivancies which require wind, Rye marshes are just the place, whilst when airships cross the channel, as easily as motors cross Romney Marsh, and that they will do in the near future, it is a practical certainty that the Rye flat country will be chosen as the site for a landing stage. It is a natural airship track, if such a term is permissable."

If Camber was not to develop as a seaside resort, perhaps it was destined to become an important flying centre! Messrs. Ogilvie and Seawright were not to have the sands to themselves for long, and in July they were joined by a Mr. Seaton Carr with his own bi-plane, but after a few not over-successful flights, he decided to experiment with a smaller sand boat instead. With so much excitement right on their doorstep, many of the townspeople of Rye travelled regularly down to Camber to get a grandstand view of these pioneer aviators, and this extra Tramway traffic made up in no little way for the poor returns brought about by the generally bad weather.

Because so many golfers wished to travel out to the links on Sunday mornings, the Golf Club decided to offer the Tramway Company a guarantee of 15 shillings if they would provide special Sunday trams at 9.30 and 10.00 a.m. between Rye and Golf Links until the end of January. [2] This was to be on the understanding that the

Dormy House Club and the Mermaid Inn paid two-thirds of the subsidy (i.e. 10 shillings between them). Once the Clubs had agreed on the subsidy the Tramway Company, pleased to oblige as ever, added a 9.30 a.m. Sunday departure from Rye [3] that was to become a regular feature of the timetable not just until the end of January, but right up to the First World War.

An amusing incident relevant to this period concerns the son of the Golf Club secretary, R. B. "Beau" Vincent and John Vidler, son of Trustee John Symonds Vidler, who were the cause of much annoyance to the more mature members of the Club with their ceaseless practical jokes. Because of their noisy behaviour, one Sunday evening the pair of them, along with their friend H. A. (Jay) Shadforth, grandson of the Rev. J. Lockington Bates, were banished from the First Class compartment to suffer the humility of having to travel with the caddies in the Third Class carriage as punishment. Not wishing to be out-done by their elders, the three pranksters devised a reprisal plan in an attempt to cause havoc for the distinguished London bound passengers and whilst the tram waited at Golf Links station, the young Messrs. Vincent and Vidler managed to un-couple the First/Second Class Bagnall carriage from the rest of the train. It was not until the un-suspecting driver arrived at Rye that he realised that half of his train had been left behind, but that was not all! As he hastily tried to run round the Rother Ironworks carriage in order to return to fetch the Bagnall vehicle, he found that the points (that were normally sprung towards the run-round loop at the northern end of the station) had been set to the main running line! Luckily for the young jokers, a message was sent to the station master at Brookland on the New Romney branch line, (there being no rail connection between Rye and London on Sunday evenings) and he held the train until the post chaise arrived from Rye with its complement of belated, angry passengers. The boys were fortunate in that they had escaped to their respective boarding schools before the storm broke, and by the time they returned to Rye at a later date they had been forgiven, although the incident was never to be forgotten. [4]

The Company's Annual General Meeting, which took place at the usual venue of the Cinque Ports Arms Hotel, Rye on Friday, 18th March 1910, was a little better attended than that the previous year. There was some sad news in that William Dawes, one of the original promoters of the Tramway, had died on Christmas night at the age of seventy. The Directors' Report quoted passenger fares for 1909 as being £587 6s.3d., a decrease of £2 compared with 1908, with season ticket sales up by £5 at £60 8s.6d.. Cuthbert Hayles commented that, considering the bad summer and the fact that in so many ways it had been an unsatisfactory year with regard to the general affairs of the country, they could not complain of the support that they had received. Repairs had cost £150 5s.9d., and it was hoped "that next year we would not have so many repairs done". With reference to the extension, the chairman advised that it had not made

much difference, but that if it had been a hot summer, they might have got more money! Once more a dividend of 4 per cent to the shareholders.

Always keen to increase its income, the Rye & Camber Tramways Company wrote to the Golf Club in April offering to lease to them the reclaimed land behind the extension embankment (so much for the South Eastern Advertiser's idea of using the "extremely valuable" land for growing vegetables!) and at their Board of Management Meeting at the Club on 9th April, this was agreed to. Messrs. Dawes, Son & Prentice (solicitors) were asked to act on behalf of the Golf Club, so long as the Tramway Company was separately represented, and in June, the solicitors wrote to the Club advising

"With regard to the Tramway Company's title and the question of the Crown's rights, we may say that when the negotiations were entered into between the Tramway Company and the Curteis Estates for the lease referred to, the Board of Trade suggested that the Crown was entitled to the foreshore below the 1872 high water mark, and although nothing further was done with regard to substantiating this claim, the Curteis Estate, in order to protect themselves, made it a condition of the lease to the Tramway Company that the latter should not hold themsleves responsible in the event of the Crown substantiating their claim, but should expressly covenant in the Lease to indemnify them from any habituity in that event.

"The Tramway Company will, therefore, we presume, sub-let this land to the Golf Club on similar terms, but we may add, on behalf of Curteis Estates we wrote to the Secretary of the Board of Trade in April 1909, and expressly repudiated the Board's claim, with the result that we have not heard anything further of this claim from the Board."

On Tuesday, 5th July 1910, the Rye Harbour Commissioners, after their Annual Meeting in Rye, travelled down to Rye Harbour (as they did every year) on the tram to see for themselves the condition of the harbour. The notice of agenda on these occasions stated that the Commissioners were to meet at Monkbretton Bridge "and then by adjournment to proceed by Tram to the mouth of the Harbour" followed by dinner at 2 o'clock. [5] It must have been no little embarrassment to Cuthbert Hayles, who was present as Clerk to the Commissioners, to be informed while the distinguished party waited at Golf Links station for their return trip to Rye, that the tram had broken down! In actual fact, CAMBER had come off the rails on the previous "up" trip within a few yards of the bridge across the Broadwater Stream, but luckily the two carriages remained on the line. With the aid of a number of men armed with long wooden planks and poles, the errant little locomotive was quite quickly returned to the rails and the service was resumed with not too much delay. Apart from inconveniencing the Commissioners and making them late for their lunch, insult was added to injury when a photograph of CAMBER being re-railed appeared in the South Eastern Advertiser on 9th July!

76904

28. VICTORIA waits patiently at the shelterless Camber Sands station on Saturday, 10th April 1909. Few people would have wished to visit the sands in the winter, so the nine month old station had been closed since the end of October and had re-opened in time for Easter the week before.

(H. L. Hopwood, L.C.G. B. Ken Nunn collection)

29. A small party of children, perhaps on a Sunday School outing, pose for the cameraman at Camber Sands station, now complete with a small wooden shelter, prior to the First World War. Visible along the tops of the windows are the brass hand rails that, with a footboard along the length of each carriage at platform level, enabled the conductor to collect fares between stations whilst the tram was in motion. To the right of the locomotive the golden sands stretch half a mile to the sea when the tide is out.

(Lens of Sutton)

The draft lease for the Tramway Company's reclaimed land on the foreshore "containing 21 acres or thereabouts as the same has been stumped out" was laid before the Golf Club's Board of Management Meeting on 9th July, and after being approved by Messrs. Dawes, Son & Prentice, it was signed and dated on 10th September. [6] The term was for fourteen years commencing on 24th June 1910, the yearly rental being £16 by equal half yearly payments on 25th December and 24th June each year. One condition was that "the Lessors will within three calendar months from the date hereof erect a sufficient fence with two gates therein on the boundary of the premises..."

Rye might not have been as busy as it might have been over the Whitsuntide weekend, but this could not be said for the August Bank Holiday. Messrs. Ogilvie and Seawright had been making regular flights since they first arrived over a year ago, and the South Eastern Advertiser wrote on 6th August 1910:

"The advent of the airmen at Camber seems to have popularised these wonderful stretches of sand. Dwellers in the district have evidently at last realised that in Camber Sands they possess one of the most bracing holiday resorts in England. The Camber air invests the most fastitidious and dainty gourmand [7] with the appetite of a farm hand. At Camber we simply must eat. This is the only disadvantage which picnic parties have to contend with at Camber - the carriage of food. If they do not take a sufficient supply of food down there, they will feel uncomfortable before the day is out. Of course, some people would not consider an enormous appetite a disadvantage at all. But, for all events, for bracing up the jaded or for bringing to the feeble-bodied all that wonderful virility alleged to be the result of taking somebody's pills, we do not think there exists a place which could do it than Camber. On Bank Holiday, seen from aloft, Camber Sands must have presented a picture akin to a honeycomb covered with a swarm of bees. 1,750 passengers journeyed thither on the Camber tram, and goodness knows how many more walked. That number constitutes a record for the trams. [8] May Camber's popularity continue. We are sure that nobody visits the sands for a day without coming back feeling as though he or she had been imbued with new life".

In October 1910 some members of the Golf Club, along with Major Horce Neve (Trustee of the Curteis Estates), inspected the ground lying to the south-east of that rented by the Club between the highest range of sand hills and the sea, east of the enclosed ground rented from the Tramway Company. Once it was confirmed that the ground in question would extend down to the high water mark, in January 1911 the Golf Club took out a further lease with the Curteis Estate Trustees, subject to Mr. Longley's grazing rights (a farmer who had taken land since 1862), existing hut rights and the Tramway lease being respected. [9] Now was it just the expansion of their links that the Golf Club had in mind, or was there an ulterior motive, for this latest lease effectively blocked any future proposals for an extension of the Tramway beyond its present terminus at Camber Sands.

Mr. Noel Prentice (of Messrs. Dawes, Son & Prentice) had, in the meantime, signed a 99 year lease with the Curteis Estate Trustees to build a house to the west of "Golf View" and just 35 ft. south of the Tramway. This involved crossing the Tramway on the level, so upon the payment of five shillings per year, for 18 years commencing on 19th May 1911, the Tramway Company gave Mr. Prentice the "full right and liberty... and all persons authorised by him" access "over and along the land... from and to the High Road leading from Rye and East Guldeford to Camber..." to and from "his messauge". Mr. Prentice was to keep this 18 ft. right of way in good and substantial repair, but should the rent be in arrears of 21 days, "the term granted shall absolutely cease and determine and this Lease shall be at an end". An error on the 30 ft. to 1 inch plan referred to in the lease showed the Tramway as being of standard 4ft.8$\frac{1}{2}$in. gauge!

Over Christmas a rumour spread around Rye that Alexander Ogilvie, the airman, was going to compete for the "Baron de Forest" prize of £4,000 for the longest cross-channel flight at the earliest opportunity. On Boxing Day morning he was observed taking short flights, and by early afternoon a large crowd of onlookers had arrived on the sands. When interviewed by a reporter from the South Eastern Advertiser, Mr. Ogilvie revealed that he intended trying for the Michelin Cup for the greatest distance over a properly marked out course, and tall flags were already in position on the sands marking out a three mile circuit. Two days later, Mr. Ogilvie's Wright bi-plane could be heard in Rye, and when the flight went on for an hour it was clear that this was no ordinary practise, and there was a mass exodus of townspeople to Camber, which must have taken the Tramway by surprise. The bi-plane rounded the course some 56 times in just under four hours and the official observer on behalf of the Aero Club confirmed that Mr. Ogilvie had flown a total of 147.25 miles, easily beating the previous record of 114 miles set by a Mr. Cody, and putting himself easily first for the Michelin Cup. What a way to end the year and, of course, it was all good publicity for Camber and Rye, and extra business for the Rye & Camber Tramway.

Whether or not it was due to the extra traffic of people travelling down to watch the airman at close hand is un-certain, but at the Tramway Company's Annual General Meeting on Friday, 17th March 1911, it was reported that receipts during 1910 had amounted to £915 12s.9d., an increase of £79 on the previous year, but expenditure had also increased to £710 19s.10d., leaving a balance in hand of £204 12s.11d.. Even so, profits had increased and the now familiar dividend of 4 per cent was again declared.

Alexander Ogilvie continued to perform regular flights from Camber until the Spring, but on Monday, 22nd May "he bid farewell to Camber Sands, and disdaining the ordinary locomotion, he flew to his new abode at Eastchurch, Isle of Sheppey". [10] With Mr. Ogilvie's departure the brief dream of Rye developing as an important airport faded, and although aeroplanes received regular mentions in the local press, they were only to be seen flying overhead en route for other destinations.

Rye was very quiet over the Whitsuntide weekend as evidenced by the fact that the magistrates at the Town Hall on Tuesday morning, 6th June, had no cases to deal with! The Sussex Express & County Herald dated Friday 9th June reported:

"Rye was not favoured with a large influx of weekend visitors this Whitsuntide, and in fact the hotels and boarding establishments did not appear to be doing so much business as at ordinary weekends. The day visitors to the town were, however, fairly numerous and Monday brought a lot from Hastings, both by rail and motor coaches. No attractions were offered in the town and the residents seemed to distribute themselves equally between Camber Sands and Hastings, the fun obtainable at the Joy Wheel of the latter place proving a strong attraction. The proximity of the Coronation undoubtedly had an influence in the lessened numbers visiting the old town".

The mention of "the proximity of the Coronation" seems a rather lame excuse for the lack of visitors to Rye over the weekend, and the reporter knocks the nail right on the head when he writes that "no attractions were offered in the town". Hastings was quite deservedly building up its popularity as a fashionable seaside resort, but what of Rye's marine suburb of Camber-on-Sea? At the opening dinner of the Royal William Hotel in October 1894, Mr. W. Carless, in his speech, had hoped for "a long line of villas, or rather a village of bungalows", but where were they? And where were the "pleasure trips to sea and musical entertainments of a more refined character" that had been discussed at the Rye Trade Association's meeting in September 1895? Other than the alterations to the Golf Course and the extension of the Tramway along the foreshore, a visitor of 1895 would have seen no change whatsoever in Camber 16 years later, so it was hardly surprising that day trippers and holidaymakers were going elsewhere to the more go-ahead resorts.

Whether the August Bank Holiday was similarly disappointing is not recorded, but in the Autumn the Tramway was faced with a problem of a rather different kind. Owing to rough weather and some exceptionally high tides in October, the embankment along the extension was severely damaged, the repairs to which cost the Company around £50. As Cuthbert Hayles explained at the Annual General Meeting on Friday, 16th February 1912, the cost of these repairs had been charged against the year 1911, and that a further sum of £77 3s.0d. had been written off against depreciation of the rolling stock. The profit, which included £82 0s.11d. brought forward from the previous year, came to only a few pounds less than 1910 at £165 8s.8d., and a dividend of 4 per cent was still paid to the shareholders. Mr.

Hayles summed up the report and accounts stating that they presented no glowing features and contained nothing at all startling. He did admit that there was one mistake in the accounts where £120 and £20 had been made to add up to £122, but the correct figures were £102 and £20, and Mr. T. G. Sharpe (the Company's auditor) confirmed that the paper that he had signed was correct, and that it was entirely a printer's error!

Hardly had the repair work to the embankment on the extension settled down when, on Tuesday night, 5th March 1912, nature struck another blow against the Tramway. So much for the prediction back in 1904 that the sea would only come up to the embankment on infrequent occasions! What was stated as being the highest tide for 30 years washed over the line beyond Golf Links station and carried away so much earth that the sleepers were left hanging from the rails in mid-air in several places. Repairs were put in hand as soon as the flood waters had subsided, with the cost being charged again to the profit and loss account for the current year.

Two years after the South Eastern Advertiser had complained of the lack of refreshment facilities at Camber [11] a large tea room was now being constructed just behind Camber Sands station. Once the Tramway had been extended in 1908, Councillor Longley's refreshment stall close to Golf Links station had become redundant and in April the Golf Club were asked if they would be prepared to purchase the building, by then known as the "Townpeople's Bungalow". The Club decided not to make an offer [12] and the building was later demolished.

Access to "Golf View" had until now passed between Charles Tunbridge's cottage situated close beside the Tramway to the south and thence to the Camber road alongside the 17th green, but at the Golf Club's Board of Management Meeting on Saturday, 1st June it was suggested that "a road be made from the high road across the shingle to Mr. Prentice's house via the back of "Golf View" and to make a hard road between the 11th green and the tramway line, cutting off from the same access to Mr. Prentice's house". However, Mr. Noel Prentice was un-willing that the work should be carried out as he understood from Major Horace Neve that in the event of such a road being made, the Curteis Estate Trustees would wish to develop the estate, building other houses, [13] which would, of course, have been beneficial to the Tramway in the long run. After further discussion it was agreed that a road should be built across the back of the 11th green to serve "Golf View" only, with posts and chains alongside the Tramway to prevent traffic going that way to Mr. Prentice's house. [14]

Early in July, John Symonds Vidler was taken ill. On Monday morning, 8th July, it was stated that his condition was more favourable, so one can imagine what a shock it must have been to the townspeople of Rye to hear almost directly after this assuring news that he had passed away, aged just 61. The South Eastern Advertiser wrote:

"With the passing of Mr. Vidler, Rye has lost one of

its most distinguished citizens, and wide is the gap that has been left".

Not only was John Symonds Vidler one of the founder members and a director of the Rye & Camber Tramways Company and a director of the Mermaid Inn Company, but a Trustee of Rye Golf Club. His interest in anything appertaining to the welfare of the town of Rye was well known, and he had occupied a prominent position in local affairs, being both a County and Borough magistrate, and for many years, a member of Rye Town Council. In 1883 he was elected for the first time as Mayor of Rye, as well as being the youngest Chief Magistrate in the kingdom. The following year he was again elected, and in 1892 he filled the office for a third time. Paying tribute to Mr. Symonds Vidler the Mayor, Councillor Joseph Adams, J.P., C.C., said

".... His strenuous advocacy of the Rother Bridge Scheme was a large factor in bringing about its accomplishment, and started the new era of prosperity attributable to the opening up of what has now become a main artery to the borough.

"To all "croakers" he gave a short shrift, and the construction of the Rye and Camber Tramways line owes not a little to his whole-hearted endeavours. Upon this latter concern depended largely either the success or failure of the Rye Golf Club, and he most vigilantly watched every turn of its wheel of fortune, his policy being one of lubrication rather than an irksome application of the skid pan...."

The funeral took place on the afternoon of Friday, 12th July, the coffin draped in the union jack, being brought up from Camber on the tram which he had used daily in life. Mr. Symonds Vidler had been a member of the firm Vidler & Sons, Ltd., general merchants and shipping agents, and many vessels on the River Rother flew their flags at half mast as the tram passed slowly by. The Borough flags also flew at half mast over the Town Hall and the Landgate Tower, and everywhere there was a general air of sorrow that contrasted strangely with the brilliant sunshine of the day. Business in Rye was suspended for the duration of the service, and almost every trade and institution in the town was represented at the graveside, including Mr. C. A. Gafford (secretary) and Mr. R. H. Hunnisett (director) of the Tramway Company. [15]

Over the year, passenger traffic showed a serious diminution of around £100, (receipts for August alone showed a falling off of around £19) mainly due to the exceptionally bad weather, so when the accounts were presented at the Annual General Meeting on Friday, 21st February 1913, the balance of profit, including the amount brought forward from 1911, came to only £107 11s.4d.. With takings down on 10 months out of the twelve, the Company had experienced its worst year since 1903. For eight years the shareholders had enjoyed a 4 per cent dividend, but with these poor results the directors regretted that the dividend would have to be reduced by 50%. Cuthbert Hayles explained that they

30. The photographer would have been standing back to and close to the Tramway just to the south of Golf Links station to take this picture of the concrete hexagonal lighthouse situated on the eastern bank of the River Rother c.1910. Its purpose was to advise shipping the depth of the river at night by showing red and green tide signals. To the right is the harbourmaster's small house and on the far side of the river a part of Rye Harbour village forms the background. According to the back of the original postcard it was "Published by R.J. Tunbridge, Propr. Royal William Hotel (The Billy) Camber, Rye", who was one of 4 sons brought up by Charles Tunbridge in the small cottage beside the Tramway close to "Squatter's Right".

(L. Bearman collection)

had had considerable trouble with the sea during the year, the exceptional high tides in the Spring having done the Company damage as well as other people. To laughter, he suggested that when the sea put the beach in the right place, they would all be free from trouble! Mr. R. H. Hunnisett had relinquished his position as Managing Director, although he was still to carry out work for the Company, and Alderman John Neve Masters, on behalf of the Chairman, Secretary and Directors, acknowledged his valuable services. In reply Mr. Hunnisett said that he considered himself to be "father of the trams", and though they had had a terrible year, he hoped that the present year would be better.

What seemed like becoming an annual, but most unwelcome event returned with a vengeance to the South-east of England on the night of Saturday, 22nd March 1913. Coinciding with a period of High Spring Tides, a raging storm whipped up the sea to such an extraordinary height at Rye Harbour that it once again washed over the Camber tramline, destroying a portion of the track. (16)

Rye was host to a large number of visitors over the August Bank Holiday weekend, although most of the locals deserted the town to witness a pageant in Hastings. Camber Sands proved to be more popular than ever, the Sussex Express & County Herald reporting ".... there being a record holiday crowd at this increasingly popular resort, and the resources of the Tram Company were taxed to the utmost in conveying passengers to and fro".

Since June 1912 the Golf Club had paid a subsidy to the Tramway Company to provide three special trams all the year round on Sunday mornings, leaving Rye at 9.30, 10.00 and 10.30. In September 1913 the Golf Club secretary had a meeting with Charles Gafford (secretary of the Tramway Company) where he queried the rate paid by the Club, but Mr. Gafford confirmed that the fares paid by the passengers, other than golfers, were taken into consideration when working out the payment payable by the Club. (17)

After the poor returns of 1912, it must have been with some relief that the directors at the Annual General Meeting held on Friday, 20th February 1914 were "pleased to report a considerable increase from passenger traffic during the past year, though the receipts from other sources have, owing to extraneous circumstances, declined". A larger profit had been made, and after writing off a further £87 3s.0d. for depreciation, an available balance of £101 18s.10d. remained, and it was recommended that a dividend of 3 per cent should be paid. Cuthbert Hayles advised that traffic receipts had increased by about £90 and commented "... to take £700 on a railway which extended just over 2 miles is very satisfactory". The amount expended on repairs remained practically the same as in 1912. Mr. R. H. Hunnisett proudly reported that the last heavy gale and tide had not affected their previous repairs, so perhaps all would be well in the fight against nature on the extension in the future.

Mr. C. A. Gafford had another visitor from the Golf Club, this time the acting secretary who, in April, asked if it would be possible for a tram to be put on that would leave Golf Links station for Rye at 5.00 p.m. on Saturdays or, at the very least, on the first Saturday of each month. If this was not feasible, he asked if a 5.00 p.m. tram could be run instead of that scheduled at 5.35 p.m., or that at 4.20 p.m., or if really necessary, both! (18) This time the club was out of luck! It was not to be until 7th June that the timetable was amended very slightly, and hardly in the interests of the Golf Club when the 4.20 p.m. was re-scheduled to run at 4.35 p.m. en route from Camber Sands, and the short-working 5.35 p.m. departure was delayed by 10 minutes to arrive at Rye at 5.55 p.m..

In June 1914 the Monkbretton Bridge that carried the main Hastings to Dover road across the River Rother close to Rye Tram Station was closed for essential repairs. Work, once started, proceeded so slowly that Joseph Adams, in his capacity as County Councillor for the Borough of Rye, attended the quarterly meeting of the East Sussex County Council at Lewes on Tuesday, 28th July where, in a long statement he advised

"..... I inspect the work daily and am much disappointed with the progress which has up to the present been made. The matter is of vital concern to the Borough of Rye, which has had one of its main arteries severed. The bridge has been closed at the most inconvenient time. People who had taken houses and lodgings in Rye, when they found that they had to travel in their motor cars five miles to the Golf Links over bad roads, in addition to paying tolls at two gates, had either refused to come to the town, or had left as soon as they conveniently could. The Council can understand that this has caused much dissatisfaction in the Borough. Anyone now wishing to take the main road from Hastings to Folkestone, or vice versa, has to pass through 3 toll gates, and this leads to ceaseless complaining...."

It is interesting to note from what Joseph Adams said that many visiting golfers were already using their motor cars to travel to and from the links at Camber. Convenient though the Tramway had been in the past, it was beginning to fall out of favour, and rather than use it, they preferred to cut their vacations short and return home.

A temporary footbridge had been erected on the south side of the Monkbretton Bridge, so that its closure to vehicular traffic had little or no effect on the number of people travelling on the Rye & Camber Tramway, and up to the end of July passenger receipts had actually "materially increased". With the outbreak of war in August, all suddenly changed, and the consequent absence of visitors to Rye resulted in a dramatic drop in the number of passengers carried. A profit was still made with a balance of just £62 5s.8d. remaining after £82 6s.0d. had been written off for depreciation, and the dividend paid to shareholders was reduced to 2 per cent, which absorbed £51 6s.0d..

Eventually, with the temporary footbridge removed, the Monkbretton Bridge was re-opened to all traffic on Tuesday, 20th July 1915, the work having taken 9 months longer than had been contracted for, but now the structure posed a new problem for the Tramway Company. The road had been raised by such an extent that it was now difficult for carts to gain access to the station! Mr. Gafford suggested to Rye Town Council that it would save alterations and expense if the Company's carts could cross the corner of the adjacent field and onto the road, in which case the Company would provide the necessary gate. His letter came up for discussion at Rye Town Council's meeting on Monday, 9th August 1915, but the surveyor (Mr. G. Henbrey) did not think it would be wise to alter the present roadway to the Tram Station and that it would be much better if the present roadway could be made up and used as far as possible. If all the broken grit that was available could be carted over, in a month or so the whole thing would be much improved, whereas if they came across the field, in the wet weather there might be "a very bad piece of roadway" which the Council might be asked to make good!

Earlier that month a curious little article appeared in the "Daily News" under the heading "Cyclist's Impressions of Rye", this section being of relevance to our narrative:

"... The sea, of course, has withdrawn somewhat from Rye. But they told us - and we quite believed them, though we did not see it - that a funny little steam tramway runs in a few minutes direct onto the sands of Camber-on-Sea; and that tramway, together with the fact that there is no "Camber-on-Sea" on any of my maps, seems to me a charming and original proof that Rye is a seaside resort within the meaning of the Act, and ought to be highly popular with the numerous people to whom the usual thing is simply obnoxious...."

Rye might not have been host to as many visitors as in previous years, but the townspeople still journeyed down to Camber on the Tram in the summertime to savour the delights of the golden sands and sea air, and the problem of some of these day trippers wandering over the links was still a thorn in the side of the Golf Club. The President of the Golf Club, Mr. Horace Avory, (later to become Mr. Justice Avory) decided that something had to be done and wrote to the Club Chairman, his letter being read out at the Board of Management's meeting on 4th September. One paragraph confirmed an earlier suspicion:

"Many years ago, on the Committee, when the tramway was extended to the sands, I predicted that this necessity would arise, and the lease over the additional land was taken in 1911 with this object....".

The entrance to the Tramway Station at Rye came up for discussion again at Rye Town Council's meeting on Monday, 6th September, when the Finance Committee recommended that it should be widened by the corners being taken off the fields leased to Mr. Ashbee and Mr. Colebrooke and that the fences and gates be adjusted. It would mean cutting about 15 ft. off of the corner of the field which came almost up to the bridge, and they also proposed to make a small improvement on either side so that the approach road would be better, not only for the passengers, but for keeping the sand traffic away from the Tramway. The report was then adopted and the work soon put in hand.

On Sunday, 3rd October the Tramway Company sustained another loss when Mr. T. G. Sharpe passed away during the afternoon, aged 70. [19] He had been a director since the formation of the Company, and had served as the Tramway's auditor alongside Mr. G. W. Strick since 1901, and had carried out the duty alone for the past 12 years.

At the beginning of February 1916, Rye Golf Club decided that the annual payment of £7 made to the Tramway Company that permitted caddies to travel for 1d. instead of 2d. should only be paid on condition that a 6 o'clock tram be run from 15th February. [20] Since December the last tram of the day had left Rye at 4.20 and Golf Links at 4.35 p.m. (4.00 p.m. and 4.30 p.m. respectively on Sundays) but they remained so until March when a daily service was added from Rye at 5.30 p.m., which returned from Golf Links at 5.45 p.m.. The Golf Club might not have got its way, but contrary to their threat, the subsidy was paid, and the caddies continued to travel for half the normal fare!

In June, the Mayor, Councillor G. F. Burnham, issued a public notice expressing the hope that shops in the town would remain open on the Monday of the Whitsuntide weekend as that day was not generally to be observed as a holiday, with the exception of school children who were not to be deprived of their short vacation. So as the war dragged on, and visitors to the town became fewer and far between, even the traditional Bank Holiday looked like becoming a thing of the past.

1. South Eastern Advertiser, Saturday, 27.3.1909.
2. Rye Golf Club Minute Book 13.11.1909.
3. Rye Golf Club Minute Book 11.12.1909.
4. "Rye Golf Club - The First 90 Years" Denis Vidler, 1984.
5. "A Maritime History of Rye" - John Collard, 1978.
6. Rye Golf Club Board of Management Minute Book 10.9.1910.
7. Glutenous, fond of eating.
8. This contradicts the report in the South Eastern Advertiser dated 11.8.1906 when it was quoted that over 2,000 people were conveyed to and from Camber.
9. Rye Golf Club Board of Management Minute Book 14.1.1911.
10. Sussex Express & County Herald, Friday 26.5.1911.
11. South Eastern Advertiser, Saturday 6.8.1910.
12. Rye Golf Club Minute Book 4.5.1912.
13. Rye Golf Club Board of Management Minute Book 6.7.1912.
14. Rye Golf Club Board of Management Minute Book 3.8.1912.
15. Sussex Express & County Herald, Friday 19.7.1912 and South Eastern Advertiser, Saturday 20.7.1912.
16. South Eastern Advertiser, Saturday 29.3.1913.
17. Rye Golf Club Board of Management Minute Book 4.10.1913.
18. Rye Golf Club Minute Book 6.4.1914.
19. South Eastern Advertiser, Saturday 9.10.1915.
20. Rye Golf Club Board of Management Minute Book 5.2.1916.

Chapter Seven
THE TRAMWAY COMES OF AGE (1916-1925)

On 13th July 1916, the Rye & Camber Tramway reached its 21st birthday, but with little to celebrate. Passenger receipts were continuing to fall, and with little building work being carried out because of the war, the sand traffic was virtually at a standstill. The summer timetable had been reduced to 8 return weekday trips compared with 10 in July 1914, although reflecting the number of locals still visiting the sands, there was one extra return tram to Camber Sands, making a total of six. The Sunday service had been reduced from 8 to 6, of which 5 ran through to Camber Sands. Unhappy with the reduction in the service, the Golf Club asked for an extra tram to be put on before or after the 10.00 a.m. departure on Saturdays, but the Tramway Company was unable to oblige. [1] The Tram was still considered as the main means of reaching the Links, and the Golf Club advertising in a local information booklet advised ".... the 18 hole course is situated among the Camber Sandhills, and is reached by the Steam Tramway in a few minutes...." (a slight exaggeration!)

From the end of October the timetable was curtailed still further and by the end of March 1917, the service had reached an all time low of 3 return trams on weekdays and just 2 on Sundays. February had been a particularly bad month with the whole of southern England being brought to a standstill under a deep blanket of snow. After the thaw, the Golf Club arranged a meeting with the Tramway Company chairman, Cuthbert Hayles, where they offered to pay an extra subsidy of £5 (in addition to the £7 already paid for the caddies to travel at half price) in an effort to get a more efficient service, and at the same time they complained of the un-punctuality of the 10.00 a.m. and 1.30 p.m. trams from Rye and the 4.45 p.m. from Camber. [2] Their complaint embraced the whole of the meagre service, but why, with so few trams running, should they have not run to time? Mr. Hayles declined the offer of the £5 subsidy, but said that the Company would agree to a payment of 5 shillings per day up until Good Friday, which would guarantee trams leaving Rye at 10.00 a.m., 1.30 p.m. and 4.30 p.m.. [3] In Mr. Gafford's letter to the Golf Club confirming these arrangements dated 9th March, he added that should the subsidy not be paid, the directors would have no alternative but to close the Tramway until the summer.

Good Friday arrived, and having heard nothing further from the Golf Club, Mr. Gafford wrote another letter that day to them as follows:

"My directors at their meeting this morning decided that owing to the small amount of traffic on the line, they will be compelled to carry out the terms of my letter dated 9th March last, unless your Club can extend the

time for payment of the subsidy of five shillings per day up until Whitsuntide, to commence on Monday next."

The letter came before the Golf Club's Board of Management at their meeting the following day, 14th April, where it was resolved "that representatives of the Board be delegated to confer with the Tram Company and representatives of the town, and have power to make permanent or temporary arrangements, with instructions that they demand a minimum of three trains (sic) a day and, that if necessary, they offer a subsidy not exceeding £30." In the meantime they agreed to continue to pay the sum of five shillings per day from Monday to the following Friday inclusive.

As a matter of urgency the meeting between the Rye Trade Association and the Golf Club took place, and the South Eastern Advertiser on Saturday, 28th April reported

"The Tramway Company's receipts have dwindled during the winter months to such an extent that the Directors, in the interest of the shareholders, seriously contemplated closing down 'til July. It was realised that such a course of action, however justifiable from the Tramway Directors' point of view, would be an unfortunate blow to the Golf Club (one of the great assets of the town) and the trade alike. The Trade Association came to the rescue and as a result of an interview with representatives of the Golf Club and a discussion of the difficulties, the necessary subsidy was immediately forthcoming to ensure a tram service for, at all events, another 12 months. Prompt action was imperative, and it was taken in the spirit of ernest determination with the result that "all's well" and everybody is pleased. Cheers for the Trade Association."

The discussion resulted in three members of the Rye Trade Association agreeing to guarantee between them £25, with the Golf Club paying a like sum. At the same time a minimum of four trams throughout the year was requested, the 10.00 a.m. being a fixed time with the times of the others to be arranged by mutual agreement, [4] but the Golf Club was to be un-successful in this respect and for the time being the timetable remained unchanged.

Back in April, whilst negotiations to keep the tram in operation were taking place, the Rye area received its one and only air raid of the First World War, and this was possibly in error! The story is told that the Zeppelin crew involved, owing to navigational errors, mistook the River Rother for the Thames and dropped its cargo of three bombs on Rye Harbour village, assuming it was London! [5] Mrs. Symonds Vidler had continued to live beside the Tramway in the flimsy "Golf View" (by then renamed "Beachlands") after her husband had died in

July 1912, and though the bombs did little damage, they frightened her enough to cause her to move away and she subsequently sold the property to one of her nieces. The neighbouring "Gorse View" possibly came off worse, having all of its windows broken!

A spell of fine hot weather in June brought a large number of visitors back to Rye for their summer holidays, and many of them spent their vacation bathing on the sands at Camber. Some of them were, perhaps, unaware of the existence of the Rye & Camber Tramway and the Sussex Express & County Herald on Friday, 15th June advised:

> ".... For the information of strangers we may point out that the journey to Camber can be taken on the tramway. Trams do not run every five minutes, and people who don't want to waste time should furnish themselves with a timetable".

Three weeks later, on 6th July, the same newspaper in its regular column "Rye Local Notes" found it necessary to report

> "There is a little matter of honour which needs the immediate attention of the traders of Rye. They all must readily admit that if the tramway to Camber was to shut down during what are regarded as the quiet months of the year, the result would be most detrimental to the town, and especially to themselves. May we be allowed to remind them that when a meeting was called some weeks ago by the Tradesmen's Association, something had to be done promptly to keep the service going. The traders present felt no hesitation in pledging their fraternity to the raising of the modest sum of £25 as a subsidy to the Tramway Company, and three or four of those present guaranteed on the spot to raise the needful cash. We are sorry to hear that the necessary small subscriptions to save the guarantors from having to pay more than their fair share have not yet come to hand. We trust this hint will be sufficient. Tradespeople who have forgotten their duty in this respect should at once relieve the guarantors. Donations sent to Mr. W. H. Delves, J.P., Mr. F. G. Smith (Vennal & Co.), Mr. Ashbee, Ald. of the Rye Trade Association, or any member of the Committee of the Rye Trade Association, will reach the proper source. We should like to add that we have not been asked to pen this note, but we overheard one of the guarantors express his intention of paying his guarantee, and we are sure traders would be sorry if this were done and that they had failed to do their little part in the matter".

The Tramway received another welcome, if brief mention in the second of two articles aimed, once again, at visitors to the "antient town" by "A. M. A." entitled "A Ramble around Rye", that was published in the Sussex Express & County Herald on 24th August:

> "... We have dealt with some of the interesting spots and buildings of Rye, but when you have done these and the eye wants a change of scene, walk around the outside of the town. Go down on the marshes or take the little steam tram to Camber Sands. Where can you find, at low tide, an expanse of clean open sand shore to compare with Camber?"

In September the Golf Club secretary was instructed to write to the Tramway Company again because, contrary to the agreement of November 1904, the caddies' fare had been increased from 1d. to 1¹/₂d., [6] and Charles Gafford was left with no alternative but to apologise, explaining that they had been overcharged in error! When the Club asked if the amount overpaid could be recouped, Mr. Gafford regretted that it would not be possible owing to the difficulty in compiling the amount [7] and, luckily for the Tramway Company, this explanation was accepted with nothing more being heard of the matter. The Golf Club further complained that accommodation had been inadequate of late, the Rev. H. C. L. Lindell commenting that on Wednesday, 5th September, 132 persons had been brought up in the two carriages, no trucks being used. [8] Mr. Gafford promised that at crowded times a 9.30 a.m. tram would be run (though the extra service was never to appear in the timetables) and that he would endeavour to secure more accommodation for the golfers, but just how he intended to do this is not revealed!

At the Rye & Camber Tramway Company's Annual General Meeting on Friday, 15th March 1918, after presenting the Directors' Report and Balance Sheet, Cuthbert Hayles explained that although at the commencement of the previous year's workings the financial position was "unfortunate", kindly attention on the part of "interested parties" saved the situation and ensured the continuation of the service. As as result, the directors had not only met expenses, but were now able to recommend a dividend of 3 per cent, and this was agreed to.

The Sussex Express & County Herald a week later on 22nd March wrote:

> "Congratulations to the Rye & Camber Tramway Co. on having succeeded in keeping their head above water. At one period the outlook was extremely bleak and the Directors were seriously thinking of "closing down" during the slack season. Thanks to the Rye Trade Association, the Golf Club and the Dormy Club, financial assistance has provered to keep things going till the clouds had rolled by. This timely aid, coupled with a good summer, has enabled the shareholders not only to pay their way but to recoup themselves with a moderate dividend of three per cent. To close down would have had a serious effect on the golf links, and local traders know too well what a valuable asset are golfing visitors and residents to allow anything to stand in the way of their enjoyment of required facilities for indulging in this fashionable game".

It may have been reassuring to see the Tramway bounce back from almost certain winter closure to publish a surprisingly good balance sheet, but it re-awakened the 1902 argument as to whether dividends should be paid out of subsidies. Unfortunately, this time opinions were not confined to the Tramway Company's meetings and there was soreness amongst certain of the

31. What a superb photograph of CAMBER and her train consisting of all of the passenger stock at Rye with Percy Sheppard and "Jokey" Rhodes in attendance c.1924. The blackboard just inside the waiting room door advised passengers "TICKETS ON THE CAR". It must have been a very hot day as every available window and ventilator is open on the enclosed rolling stock. *(H. Sheppard collection)*

32. As shadows lengthen, CAMBER propels her two carriages into the carriage shed at Rye for the night. Her bunker has already been filled with coal in readiness for the following day's services. *(Wilfrid Shearan)*

local traders (some of these being shareholders) who, whilst they were prepared to do their bit to keep the Tramway running, did not like the idea of subscribing to provide fees and dividends.

On the Whitsuntide Bank Holiday, which was reinstated in Rye in 1918, the sun shone and "many people spent the greater part of the day at Camber. The tramway did good business and visiting golfers were much in evidence and comprised many officers who were recuperating after a long spell of war work". [9] The Golf Links at Camber were host to some Royal visitors in August when they were played over by two future Kings of England, the Prince of Wales and Prince Albert, the Duke of York. Needless to say, they travelled to the Club by road, and did not patronise the humble tram.

Throughout the summer the Tramway remained busy, but the continued overcrowding of many of the services was considered to be too much of an inconvenience by the Golf Club and the subject was again on the agenda of their Board of Management meeting on 24th August 1918. Sir Thomas Parkyns thought that "it was only just" that places should be reserved for golfers on the 10 o'clock Sunday tram, particularly as it was paid for by the Club! The Board were so fed up with the "general attitude of the Tramway Company towards the Club" that the secretary earlier that month had visited the Petrol Engine Company at Monkbretton Bridge with a view to the possibility of engaging a motor boat service from the bridge to the ferry at Rye Harbour, thus eliminating the Tramway altogether. In this respect he had already written to the petrol department of the Board of Trade for a permit to use petrol, but the Club was, in this instance, to be out of luck, and their request for the permit was refused. The Petrol Engine Company did offer to run a boat on paraffin and place it at the Club's disposal, but their offer was not taken up. [10]

Whereas the Tramway Company's "general attitude" is not explained, it is clear to see why there was a growing friction between them and the Golf Club. When the Tramway first opened it was the most convenient and quickest means of travelling to and from the Links and indeed, it was run mainly for the benefit of golfers. For many years the Tramway Company had been happy enough to have been at the Golf Club's beck and call, but as time went on, with more and more well-to-do golfers (mainly non-resident members, but it was they who made up the majority of the Club membership) preferring the privacy of their own motor cars, it was now the holidaymaker and day tripper that had become the Company's bread and butter.

At long last, on 11th November the First World War came to an end. War or no war, the number of day trippers using the Tramway remained much the same, subject to good weather in summertime, and the timetable for June 1919 was similar to that of the previous year. Expenses had increased to such an extent (for instance, Rye Town Council that year commenced charging 1/4d. per 100 gallons for the supply of water, a rise of 33%) that from Sunday, 8th June, fares were put up for the first time since the extension to Camber Sands had opened in 1908, Second Class being abolished at the same time.

Peace Day was celebrated in Rye on Saturday, 19th July 1919 as a General Holiday with processions round the town, sports, dancing and a firework display. The Tramway enjoyed a break from its usual routine as detailed in the following notice published in the Sussex Express & County Herald the previous day:

PEACE DAY TRAM SERVICE

Mr. C. A. Gafford, the secretary to the Rye and Camber Tramways Company, informs us that for the information of the public and especially golfers, that the ordinary service will be suspended on Peace Day when only the following trams will run:

Rye	Golf Links	Camber Sands
a.m.	a.m.	a.m.
10.00	10.25	10.20
11.30	11.55	11.45

By 1920 the Rye Trade Association, still fulfilling its original objectives, had changed its name to the Rye and District Chamber of Commerce, and Mr. J. Smith at their meeting at The George Hotel on Monday evening, 8th March 1920, suggested that the Tramway timetable needed revision as the trams started from Rye and returned from Golf Links too quickly to enable people to avoid having to walk back. He explained that the 10.00 returned at 10.20, the 1.30 at 1.43 and the last journey, the most convenient, came back at 4.35 p.m.. He believed that the reason why the return journey was made so soon was "because of the sand blowing and being a detriment to the engine" and thought that, to avoid this, the tram should go up the line a little and wait at a spot near "Beachlands". He moved a resolution to the effect that a longer wait at the Golf Links would be a benefit to the public and lead to increased traffic. Mr. H. Ashbee confirmed that when goods were sent to Camber for delivery, the man often had insufficient time to do his business and catch a return tram and Mr. Donald Jones spoke in favour of a better service on Tuesday afternoons (early closing day for most businesses) and Sundays as the present 1.30 p.m. tram was too early for those who dined in the middle of the day.

The Mayor, Councillor J. L. Deacon, agreed that anything that stimulated the Tramway Company to give an improved service would be so much the better, and he had every confidence that the Company would listen to any reasonable request from their Chamber of Commerce. In Mr. Milsom's opinion it was a question of money and management. A short time ago they "went round with a hat" in order to get the service improved and Mr. F. G. Smith admitted that three of them had to pay up themselves, confirming that the previous newspaper article had not touched certain traders' consciences as had been hoped. Mr. T. Bushby contended that if the Company ran "at more popular

33. A fine portrait of CAMBER and her train waiting patiently at Camber Sands station on a dull summer's day some time in the early 1920s. *(Lens of Sutton)*

34. The sun shone for VICTORIA, polished to perfection, when she posed similarly for the photographer at Camber Sands station around the same time.
(Colonel Stephens Railway Museum & Archives, Tenterden)

35. From rail level a passenger chats with CAMBER's driver, whilst others look for a space in the already crowded open passenger wagon at Camber Sands in the summer of 1924. The locomotive's badly cracked nearside rear spectacle plate still awaits repair after some twenty years! *(Wilfrid Shearan)*

prices" they would get more customers and obtain a better return. The Chairman of the Chamber of Commerce, none other than Cuthbert Hayles (who still held his position as Chairman of the Directors of the Tramway Company) confirmed that, if the resolution was passed it would be considered and reminded members that the trams only paid during four months of the year, and that it would pay them better to "shut up" for six months out of twelve. The resolution was then put and carried.

Other than for the privileged minority who owned a private motor car the Tramway was the only way to get to and from Camber, the only alternatives being to walk or cycle. This situation, however, was soon to change, as witnessed by the advertisement that appeared in the Sussex Express & County Herald on Friday, 26th March 1920:

CHAR-A-BANC TRIPS TO CAMBER
"E. Bryan's summer motor service will commence on Sunday next, March 28th.. Cars will leave "The Garage" at the following times:
Leave Rye 9.45 a.m. 2 p.m. 3 p.m. 5 p.m.
Leave Camber Sands 2.30 p.m. 4.30 p.m. 5.30 p.m.
Leave Golf Links 10.15 a.m. 2.35 p.m. 4.35 p.m. 5.35 p.m.
Single Fare Golf Links 9d.   Camber Sands 1/-
Book your seats early"

"The Garage" was situated in King Street, Rye, (now known as Landgate) from where Mr. Edward Bryan had founded a bicycle manufacturing business back in the early 1890s, which he later expanded to include motor engineering. Cunningly aimed at the golfers staying at the Dormy House Club just a hundred yards away, the morning departure was timed to run a quarter of an hour ahead of the Tram service, but the journey would cost more than double the Tramway's First Class fare. (So much for Mr. T. Bushby's recent remark that the Tramway might get more passengers if they charged "more popular" prices!)

With reference to the resolution passed at the March meeting of the Rye Chamber of Commerce, the Rye & Camber Tramways Company replied that during the summer months an improved service would be run, but confirmed that the quick turn-round of the tram at Golf Links was to prevent sand blowing into the engine. His not un-reasonable suggestion that the locomotive might wait up the line close to "Beachlands" seems to have been conveniently ignored!

There was a subtle change in the local newspaper's description of the Whitsuntide holiday in Rye when it was reported that "a good many golfers were on the Camber course throughout the day, and the *motor service* had a busy time in conveying people to and from "Camber Sands". There were no special attractions to keep Rye holiday folk in the town, and a large number went over to Hastings, whilst others availed themselves of the motor service to Tenterden and other places on the route". [11] Perhaps after 25 years the Tram had become too much a part of everyday life to be worthy of a mention, but surely it, too, must have taken its fair share of holidaymakers to the sands. Mr. Bill Cutting recalled

that round about this time he and a friend, on at least one occasion, travelled between Rye and Golf Links (unofficially) on the roof of the carriages as the tram was so full!

Mr. Edward Bryan's char-a-banc service to the Golf Links and Camber Sands was withdrawn by the end of the summer season and was not re-instated in 1921. Rather than breathe a sigh of relief, the Tramway Company should have heeded this warning that they might not have the monopoly on the Camber holiday traffic for much longer. As it was, many of the local golfers now also preferred to drive to the Club House in their new motor cars, even though the road took a very roundabout route from Rye with the added inconvenience of three toll gates to pass on the way. Hickman's Gate was close to St. John's Cottage at East Guldeford, with Tree Gate a few hundred yards beyond at the first right-angled bend, whilst Broadwater Gate was situated just around the sharp left-hand corner soon after the road had crossed over the stream of that name. The main purpose of these gates was to keep sheep in their respective fields, but a few pence had to be paid to pass each one.

Thanks to the long, dry, hot summer, the Tramway had an extremely busy season, but a possible new threat arrived in the area during the Spring of 1922 when the East Kent Road Car Company acquired premises in Fishmarket Road, Rye on which to construct a small dormitory shed for their buses. The Company had been formed on the amalgamation of Folkestone District, Deal & District, Margate, Canterbury & District and Ramsgate Coaches back in August 1916, and it had extended its stage carriage services as far westwards as Hastings by 1920, [12] their route between New Romney and Rye taking the more inland main road via the small village of Brookland.

After a three year reprieve, the Rye & Camber Tramways Company must have realised that sooner or later motor buses would set up in business against them. Surprisingly, the competition was not to come from the East Kent Road Car Company, as this notice appearing in the Sussex Express & County Herald on Friday, 7th March 1924 explained:

"NEW MOTOR SERVICE.- In order to supply a long felt want, Messrs. Wright & Pankhurst of Rye, who deserve to be congratulated upon their enterprise, are instituting a motor service from Rye to the Camber Golf Links and Rye Harbour. The interior arrangements and seating accommodation of the vehicle (which holds about 25) is excellent, so as to ensure the comfort of passengers. The inhabitants of Rye Harbour will in particular find the service a great boon, as hitherto they have been very isolated and practically cut off from the rest of the world. If the service proves a success, it is hoped to extend it further along the coast to such places as Lydd and New Romney".

Already well established as "motor car proprietors" since 1911, the Company, one of the oldest in Rye, had been started around 1850 by Mr. Isaac Wright carting

36. For 29 years the Rye & Camber Tramway had more or less held the monopoly of taking passengers to Camber until, in March 1924, Messrs. Wright & Pankhurst of Rye commenced operating this 'bus between Camber and Rye Harbour via Rye. The driver, Mr. Amos Wright, proudly poses with the new vehicle and his sisters Doris, Lillie and Alice outside the Royal William Hotel opposite the Golf Club House.

(A. N. Wright collection)

goods to and from London with a horse and wagon. With the arrival of the South Eastern Railway in the town he was appointed its agent and he ran a carrying business to the local villages. At the turn of the century he handed over the Company to his son, William Newton Wright and his son's cousin, T. G. Pankhurst, the present owners. The new 'bus was based at Messrs. Wright & Pankhurst's "Fireproof Furniture Repository" in Tower Street, and operated from their office in Cinque Ports Street to Rye Harbour and Camber as two distinctly different services. An unusual finishing touch to the vehicle's bright blue and white livery was the addition of a painting of Rye's Landgate Tower on its rear panel by the local Iden artist, Frederick James Hackman. Unlike the Tramway, the bus was able to offer an almost door to door service, taking its passengers right into the town of Rye [13] rather than leaving them half a mile short of their destination on the wrong side of the River! One would have expected the Tramway Company to have fought back, but no! Their timetables that had appeared in the

37. This well-known postcard featuring VICTORIA with all of the passenger rolling stock at Camber Sands c.1922 was published in several editions, including one that was colour enhanced. As if to emphasise how popular the open passenger wagons were, they are both filled to capacity, whereas the two closed carriages appear to be empty!

(Clifford Bloomfield collection)

local press until the beginning of the decade were not re-instated. Although their fares remained a half of those charged on the 'bus, how many visiting holidaymakers must have travelled out to Camber not even realising that there was a much more comfortable tram service that would have taken them directly to the sands?

The price of coal had more than doubled since 1914 and CAMBER and VICTORIA were proving to be more expensive to maintain than ever, so on the recommendation of the Tramway's engineer and director, Holman F. Stephens, (by now Lieutenant Colonel, but who had already became known as "The Colonel") a small petrol locomotive was purchased from the Kent Construction Company of Victoria Street, Ashford, Kent. She may not have been everybody's idea of what a railway locomotive should look like, lacking the classic lines of her stablemates, but she proved to be quite capable of hauling the two passenger carriages, though she did struggle a little when two open passenger trucks had to be added to her train on busy days!

For some un-explained reason, the Tramway Company failed to notice that the Golf Club's lease on the re-claimed land behind the extension embankment had expired on 10th September 1924. Surely, with 'bus and car competition eating into its meagre profits, the Company needed ever penny it could lay its hands on. The Golf Club conveniently "forgot" to negotiate the renewal of the lease and continued to occupy the land free of charge, whilst still sub-letting a part of it to the local farmer, Mr. Longley!

Whether it was the introduction of the petrol locomotive that enabled the Tramway Company to lower its already reasonable fares is not clear, but in April 1925 they were reduced to the equivalent of the 1908 Second Class tariff, but now one class only. In future CAMBER and VICTORIA would only be used on the busiest weekends and Bank Holidays when traffic was expected to be the heaviest, or on the rare occasions that the petrol locomotive failed.

Successful the Golf Club may have been in the past controlling development in the proximity of their Links by buying up threatened plots of land "with a view to preventing further building", but half a mile east of the coastguard cottages, over the past few years bungalows had been "springing up in all directions, and caravans are dotted here and there as there are not enough houses in Camber". [14] Seaward of this un-controlled development a short, but tiring walk away across undulating sand dunes, stretched the best part of the golden Camber Sands. There was to be a profitable business in selling refreshments to the thousands of summer visitors, and soon several tea rooms were being hastily constructed, one of the first advertising: [15]

"The Cottage Tea Rooms, close to the main road and adjoining the Sand Dunes, are now open. The motor 'bus stops at the door, and a speciality is the supply of good home-made confectionery and refreshments at popular prices, and luncheon parties are catered for. Park for cars".

On Saturday, 23rd May 1925, Messrs. Wright & Pankhurst extended their operations by opening another bus route between Camber and Winchelsea Beach via Rye, [16] this having been made possible by the acquisition back in November of a second saloon bus. Such was the great interest shown in the local picture on the rear of the original vehicle that Frederick Hackman was asked to paint a picture of the "Ypres Castle" on this new arrival, and subsequent deliveries had "Rye Church and the Striking Boys" and "Camber Castle" added respectively, the latter being reproduced in several of the London pictorial newspapers. The new route brought the Company's mileage to the grand total of eight, and though their stage carriage services were proving to be a great success, the previously suggested extensions along the coast into west Kent were left to more ambitious operators.

Now that there was a bus service that left Cinque Ports Street, Rye for Camber at 9.45 on Sunday mornings, the secretary of Rye Golf Club raised the question as to whether it was worth the Club continuing to share with the Dormy House the expense of running the 10.00 a.m. Sunday tram to Golf Links during the winter months. If no one used the service, as was sometimes the case, it cost the Club 7/6d, but after discussion, it was decided to continue paying the Tramway Company this amount. [17]

At the beginning of October, Charles Gafford wrote to the Golf Club asking them if they would increase their subsidy to £50 "to help defray the cost of running a curtailed winter service" with the usual threat that if the subsidy was not forthcoming, the Tram service would have to be abandoned until the following summer. The letter was discussed at the Golf Club's Board of Management Meeting on 10th October, but as the Tram had out-lived its usefulness as far as the Club was concerned, they replied that they "could not see the way to grant this subsidy". The £38 subsidy paid by the Club the previous winter would ensure a service up to the end of 1925, but commencing with the New Year the Tramway service became seasonal only.

1. Rye Golf Club Minute Book 12.8.1916.
2. Rye Golf Club Minute Book 3.3.1917.
3. Rye Golf Club Board of Management Minute Book 14.4.1917.
4. Rye Golf Club Board of Management Minute Book 12.5.1917.
5. "Rye Golf Club - The First 90 Years" - Denis Vidler, 1984.
6. Rye Golf Club Board of Management Minute Book 8.9.1917.
7. Rye Golf Club Board of Management Minute Book 10.11.1917.
8. Rye Golf Club Board of Management Minute Book 8.9.1917.
9. Sussex Express & County Herald, Saturday 25.5.1918.
10. Rye Golf Club Board of Management Minute Book 12.10.1918.
11. Sussex Express & County Herald, Friday 28.5.1920. The motor service, which ran twice per day, was operated by a Mr. Standen.
12. "The Motor Bus Services of Kent & East Sussex" - Eric Baldock, 1985.
13. 'Buses and char-a-bancs were (and are still) not allowed in the narrow High Street and had to pick up and set down their pasengers in the wider Cinque Ports Street.
14. Sussex Express & County Herald, Friday 11.8.1922.
15. Sussex Express & County Herald, Friday 22.5.1925.
16. Sussex Express & County Herald, Friday 22.5.1925.
17. Rye Golf Club Board of Management Minute Book 12.9.1925.

Chapter Eight
CHANGING FORTUNES
(1926-1939)

For thirty years the Tramway had provided a regular daily service between Rye and Camber, but now, like so many minor railways at that time, it was falling victim to the motor car and bus. Who could have blamed anyone for preferring the comfort of a direct 'bus ride from Rye Harbour into Rye rather than suffer the inconvenience of being rowed across the River Rother in a primitive open boat, only to have to wait on the draughty platform at Golf Links station for the Tram? After a sunny start to the New Year, snow made an un-welcome return to the Rye area on Thursday, 14th January 1926. Cars were soon in trouble on the slippery roads and the 'bus services, which were all that ordinary working folk now had to rely on, were discontinued, giving intending passengers no alternative but to stay at home, or brave the arctic weather on foot. [1]

Having occupied the Tramway's reclaimed land (referred to by the Golf Club as the "practise ground") rent free for almost two years, the Club brought up the matter of renewing the lease with their solicitors, but their advice was to leave things as they were and not to say anything to the Company! [2]

Joseph Adams read an interesting paper that he had written specially for the meeting of the Rye Literary Society on Monday evening, 14th November 1926, in which he described his memories of the town dating back to when he had moved there from Hastings as a young boy. After describing the Monkbretton Bridge as a "gingerbread structure" in view of the way "it became necessary to practically rebuild the contraption in less than a quarter of a century", he went on to say that few realised at the time what " a remarkable harvest would be reaped by this further spanning of the River Rother within the confines of the Borough [3] which, coupled with the enterprise shown in what visitors describe as our "toy railway", brought Camber and Rye Harbour within measurable distance". But now, thanks to that same bridge, the ever conquering motor vehicle had brought those villages even closer, to the detriment of the Tramway.

It might have been assumed that the Camber Tea Rooms, situated immediately behind Camber Sands station, would have fallen out of favour with the exodus of day trippers to the sands further to the east, but this was not the case. Most local people continued to patronise the tram, and preferred to congregate on the large shingle bank near the station, and the refreshment room continued to be a lucrative business. The lease on the Tea Rooms came up for renewal on Christmas Day, but rather than renew it for a further period of 7 years, the Golf Club, (who had recently purchased the freehold of their Links from the Curteis Estate Trustees) was only

prepared to grant a yearly tenancy, although Mrs. Wilson, the lessee, was given permission to use the building as a bungalow. [4]

1927 got off to a sad start when, on 7th January, Alderman Frank Jarrett passed away. Thanks mainly to his efforts, the Tram had been kept running throughout the winter of 1900-1, and from then onwards he had served as a director of the Company. His funeral took place at the parish church of St. Mary the Virgin, Rye the following Wednesday, and having been a very popular man who had done much good for the town, a large number of people attended the service to pay their last tokens of respect. Among the many floral tributes was one from his fellow Tramway directors.

The Tramway broke its long silence in the local press when the Sussex Express & County Herald dated Friday, 6th April briefly advised

"The Rye & Camber Tramways Company announce the resumption of the service to and from Camber Sands on Monday, 11th April when a frequent service will be run."

No further information was given, and it was left up to the prospective passenger to find out details such as times etc. for himself. This generally un-helpful attitude, though surely not intentional, can hardly have helped the Tramway win back custom from the buses!

The General Strike of 1926 had dealt a fatal blow to the Rye Harbour Commissioners, and with no other local body possessing the knowledge or resources to run the harbour, it had been inherited by the Commissioners of the Levels who, naturally, were more interested in land drainage than navigation. [5] Combining with the Borough of Rye and the Kent and Sussex Councils, with the Ministry of Agriculture contributing half of the cost, they put in hand an ambitious scheme, devised by Mr. M. du Plat Taylor, M.Inst. C.E., to keep the harbour mouth clear of shingle, and at the same time re-claim a considerable area of land between the Tramway and the sea east of Golf Links station. At every high tide the muddy flats would be inundated to such an extent that silt, much of which had been dredged from the river bed, was washed over the stonework and back into the river. Starting in September 1927 on what was to be a 2 year task, a dam was built across the lower end of the mud flat to keep back the sea, and the stonework from a position near Golf Links station to a point close to the river mouth was raised by about 2 ft. so as to prevent the silt from being washed back into the channel. [6] Never again would the Tramway extension be damaged by the sea! Another part of the Rother Improvement Scheme involved dredging the river from its mouth as far as Scots Float (to the north-east of Rye) and some of the estimated 185,000 tons of material removed was pumped ashore into the Council owned field that marked the Borough Boundary close to the Broadwater Stream. This had the effect of raising the level of the land to that of the Tramway that had previously been carried across that part of the field on a low embankment. The Monkbretton Bridge again required attention when its foundations had to be under-pinned and deepened, but on this occasion the work was carried out without disruption to the road traffic.

Included in the land purchased by the Golf Club from the Curteis Estate Trustees were extensive areas of gravel deposits and in October 1927, Mr. G. T. Jennings approached the Club stating that he was desirous of obtaining from them the sole right to take shingle from their property at Northpoint Beach. At the Golf Club's Board of Management Meeting on 15th October the rates and amounts of shingle that could be removed were agreed and a 7 year lease was granted to Mr. Jennings on 14th July. Situated between the Rye & Camber Tramway and the Camber road a quarter of a mile east of the Broadwater toll gate, the beach works subsequently constructed its own internal 2ft.0in. gauge tramway which was gradually extended as the business expanded, the shingle being shovelled by hand into William Jones' "Excelsior" side-tipping wagons. The original motive power would appear to have been provided by an unusual machine called PAT, that consisted of a Morris Cowley "Flatnose" engine, bonnet and radiator (and possibly the gearbox) mounted on a Jones' skip chassis which boasted the "luxury" of a wooden cab with a curved tin roof! It was not until 1952 that this strange contraption was joined by two standard Motor Rail Simplex petrol locomotives (Works nos. 7021 and 7025) that had been obtained from the neighbouring Rother & Jury's Gut Catchment Board who had purchased them new for use on their line between Rye Harbour and Pett Level in 1936.

Camber was still developing in its haphazard way, helped now by Mr. William Newton Wright (the senior partner in the Company of Messrs. Wright & Pankhurst) who, taking advantage of the Hastings Tramways' decision to abandon its ageing electric tramway system in favour of new and quieter trolleybuses in 1928, brought a considerable number of their un-wanted tram bodies to Camber where they were converted into much needed living accommodation. In doing this, not only did he help the growing village, but at the same time provided more custom for his Company's bus service into Rye! Seven further tram bodies were purchased by Mr. R. J. Tunbridge which, named after different sea birds, he placed on the sands to lease to visitors.

In September 1928, the Tramway Company applied for the renewal of its lease for their line over the now Golf Club property which was due to expire on 25th May 1929. As they were extending a lease that had already run for 21 years, it was thought that "the rent should be reduced", but the Golf Club firmly advised "this suggestion cannot be entertained" and the lease was subsequently renewed for a further period of 21 years at the same rental of ten guineas per annum.[7] The "practise ground" was excluded from the new lease and became the property of the Golf Club, and as the latter believed (incorrectly) that the fence between the reclaimed land and the Tramway had only "been erected to keep in the Lessors' tennant's sheep", the Tramway Company was saved the future trouble of maintaining it. Because thistle down had been causing a nuisence blowing over the Links from the "practise ground", an extra clause was added to the Rye & Camber Tramway's Agreement ordering the Company "to keep all the demised land, including the banks of the Tramway, free from thistles and other noxious weeds", but a scribbled note in the margin of the Draft Lease cheekily suggested that "If the Lessees are to keep down thistles, the Lessors must do their part on the ground where they grow"!

The Tramway Company's application to renew its lease with Rye Corporation had come up for consideration at the Town Council's meeting on 3rd September and on 1st October the Leasehold Committee advised

"We have carefully considered the application of the Rye & Camber Tramways Company Ltd. for the renewal of their lease which expires on the 25th day of March next and recommend that such a lease be renewed on the same terms as before, namely, for a period of 21 years at the annual rent of £6 10s.0d. subject to the same conditions".

The Common Seal of the Council was affixed to the document on 10th June 1929.

1930 was to be a particularly sad year for the Rye & Camber Tramway as they were to lose several of their closest friends. This was only to be expected for those "middle-aged" men that had set up the Company thirty five years before, were now into their seventies, not that that made their departing any easier. The first to pass away was one of the original shareholders, Joseph Adams who, after only a short illness, died at his home at Barchester Tower, St. Leonards-on-Sea, Sussex on Friday, 6th June 1930 at the age of 71. Mr. Adams had been elected as the Mayor of Rye no less than 4 times, occupied a seat on the Borough Bench, being added to the permanent roll of Borough Justices in 1910, represented the town on the East Sussex County Council for 20 years, and at the Coronation of King George the Fifth he received the honour of being made a "Baron of the Cinque Ports". Not only had he been a strong supporter of the Tramway Company, but he had also materially assisted in the formation of Rye Golf Club. His funeral took place at Rye Parish Church on the afternoon of Wednesday, 11th June and was attended by many of his colleagues in public life from all over Sussex including the Mayor, Councillor J. Molyneux Jenkins and the Corporation in state.

Six weeks later, on 19th July, Mr. E. P. S. Jones, proprietor of the Rother Ironworks for over 40 years, departed this life at Walmer in Kent, where he had lived for the past seven years. Along with Lt. Colonel H. F.

38. Royal William Hotel viewed from outside the Golf Club House in 1926. Apart from the wonderful assortment of golfers' cars, note the appalling condition of the East Guldeford to Camber road.
(Rye Golf Club)

39. A Wright & Pankhurst 'bus (centre, right) heads through the developing plotland village of Camber on its way back to Rye in the mid-1920s. Camber Sands station was inconveniently situated more than half a mile away out of the picture to the left.
(Laurie Band collection, courtesy of Rye Museum)

40. The Rye Harbour ferryman, with one lady passenger, arrives at Rye Harbour village in the round-keeled vessel he uses at high tide. On the eastern bank of the River Rother are (left to right) Golf Links station, the ferry steps, the harbourmaster's cottage and the hexagonal concrete lighthouse. The steam crane in the background was probably employed on raising the stonework by around 2 ft. between here and the river mouth to prevent silt from being washed back into the channel, and would suggest a date of 1928-9. *(Hastings Library)*

Stephens, he had held the position of the Tramway's engineer, and his works in Fishmarket Road performed all of the heavier repairs to the Company's locomotives and rolling stock. According to one reliable source, it was Mr. E. P. S. Jones who actually paid for CAMBER and VICTORIA and the Tramway Company reimbursed him as and when they were able to.

Although now 73 years old, Cuthbert Hayles was still living a very active life and on Thursday, 4th September he was carrying out one of his many regular appointments as Deputy Registrar for Hastings County Court. For the past few years he had lived with his daughter at "The Reculvers", Old London Road, Hastings, but the following morning she was alarmed to find that her father's bed had not been slept in. To her horror she found him dead on the kitchen floor. Mr. Hayles was the senior ex-Mayor of Rye, being described as "one of the best Mayors that had ever occupied the civic chair in the Ancient Borough", and he had served as Clerk of the Peace from 1919 right up to his sudden death. "Service before self" was a maxim that he strikingly illustrated throughout the whole of his public career and he never had an unkind word to say of anyone. "Extreme simplicity characterised the funeral on Wednesday afternoon at the Hastings Borough Cemetery. In accordance with Mr. Hayles' own wish there were no flowers and the service, conducted by the Rev. B. H. Pemberton, vicar of All Saints, Clive Vale (Hastings) was brief and almost austere in its quiet dignity. A number of Mr. Hayles' associates in his many public and legal offices, both in Hastings and Rye, attended to pay a last silent tribute to his long and useful service to both towns". Among the many mourners was Mr. C. A. Gafford, representing the Tramway Company of which Mr. Hayles had been the chairman of the directors since its opening. "Mr. Hayles was laid to rest on the side of a gentle slope, overlooking the beautiful sweep of the Rye levels, with the red roofs of the ancient town, which was always so near to his heart, just visible in the hazy distance." [8]

Following the death of Messrs. Wright & Pankhurst's senior partner, William Newton Wright, on Sunday, 10th August, it was decided to close the bus side of its business and on Wednesday, 1st October the East Kent Road Car Company took over the firm's Rye Harbour, Winchelsea and Camber services. [9] Five vehicles were involved in the take-over, and at least two of them must have carried the East Kent livery of rich red and cream as they remained with their new owner until 1935. The other three were believed to have been out of use from the end of 1930 and had been sold by September 1931. [10]

It almost seemed as if with the passing away of the likes of Cuthbert Hayles and Joseph Adams, the Tramway Company had given up the will to succeed, and when the figures for 1930 were published they showed a loss. In an effort to reduce maintenance costs the run-round loop at Golf Links (which had long since become surplus to requirements) was removed, the steam locomotives' elevated water tank had been dismantled at Rye by the

Spring of 1931, and with no coal being purchased during that year, it would appear that CAMBER and VICTORIA were already out of use. With passenger receipts amounting to only £439 9s.10d., mainly as the result of a poor summer weatherwise, a loss had been sustained for the second year in succession, both years added together totalling £109 4s.5d.. In place of Cuthbert Hayles, Mr. C. Ashton Selmes had been elected as Chairman of the Directors.

The run of deaths of those closely associated with the Rye & Camber Tramways Company continued when Lt. Col. Holman Fred Stephens died at the Lord Warden Hotel in Dover on Friday, 23rd October 1931, after a long illness in which he had suffered a number of strokes. Although officials from the Southern Railway and many of the Colonel's lines attended the funeral at St. Peter's Church, Hammersmith on Wednesday, 28th October, the Rye & Camber Tramway was not represented. The Directors' Report published at the Annual General Meeting held at the Railway Hotel, Rye on Tuesday, 29th March 1932 advised

"We have suffered a further loss on the Directorate through the death of Col. H. F. Stephens, who was the Consulting Engineer to the Company at its formation and had served the Company with his advice and help ever since, and we regret the loss the Company has sustained."

Colonel Stephens' assistant, William Henry Austen, took over the post of consulting engineer, and continued to advise the Tramway Company, at least until the commencement of the Second World War in September 1939.

Despite the increased motor traffic and the occasional shattered windscreen (as many as 4,000 cars per day were using the East Guldeford to Camber road in the summer of 1931) 5^1/$_2$ years were to lapse before the Golf Club, at a Special Meeting of the Board of Management on 13th January 1932, reluctantly passed the plans of Golf Architect, Mr. T. Simpson, to alter the Course. [11] They would have preferred to have had the road diverted inland to the north, but this had proved to be too expensive. Once the decision to alter the Course had been made, work progressed rapidly and by the end of the year the new holes had been completed and were in play. Still concerned at the number of people trespassing on their property, the Golf Club invited Sir Laurence Chubb, secretary of the Commons, Open Spaces and Footpath Protection Society, to visit their Links in August 1932 to ask his opinion as to what should be done to alleviate the matter. His (obvious) advice was that the property should be fenced, leaving 3 means of access to the sands for the public, namely at the back of the 6th tee, past the coastguard cottages (probably a right of way for foot passengers) and from the Royal William Hotel to the Rye Harbour ferry. [12]

Upon receipt of Sir Laurence's report of his visit, the Golf Club took his advice and proceeded with the erection of fencing consisting of concrete posts with wire in the sand hills and along the shore, with chestnut

41. Unusually, the petrol locomotive waits with both carriages, but only one of the open passenger wagons at Rye station c.1930. The elevated water tank behind the shabby-looking engine shed has already been dismantled, but notice how neat and tidy the rest of the station area is with no clutter or weeds in sight.
(Lens of Sutton)

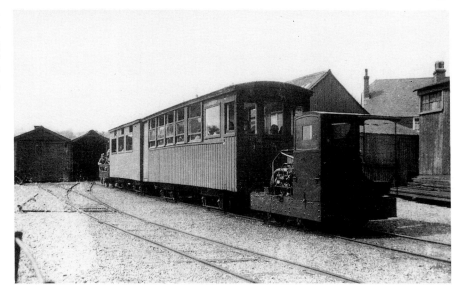

42. In the last years of the Tramway's existence, a gentleman dressed in trilby hat and plus-fours stands back to allow the ladies to board the tram at Rye station.
(John Scott-Morgan collection)

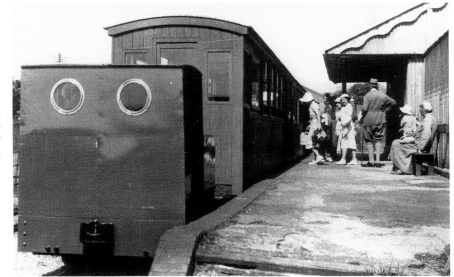

43. Everything is very quiet as the spotless petrol locomotive and solitary Bagnall carriage wait for passengers at Rye.
(J. M. Jarvis)

pailings beside the road, a distance of about 1¹/₂ miles. [13] No sooner had the work been carried out when the Tramway Company accused the Golf Club of erecting some of the new fencing on the land leased to them. This would have been on the (by then) lifted spur beyond Camber Sands station into the sand hills. The Golf Club's reply to their letter of complaint advised that this was not the case, but that "if the fencing has been erected over the land over which you have the right to extend your line we would set the fence back". [14]

Over the past few years a new secondary school built by Messrs. Bainbridge of Eastbourne, had been taking shape alongside the Tramway station in Rye, and on 31st May 1933 East Sussex County Council wrote to Rye Town Council advising that arrangements had been made for the construction of a footbridge on the south side of Monkbretton Bridge and that work would be put in hand at an early date, subject to a grant being received from the Ministry of Transport. The grant must have been forthcoming as the footbridge was in position in time for the opening of the school on 27th September that year, thus providing, at last, safe access for Tramway passengers as well as those attending the school.

Some time during the mid-1930s the Rye & Camber Tramways Company experienced a slight upset to its normal routine when on a summer Saturday evening the petrol locomotive was de-railed on the bridge across the Broadwater Stream where the heat had caused the rails to close up. The tram was delayed while the driver and conductor fetched some replacement timbers from one of the shipyards in Rye and, on their return, they cut out a part of the troublesome rail with a hacksaw. [15] In July 1935 some "Tramway employees" (probably men hired on a casual basis to help out during the summer) cut down three trees which may have been on the embankment approaching Golf Links station but were, nevertheless, the property of the Golf Club. When approached by the Club, Charles Gafford could only admit that the work had been carried out unknown to him by mistake (!?) and he hoped that the Committee would accept the Tramway Company's apologies. [16]

Because the Drainage Authority had restricted the depth to which gravel could be excavated from Northpoint Beach in its original permission of 1928, the workings were approaching the end of their life, so Mr. G. T. Jennings asked the Golf Club for permission to

Rye Golf Club's Map showing proposed deviation of Tramway at Camber Sands, 1937.

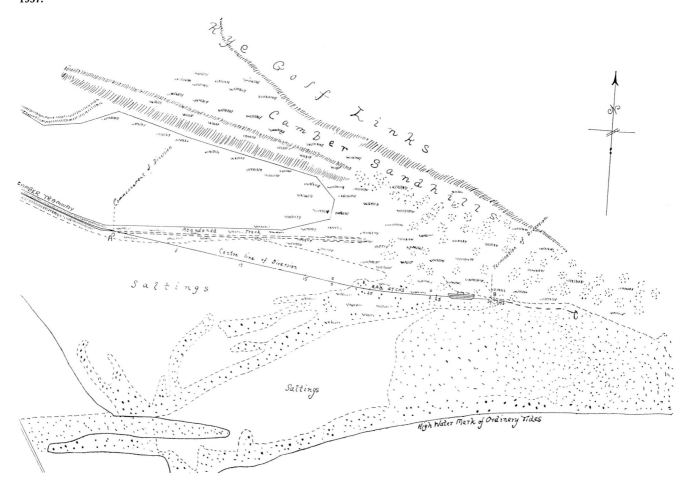

construct a concrete culvert under the Tramway to provide access to the shingle to the south of the line. The Golf Club approached the Tramway Company on the subject, and as they had no objection to Mr. Jennings' proposal, the secretary advised him accordingly. [17]

Most of the 1932 alterations to the Golf Course had been well received, but when asked to suggest ways of improving the short 4th hole, Golf Architect Sir Guy Campbell suggested that it might be better to alter the Course in other ways. The Committee were shocked at such a suggestion and in October advised him that they "could not approve of any major alterations to the Course at the present moment". [18] However, Sir Guy had many supporters for his imaginative re-building of the first half of the Course, and when his plans were put before a Special General Meeting a year later, they were passed. [19] His proposals would extend the Course away from the narrow strip of land beside the Camber road, over the first range of sand hills and down towards the Tramway, thus bringing about what must be a unique occurrence in the annals of British (if not world) railway history - the moving of a station to improve a Golf Course!

Negotiations commenced when the Golf Club wrote to the Tramway Company secretary, Charles Gafford, on 19th April 1937:

Dear Sir,

"I am instructed by the Board of Management of the Rye Golf Club, to put forward for your consideration a proposal for the diversion and extension of your track of about 375 yards, which would result in bringing the terminus to a point considerably nearer to the Coast Guard Station.

"You will no doubt recollect that this was a future project which was occupying your attention as early as 1928....

"....It is thought that there may be two lines of dealing with this matter.

"The first would be to accept the Golf Club's proposal in principle in which case an agreement would have to be reached as regards the financing of the extension.

"Secondly, as it is understood that from a profit earning point of view, your Company has not been faring too well and further that the condition of the track etc. is such as to warrant the expectation of considerable expenditure in the near future, it may be that your Directors might care to consider some arrangement by which your Company would be liquidated and satisfaction given to your debenture holders.

"We trust that these observations will not be taken as suggesting that we wish to influence the policy of your Company in any way, and .... I should be very glad if your Directors could put forward some concrete proposal as soon as possible.... "

"I enclose a map of the ground in question showing the proposed alteration.
Yours etc."

On 30th May the chairman, C. Ashton Selmes, and Charles Gafford met the Golf Club sub-committee where, judging by the Golf Club's letter the following day, they must have given the impression that the Tramway Company would be quite prepared to accept the Club's second option:

31st May 1937.

The Secretary,
Rye and Camber Tramways Co. Ltd.

Dear Sir,

"With reference to the conference held on the 30th inst. at the Rye Golf Club between the Chairman and Secretary of the Tramways Co (sic) and the Sub Committee of the Golf Club appointed to deal with this matter, the Sub Committee are prepared to recommend to the Board of Management of the Rye Golf Club that an agreement be made with the Rye and Camber Tramway (sic) Co by which the Rye Golf Club buy out the interest of the Tramway Co on the following terms:

a. That the Rye Golf Club pay a minimum of £500 plus the difference if any between the profits of the Tramway to Oct next, plus the proceeds of liquidation, and the amount necessary to pay off the debentures of the Tramway Co and 10% on the ordinary shares.

b. The Tramway Co to go into liquidation for the purpose of carrying out the above as soon as possible.

c. The Tramway Co to remove as soon as possible all property belonging to them in connection with the Tramway undertaking, the benefit of all fixtures going to the Tramway Co. The Golf Club being entitled to remove at the Tramway's expense any fixtures etc. if not removed by the Tramway Co.

d. The Rye Golf Club will if required take up the liability of the Tramway Co, (except as regards arrears if any now accrued) to the Rye Corporation for rent in respect of the lease of the Corporation portion of the tramway track for the remainder of the lease.
Yours etc."

The Golf Club must have now felt sure that they would soon be rid of the Tramway, with its associated day trippers and holidaymakers, once and for all, but they were to be disappointed because, at a meeting of the Tramway Company's shareholders on 12th August, it was resolved "That the offer of the Rye Golf Club of £500 be accepted towards the extension of the line, this being subject to the Golf Club and the Rye Corporation agreeing to accept a surrender of the present leases, and granting of a lease by both parties for a period of 25 years, also subject to a further sum of £200 being raised within two months by the Tramways Company".

At a meeting on 14th August 1937, the Golf Club Finance Committee agreed in principle to the suggestions made in the Tramway Company's letter of 13th August, but they would still have to be ratified by the General Meeting of the Club that was to be held on

44. The petrol locomotive, with all the passenger stock well loaded, approaches Golf Links from Camber Sands, 12 July 1931. A visitor occupies the privileged position on the locomotive with George Wratten. *(H.C. Casserley)*

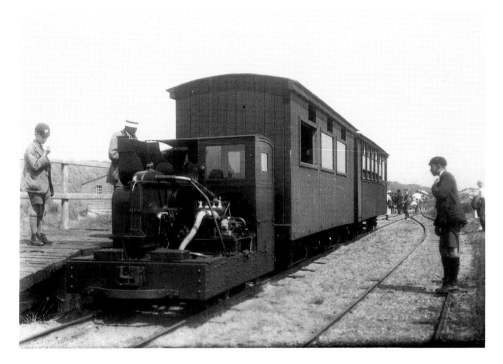

45. Two schoolboys and an older gentleman look intently at the petrol locomotive at Camber Sands station while day trippers wander over the running lines in the background on a hot September's day in 1926. The locomotive's bonnet is open to reveal the Dorman 2JO engine, and its exhaust pipe has yet to assume a neat curve downwards through 90 degrees between the engine compartment and the footplate. *(Wilfrid Shearan)*

6th October. Writing to the Tramway Company on 18th August they advised that they would require the undertakings:

(1) That as soon as the agreement is ratified your Company should forthwith proceed with the work of removing the station and line.
(2) That the £500 should be payed (sic) according to the progress of the work, at intervals as may be agreed.
(3) That no embankment be removed that gives the Course protection from the sea.

The letter concluded ".... We also assume that you will take the necessary steps to get the agreement with the Corporation, and no doubt you are aware that these steps should be taken as soon as possible". Copies of the Special Committee's Report, together with Lithographs of Sir Guy Campbell's scheme for the alteration of the Golf Course, were then sent out to all Club members.

Early and late season there might only be a handful of passengers utilising the tram on some services, but amongst these would be a few golfers who were to remain faithful right to the end. However, during the summer, the Tramway was still being well patronised as confirmed by one visitor who arrived at the Rye terminus as the tram, consisting of both carriages and the two open passenger wagons, was about to leave. Travelling out to Camber Sands he noted that "the speed was brisk, and the riding quite tolerably smooth". He returned straight away "at what was evidently a rush hour, for a large proportion of the inhabitants of Rye appeared to be on the platform; most of the would-be travellers also succeeded in boarding the train, which started with the saloons packed to standing, and passengers roughly two deep on the seats of the open trucks". Two other independent railways were not doing so well for he added that "this was in extreme contrast, from the passenger point of view, to the experiences of the deserted trains of the Kent & East Sussex and East Kent lines". [20]

Although the proposed re-siting of Camber Sands station was not to be confirmed until the Golf Club's meeting on 6th October, Charles Gafford wrote a letter to Rye Town Council on 3rd September asking if, upon surrender of the present lease held by the Rye & Camber Tramways Company dated 24.6.1929, would they be prepared to grant a new lease for 25 years on the same terms. At the Council's meeting on 13th September it was recommended that the application should be granted and "that the new lease coincide with the new lease which it is understood is to be granted by Rye Golf Club". Having heard nothing to date, the Golf Club wrote again to the Tramway Company on 30th September, reminding them that with their Extraordinary General Meeting taking place on the following Wednesday, would they please advise the intentions of their Directors with regard to the removal of the present station at Camber and the diversion of the line, pointing out that a definite agreement was not necessary, but that they had to have something in writing prior to the meeting. Mr. Gafford replied on 4th October that they had been waiting for the confirmation of the Club's proposal that was to be ratified at their meeting on 6th inst.! He concluded his letter

".... In the meantime I would say that the Rye Corporation have agreed to a surrender of the present lease and granted a fresh one for 25 years, the date to coinside (sic) with yours, on hearing from you I will immediately get in touch with this Company's Engineer as to the commencement of the alterations."

As expected, the Golf Club's Special Meeting confirmed the proposed arrangements and on 15th October their solicitor was instructed to prepare a formal document embodying the agreement which, in the Club's opinion, "should be done as a modification of the leases involved". A month later, no progress whatsoever appears to have been made and at the Golf Club's Board of Management meeting on 13th November Mr. George Marsden and Mr. Ronald Smith were instructed "to meet the Tramway engineer and negotiate the shifting back of the line as cheaply as possible". The same two gentlemen were authorised to go into the Agreement with the Tramway Company and sign it on behalf of the Committee. [21] The estimated "cost of erection" of the new Tramway was £767 2s.9d., with the Golf Club to pay £500 and the Tramway Company the remainder. If the actual cost of construction worked out less than estimated, an abatement pro rata was to be made between the two parties, but if the actual cost exceeded £767 2s.9d., then any such excess should be borne entirely by the Tramway Company.

On 4th March 1938 the new document was duly signed and sealed, not by Messrs. Marsden and Smith as authorised above, but by Doctor E. W. Skinner and Rev. H. C. Lennox Tindall (Trustees) and Colonel J. E. Cairns DSO (Secretary) on behalf of the Golf Club, and Messrs. C. Ashton Selmes, L. G. Pankhurst (Directors) [22] and C. A. Gafford (Secretary) for the Tramway Company. Although their sand traffic had ceased many years previously, for some unexplained reason, permission was granted for the Tramway to be extended beyond its new Camber Sands station without payment of extra rent!

In May, the Camber Chalet Holiday Camp opened at the eastern end of the village, but being a good mile from Camber Sands station, the Tramway would benefit very little from the new enterprise, other than perhaps providing a novelty train ride into Rye for some of the holidaymakers. Needless to say, within a month of the opening, the East Kent Road Car Company had extended its bus service to serve the new Camp.

Mr. G. T. Jennings repeated his request to build a subway under the Tramway in a letter to the Golf Club in November 1938 as "he was obliged to make arrangements to take shingle from the south side of the Tramway". Once more his request was granted, and in the following June he was granted a 21 year lease on the new land from which the shingle was to be taken. [23]

Once the Tramway had closed down for the winter in

October, work on building the deviation embankment soon started with additional labour being supplied by some un-employed men. The plans for the deviation had been prepared by William Holman Austen [24] and he personally supervised the work on instructions from his father, William Henry Austen, the Tramway Company's consulting engineer. The Camber Tea Rooms behind Camber Sands station, which had been out of use and stood derelict for several years, had already been demolished, and now two beach huts that were in the way had to be removed, one to the sands to continue to fulfil its original purpose, and the other to suffer the indignity of becoming a pig sty.

The Tramway deviation was constructed on a 3 ft. high embankment like its predecessor, with a widening of the formation at the new terminus to accommodate a sleeper-built platform and the run-round loop, and all was ready for the re-opening of the line for the Easter weekend on Thursday, 6th April 1939, the new holes on the Golf Course also coming into play that Spring. Doctor E. W. Skinner, who had had so much to do with these latest major alterations to the Golf Course, regrettably did not live to see the completion of the works as he passed away in March 1939. He had been one of the original Tramway Company directors, but although he resigned the post in March 1901, he remained a share-holder and strong supporter of the Tramway throughout his life.

Obtaining the new 25 year leases from the Golf Club and Rye Corporation certainly gave the Tramway Company a new lease of life, and the peak summer timetable for 1939 of 9 return trams compared very favourably with the rival East Kent Road Car Company's 13 weekday return trips on their service 116 between Rye and Camber. For many years the full-time Tramway staff had been reduced to just two men, driver George Wratten and Percy Sheppard the conductor. Percy would issue tickets to those in the open passenger wagons prior to departure from Rye, but some local lads found that they could avoid paying the 2d. fare if they jumped aboard as the tram pulled away from the station. W. G. "Blower" Pierce was one of these boys, and he recalled that on several occasions, George Wratten would stop the tram with the passenger trucks positioned on the bridge over the Broadwater Stream and shout unseen from his cab "Bill, I know you're on there!" In spite of having been caught red-handed, "Blower", much to the annoyance of Percy Sheppard, would still leave the tram at Golf Links without paying! [25]

Storm clouds had been gathering across the English Channel in Europe for some time, and then, on 3rd September 1939, for the second time this century, War was declared. Rather than terminate its summer service in the middle of October as had become the custom in previous years, the Rye and Camber Tramway closed prematurely, and without warning the very next day.

1. Sussex Express & County Herald, Friday 15.1.1926.
2. Rye Golf Club Board of Management Minute Book 12.6.1926.
3. The first bridge had been the South Eastern Railway's single track swing bridge opened in 1851 a few hundred yards upstream of the Monkbretton Bridge, which was superseded in 1903 by the present fixed double track steel structure.
4. Rye Golf Club Board of Management Minute Book 8.5.1926.
5. "A Maritime History of Rye" - John Collard, 1978.
6. Sussex Express & County Herald, several editions, September 1927.
7. Rye Golf Club Board of Management Meeting 15.9.1928.
8. Sussex Express & County Herald, Friday 12.9.1930.
9. Sussex Express & County Herald, Friday 3.10.1930.
10. M & D and East Kent Bus Club, letter from Nicholas King, 13.8.1990.
11. "Rye Golf Club - The First 90 Years" - Denis Vidler, 1984.
12. Rye Golf Club Board of Management Minute Book 13.8.1932.
13. Rye Golf Club Board of Management Minute Book 12.11.1931.
14. Rye Golf Club Board of Management Minute Book 1.4.1933.
15. "The Tenterden Terrier", No. 10, Summer 1976, House Journal of the Kent & East Sussex Railway.
16. Rye Golf Club Board of Management Minute Book 13.7.1935.
17. Rye Golf Club Board of Management Minute Book 14.12.1935.
18. Rye Golf Club Minute Book 10.10.1936.
19. "Rye Golf Club - The First 90 Years" - Denis Vidler, 1984.
20. "Railway Magazine", January 1938.
21. Rye Golf Club Board of Management Minute Book 15.1.1938.
22. Mr. L. G. Pankhurst had been elected to the Directorate in the early 1930s.
23. Rye Golf Club Board of Management Minute Book 17.6.1939.
24. William Holman Austen (1902-1981) was the god-son of Holman Stephens and a position was made for him at 23 Salford Terrace, Tonbridge in 1932 where he was mainly employed on outside work until 1948.
25. "Blower" received notoriety by graduating from caddying in the 1920s at the age of 9, to dominating Artisan and Sussex Golf in the 1950s and 1960s, and he received the honour of being made an Honorary Life Member of Rye Golf Club alongside a select few that included Sir Winston Churchill.

Chapter Nine

"PERADVENTURE IT SLEEPETH & IS NOT DEAD" [1] (1939-1949)

With less than two years having expired on the re-negotiated leases with the Golf Club and Rye Town Council, the Directors of the Tramway Company must have been hoping that the War would be a short one, unlike that fought between 1914 and 1918. Perhaps they even regretted closing their line with such indecent haste as life around the "Antient Town" carried on much as normal, and even the first few months of 1940 gave the country little indication of the disasters which lay ahead. Local members still frequented the Golf Club during the week and officers from the newly-formed R.A.F. Training Centre in Hastings played there regularly at weekends, but come the Spring and the atmosphere changed, for with only the English Channel separating the enemy from our shores, the south coast of England became a prime invasion target. As a safety measure the pupils of the new secondary modern school in New Road were evacuated to Bedford and the timber board walk of the footbridge alongside Monkbretton Bridge was removed for the duration so that, once more, pedestrians had to use the narrow roadway.

Unlike the Tramway, the East Kent Road Car Company did not panic at the outbreak of war, but in anticipation of fewer people wishing to travel, they reduced their service 116 between Rye and Camber from the previous hourly weekday summer schedule to 7 return trips, and the autumn timetable was similar to that operated in peacetime with 8 weekday return buses. Their fares were still well in excess of those charged on the Tram, but now, other than the motor car, they had no competition whatsoever. From Rye to the Golf Club was 7d. single and 10d. return, to the Camber Post Office 9d. single and 1/1d. return, whilst the "service will be extended to CAMBER CHALET CENTRE when required" for 10d. single and 1/3d. return.

On 22nd July 1940, with the exception of a few isolated farmers, everyone was given 48 hours to evacuate Camber and as the last families moved out at midnight on 24th July, armed sentries were already manning the barriers that were in position across the road close to the coastguard cottages. Under the command of Major F. E. Shrimpton some 4.5 howitzers were positioned next door to the Rother Ironworks in Rye, an observation post was set up in the Martello Tower called "the Enchantress" at Rye Harbour village, and mines were laid in the sand dunes, on the fairways of the Golf Course and along the coast to east and west. A concrete pill box was constructed close to the Tramway on the southern side of the Broadwater Stream, and another overlooked the site of the original Camber Sands station from the ridge of sand hills to the north. The coastguard cottages were requisitioned and the Golf

Club property beyond them was transformed into a battle school. Three large concrete fuel tanks were sunk into the 18th fairway and an old 75 m.m. French gun was positioned alongside the 11th green, near "Squatter's Right" (formerly "Beachlands"), though there is some doubt as to whether there was any amunition to fire it! [2] The mouth of the River Rother was not mined, but was protected by an anti-invasion blockade comprising a barrage of tree trunks, and vessels entering and leaving the harbour had to negotiate these obstacles via an unmarked gap. As it was, despite the major works carried out between September 1927 and 1929, silting had reduced the width of the river from 100 ft. to 60 ft. and the shingle bank on the western side was so high, it had become impossible to see the sea from Rye Harbour village.

Railway-wise there remained one vulnerable spot in the south coast defences between Dungeness and Rye, and to fill this gap Major Kenneth Cantlie, the Director of Military Railways in the invasion area, was tempted to single the 15 inch gauge Romney, Hythe & Dymchurch Railway between New Romney and Dungeness, and use the lifted track to extend that line, utilising the track bed of the Rye & Camber Tramway for the final approach to Rye. Major Cantlie very nearly arranged for the extension to be built, but as the threat of invasion diminished, so the scheme came to nought. [3]

Conveniently (or otherwise) the Tramway Company had not paid its share towards the re-siting of Camber Sands station back in 1939, but then, through no fault of their own, they had only been able to use the new deviation for one shortened season. Neither was it the fault of the Golf Club, but they received a letter in September 1941 from their solicitors, Messrs. Dawes, Son & Prentice, asking if they would be prepared to pay the Tramway's share of the cost incurred. The solicitors, surely, must have anticipated the Club's reply that as they had already paid their share, they could not make any payment on behalf of the Tramway Company! [4]

To return to Europe and defeat the enemy on their own ground was the ultimate aim of the British Government, and to prepare Rye Harbour for when it might be needed in the great offensive, in the Autumn of 1941 Messrs. Mears Brothers, with Mr. Jack Evans as civil engineer, were awarded the contract by the Admiralty to restore navigability to the River Rother. Mr. Jack Doust, who had become Harbourmaster in 1936, had single handedly removed the anti-invasion blockade from the mouth of the River, and Messrs. Mears Brothers (after several false attempts owing to the inadequate equipment with which they had been provided) as the first part of their contract cleared the shingle and silt

46. In 1946, the petrol locomotive and both carriages stand outside the large shed at Rye. Looking at the poor state of the rolling stock alone, it is hardly surprising that the directors made the decision to wind up the Company. *(Lens of Sutton)*

47. With every window broken, the once proud Bagnalll carriage stands amongst the weeds beside the platform at Rye on 10 April 1946. With a part of the panelling missing, we get the chance to see how the seating was carried across the end bulkhead when the carriage was re-built after the First World War. The Rother Ironworks carriage is just visible in the engine shed.
(S. C. Nash)

48. In July 1954, the bridge across the Broadwater Stream still had a short length of track laid across it on longitudinal sleepers, and as per the agreement with Rye Corporation of 21st May 1895, the iron fencing on the western side of the Tramway has been left in situ. *(J. G. Vincent)*

sucessfully from the river with the aid of a converted Thames barge fitted with 8in. suction pipes. Their second task was to build a concrete slipway at the Rother Ironworks that would be available at all states of the tide, complete with a turntable for turning motor gun boats. The third phase of their contract (and of more interest to our narrative) was to construct what was to become known as the 1,350 ft long "Adniralty Jetty", and this was achieved by joining together the wooden stages on the Camber side of the River Rother opposite Rye Harbour village.

For over three years the new senior school in New Road had remained un-occupied, but now the building, along with 20 nissan huts that had been sited in the narrow space between the Tramway and the Camber footpath just outside Rye Tram Station, became a small Royal Naval establishment known as H.M.S. Haig. The Tramway had also been quietly slumbering, completely oblivious to what was going on around it, but early in 1943, with no vehicular access to the Admiralty Jetty site, permission was sought to use the Tramway to transport men, equipment and stores between Rye and Golf Links station. Authority was received fron Tramway Company director Mr. J. L. Pankhurst, acting in his capacity as a Rye Harbour Commissioner.

Despite being out of use for so long, the permanant way remained in reasonable condition and only the latterly constructed crude bridge carrying the Tramway over Mr. G. T. Jennings' gravel works on Northpoint Beach required major attention to make it safe. At Golf Links the run-round loop was re-instated and a siding, $4^{1}/_{2}$ chains long, facing Camber Sands was crudely constructed from off the loop to serve a wooden jetty on the River Rother. On a falling gradient, the siding, laid directly onto the sandy soil, curved sharply to the left on a radius of $2^{1}/_{2}$ chains, to run onto the jetty at right-angles to the stonework. The sleepers were spiked directly onto the longitudinal timbers of the pier and a post and chain link fence provided a little protection on the south side of the structure only. The Admiralty had no use for the Tramway beyond Golf Links, and the turn-out for the new siding could well have been that previously sited at the west end of the run-round loop at Camber Sands station.

Messrs. West's Engineering (whose main business was to repair agricultural machinery at their premises adjoining the Camber road at G. T. Jenning's gravel pit) sent their fitter, Ken Hickman, to the Tramway Station at Rye who, being responsible for keeping the gravel pit's crude "Morris Cowley" locomotive PAT in operation, soon had the Kent Construction Company petrol locomotive running. The body of the Rother Ironworks carriage was also carefully removed so that its chassis could be used as a bogie flat truck for carrying the longer lengths of timber. All the materials were stacked just beyond the platform to the east of the running line at Golf Links station, and the building at long last served a useful purpose by becoming a mess room for the men, and later, rumour has it, a mortuary! At Rye the booking office also found a new lease of life as a Guard Room. The Tramway did not have a monopoly in carrying goods to the site, and to enable motor vehicles to reach the jetty, the access road to "Squatter's Right" (un-inhabited at the time and in use as a store) was concreted over, as was either side of the tramline between there and Golf Links station, and an area in front of the station itself.

Day in, day out, the Tramway was now working as hard as it ever had done in peace time, and at least Colonel Brookfield would have been impressed; remember the part of his speech at the opening ceremony in 1895 when he suggested, tongue in cheek, that the Tramway might be used "against their foes on the other side of the Channel"? Often German aircraft would fly so low overhead from across the sea with their deadly cargoes en route for London, that the pilots could be clearly seen in their cockpits. These flights became such a regular occurrence that no notice was taken of them until one day, as Mears Brothers' general foreman Mr. L. Buttle recalled, one of them opened fire on the tram as it was returning to Rye from Golf Links. The driver quickly stopped the tram and those on board took cover beneath the Bagnall carriage and luckily, no damage was done to men, rolling stock or property. On another occasion the tram accidentally struck a sheep near "Squatter's Right", killing it instantly. Within minutes, the men on duty in the sand hills had removed all evidence of the incident, the unfortunate animal being destined to become a very welcome, but un-official Sunday lunchtime treat! The evidence may have been quickly disposed of, but Mr. Saunders, the farmer who rented the Golf Links as grazing ground throughout the War during the winter months, was well aware that he was one sheep short (of course it had to be a "prize sheep"!) and Messrs. Mears Brothers had to pay him £5 compensation for the loss!

The Tramway's Admiralty duties came to an end all too soon, the Rother Ironworks carriage body was re-united with its underframe and the petrol locomotive and rolling stock were returned to the safety of the large double shed at Rye station. This, supposedly, should have brought the Tramway's brief second life to an end, but whilst stationed at H.M.S. Haig between 19th August and 15th September 1943, some sailors ".... discovered in a shed a small railway engine and carriages; having got the engine into running condition we used it, un-officially I believe, to get to and from the jetty.... We used to race up and down the line whooping and cheering like a lot of children.... Great fun!" [5] So perhaps this part of the Tramway's wartime duties was more akin to its happier peacetime duties..

In early 1944 the Tramway was used for just one more operation, that of bringing up shingle from Northpoint Beach that was to be raked around the nissen huts beside the line approaching Rye station. The train comprised one ballast wagon with the petrol locomotive coupled permanently to it at the southern end. Having received no maintenance whatsoever over the past year of heavy

49. This was the simple bridge that had to be re-built before the Admiralty could use the Tramway in 1943. One of Messrs. G. T. Jennings' gravel works 2ft. 0in. gauge side tipping wagons is just visible beyond the bridge that passed under the Rye & Camber Tramway after 1939 to reach the shingle on the south side of the line. *(S. C. Nash)*

50. With the Rye & Camber Tramway bridge in the background, W. E. Colebrooke's locomotive PAT, is seen on 21 September 1946. *(E.S. Tonks)*

51. Later, Colebrookes acquired this Motor Rail Simplex diesel locomotive, no. 7025, from the Rother & Jury's Cap Catchment Board, July 1954. *(J.G. Vincent)*

traffic, the track was now in such an appalling state that the loaded truck would regularly fall between the rails from whence it had to be bodily lifted out by the six man crew. Even this arduous, back-breaking work of lifting and shovelling was preferable to the regular marches to Tenderden and back, a round trip of some 20 miles!

During the night of 20th October 1943 a bomb fell in the mine field to the east of Golf Links station and south of the 13th green, destroying a section of the Tramway extension embankment, and breaking several windows in the Golf Club House. After "D" Day (6th June 1944), with Britain being bombarded by "V.1" flying bombs, the largest concentration of artillery in the country, consisting of 1,300 gunners, was stationed between Rye Harbour and Camber. By mid-August the "doodle-bug" [7] had been virtually mastered, and on 28th August alone, 90 out of 94 approaching the coast en route for London, were destroyed. [8] Unfortunately, one of the 90 that afternoon fell and exploded on the 15th fairway just 50 ft. from the Club House. [9] The southern side of the building took the full impact of the explosion, tearing the roof sheeting off, and for four long years the Club House was to remain a roof-less ruin. As luck would have it, the owner of the Royal William Hotel decided not to re-instate it as a hotel when it was de-requisitioned in May 1945 (most of the Golf Club's property was de-requisitioned at the same time) and the Golf Club was able to purchase the property, it serving as the temporary Club House until the original building, enlarged slightly and improved, came back into use in 1950. The first residents were allowed to return to what remained of the village in 1945, for many houses, together with the church and memorial hall, had been destroyed by bombs.

When the Tramway was handed back to its rightful owners at the end of the War, both Rye and Golf Links stations remained intact, although many of the sleepers en route had perished and would need replacement. For the first quarter of a mile or so beyond Golf Links the track, understandably overgrown after more than 5 years' disuse, was still in situ, but the deviation grass-covered shingle embankment had disappeared on the last curve towards the new station owing to bomb damage, and at the terminus just two parallel rows of vertical wooden platform supports remained in place to show where the short-lived station had stood. There was a possibility that the Tramway may have been used in connection with some further work at Rye Harbour, for on the recommendation of Charles Dobbie, the engineer to the Rother & Jury's Gut Catchment Board (who had taken over the legal responsibilities of the Harbour and River Rother from the Commissioners of the Levels in 1932), Messrs. Mears Brothers received the contract to extend the jetties a further 1,200 ft. on either side of the River to the south of Golf Links station. Unfortunately, owing to immediate post-war cut-backs, the Government had to cancel the contract, and Messrs. Mears Brothers were to spend the next 3 years constructing a new sea wall a few miles away to the south-west at Pett Level instead.

In June 1945, Charles Gafford wrote to the Golf Club asking if they would have any objection to the Tramway Company receiving compensation from the Admiralty regarding their laying of concrete on either side of their line on Golf Club property between "Squatter's Right" and Golf Links station. Mr. Prentice, the Club's solicitor, advised that the Club should raise no objection providing that the Tramway Company's rent arrears were paid up to date. This "new cement track" was being regularly used "by fishermen and others" to gain access to Rye Harbour, and Mr. Prentice was asked to ascertain whether a question of trespass arose. [10]

Apart from putting a lick of cream paint on the engine and coal sheds at Rye, so far the Tramway Company had made no apparent attempt to put its line back into working order and, fed up with the lack of progress, in November 1945 the Golf Club instructed their solicitors to request them "to arrange for the repair to the Gap in the embankment at the 8th hole as early as possible". [11] Four months later, still nothing had been done, and Charles Dobbie offered to fill in the gap on condition that the estimated cost of £85 be paid by the Tramway Company, [12] but the work was destined never to be carried out. By now the Tramway was rapidly deteriorating. At Rye, with weeds covering the whole area, (something never seen prior to 1940) the scene was one of dereliction with the right hand door of the engine shed hanging open on just its top hinge, whilst the later shed alongside teetered drunkenly to the east. Within the shelter of the engine shed the Rother Ironworks carriage rested, but closer inspection revealed that part of its northern end was missing altogether. Beside the platform, the Bagnall carriage stood in the open with all of its windows broken and some panelling missing, but in contrast, the petrol locomotive on the sand siding in front of the large 1922 shed seemed to be in reasonably good order. Towards the front of this shed, behind the broken doors on what had been the petrol locomotive and open passenger wagons' siding, CAMBER waited with more hope than certainty for the holidaymakers and day trippers to return, whilst two flat wagons completed the sad scene. [13]

The Tramway Company duly received its compensation from the Admiralty, but to date they had not begun to remove the concrete from either side of their line on the last few hundred yards approaching Golf Links station. The payment also included the cost of restoring the road alongside the 11th green to its original condition. Not wishing to wait any longer, the Golf Club Board of Management, at their meeting on 9th June 1946, instructed their secretary to obtain a copy of the Tramway's Lease and suggested that Mr. Murton-Neale "should go into the obligations of the Tramway Company to remove the concrete". This must have been the last straw, and in view of the heavy cost that would be incurred in making the line operational once more, together with the meagre receipts that might be forthcoming if services were resumed, the Tramway

52. On behalf of the Admiralty Messrs. Mears Brothers laid concrete on either side of the Tramway along the embankment from "Squatter's Right" to Golf Links station and in front of the platform to allow lorries access to the Admiralty Jetty being built on the River Rother, the siding to which veers off to the left from the reinstated run-round loop. The original sash windows of the station building have been replaced by two whose upper panes open outwards. *(S. C. Nash)*

53. Note how crudely the sharply curved siding onto the jetty has been laid in this view looking from the River Rother towards Golf Links station. *(S. C. Nash)*

Company threw in the towel and asked the Golf Club for permission to terminate their lease. The Golf Club readily agreed to the Company's request, subject to a satisfactory arrangement being made regarding the removal of the concrete road. [14] Rye Town Council were similarly approached asking if they would be willing to "accept the surrender of the lease dated 24th June 1929, as the Company are anxious to wind up the business", and this was agreed by the Property, Leasehold and Houses Committee at the Council's meeting on Monday, 21st October 1946. The reference to the lease dated 24th June 1929 is curious. What happened to the re-negotiated lease that was authorised by the Council on 13th September 1937?

Since the closure of H.M.S. Haig at the New Road secondary school in January 1945, the premises and the 20 nissen huts alongside the Tramway Station had remained un-occupied. Rye Town Council fully appreciated that in the post-war housing shortage, those "Naval huts" would make ideal temporary living accommodation, and in December 1946 an application was sought and agreed by the Ministry of Health to convert them into houses for a period of ten years. The Camber footpath between the school and the huts was widened from 4 ft. to 7 ft. and when concreted over it was named Bretton Road.

As the Rother & Jury's Gut Catchment Board required access to the harbourmaster's house and the river mouth, which involved crossing Golf Club property, several discussions were held, resulting in agreement being made that their employees be granted permission, limited to 10 years (but later amended to 20) to use the concrete track along the Tramway to Golf Links station "or until the new by-pass is constructed (if ever) whichever is shorter" and "that if any widening of the track were needed, the widening should be on the seaside of the tramway embankment" (i.e. the western side). The Catchment Board were also required "to prevent any other persons from using the access, even to the extent of having a man on duty and to fence it, and if possible, to pay an acknowledgment rent". [15]

A Golf Club sub-committee met the Tramway Company directors in the New Year when they agreed to accept £350 compensation in lieu of taking up the concrete, and that the Tramway Lease should be determined once the rent had been paid up to the date of termination. [16] The necessary payment was soon made and Messrs. M. E. Engineering of Cricklewood, North London, were brought in to dismantle the Tramway, the work being supervised by their director Vincent G. B. Atwater. When the course of the line was visited on 23rd March 1947, only a short isolated length of track across the Broadwater Stream bridge and the concreted section between "Squatter's Right" and Golf Links were left in situ. All of the rolling stock had been removed without trace from Rye station with the

exception of CAMBER's chassis which stood upright on the bare ground with her boiler and firebox to one side and her cab in pieces several yards away, and nothing remained of the engine shed and other buildings apart from their concrete foundations. [17] The Rye & Camber Tramways Company, still with its registered office at Bank Chambers, High Street, Rye, Sussex, was finally dissolved on Monday, 7th February 1949.

The Golf Club had asked that Golf Links station should not be removed and at the Club's Board of Management Meeting back on 6th September 1947, a letter was read out from a Mr. A. A. Hall asking if he might be granted permission to lease the building for the storage of yachting equipment. Unluckily for Mr. Hall his request was turned down, as was a later proposal from a Mr. Tany to purchase the Tram Station in May 1952. [18]

As agreed in May 1895, the much-discussed iron fencing across the fields from Rye Tram Station became the Corporation's property on the determination of the Tramway's lease. The two parallel fences somehow managed to escape the drive for scrap metal during the Second World War, and remained as a last visible link with the Tramway in Rye, heading away defiantly towards the sea, until they were removed in the mid 1950s.

The former naval huts alongside the Tramway station at Rye, refurbished and disguised by the addition of new gabled roofs being constructed over their semi-circular originals, were to last until the early 1960s when their occupants were re-housed in new council accommodation. Once these huts had been demolished, the "Camber fields" resumed their appearance of pre-Tramway days some 70 years before. Around this time there were several schemes put forward to re-instate the Tramway as a tourist attraction, but whereas the Council were in favour of the proposals, the Golf Club, quite understandably, was reluctant to have the line re-built across its property with all the old problems of trespass that holidaymakers and day-trippers would bring. The Rye & Camber Tramway had finally been laid to rest.

1. Kings 1, Chapter 18, verse 17.
2. "Rye Golf Club - The First 90 Years" - Denis Vidler, 1984.
3. "The Tenterden Terrier" No. 11, Winter 1976, House Journal of the Kent & East Sussex Railway.
4. Rye Golf Club Board of Management Minute Book 13.9.1941.
5. Letter from Mr. M. A. Hillebrandt dated 30.1.1990.
6. Rye Golf Club Board of Management Minute Book 20.11.1943.
7. Nickname of the "V.1" flying bomb, an expression first coined by New Zealand fighter pilots.
8. "A Maritime History of Rye" - John Collard, 1978.
9. Rye Golf Club Board of Management Minute Book 16.9.1944.
10. Rye Golf Club Board of Management Minute Book 16.6.1945.
11. Rye Golf Club Board of Management Minute Book 11.11.1945.
12. Rye Golf Club Board of Management Minute Book 30.3.1946.
13. "Railway Observer", June 1946.
14. Rye Golf Club Board of Management Minute Book 27.7.1946.
15. Rye Golf Club Board of Management Minute Book 28.12.1946.
16. Rye Golf Club Board of Management Minute Book 18.1.1947.
17. "Railway Observer", May 1947.
18. Rye Golf Club Board of Management Minute Book 3.5.1952.

54. In this ariel view of Rye taken from the west on 25th March 1931, the petrol locomotive with both carriages can just be made out (above the parish church of St. Mary the Virgin, centre right) running the last few hundred yards towards the terminus. The former South Eastern Railway's station is situated centre left, a good 8 minutes walk from the Tram station, whilst the Rye Harbour goods only branch veers away to the right in the foreground.

(Aerofilms)

Chapter Ten

A DESCRIPTION OF THE TRAMWAY

The Rye & Camber Tramway station was rather inconveniently situated on the "wrong" side of the River Rother and a good eight minutes walk from the centre of Rye and the main railway station. It was approached from across the River by the iron Monkbretton Bridge which, with the wide and straight thoroughfare known then as Guldeford Road, had been built in 1893. To begin with, access to Rye Tram Station was for foot passengers only, but within a month of the opening in 1895, a proper approach road was constructed. The unmade track, protected by a large white-painted gate, dropped steeply some 8 ft. from beside the south-eastern abutment of the bridge to the level of the marsh, with spare ground fenced off to the right alongside the engine shed. The grade was made even steeper following the re-building of the Monkbretton Bridge in 1914-5, and remains so to this day. Being so close to the River, and only 10 ft. above sea level, it was not uncommon for the whole station area to be flooded at high tides and during prolonged wet weather! A public footpath with its own small gate left the higher level at the entrance and after passing behind the engine shed separated, one route continuing along the built-up eastern bank of the River, whilst the other, after negotiating nine downward rustic steps, ran alongside the engine shed before heading across the field away from the station.

The track layout could hardly have been simpler, consisting of a short run-round loop, the western end of which was extended to enter the original engine/carriage shed that was constructed of corrugated iron on a wooden framework mounted on a base of concrete. Light was more than likely provided inside the shed by windows on the northern wall in addition to a 12-paned one at the rear, above which was a louvred ventilator that matched a similar one above the entrance doors. A single roof mounted ventilator was situated at the western end of the shed, and towards the eastern (front) end an inspection pit was situated between the rails. Towering above and behind the north-west corner of the shed, some 12 ft. above ground level, a water tank for replenishing the locomotives' boilers was mounted on a diagonally-braced wooden framework, the pipe from which ran the full length inside the shed to a flexible hose on the outside and to the right of the conventional outward-opening double front doors. A wooden barrel placed under the hose prevented any wastage of water. Originally the whole building, including the roof, had been painted in a uniform light colour, probably cream.

For some un-explained reason, the short platform was not placed centrally alongside the run-round loop,

but commenced half way along it and it extended beyond to the west alongside the engine shed. Constructed of earth, it was concrete faced with bricks lining the upper edge, and was 2ft.0in. high. Although Holman Stephens in his letter to the Board of Trade dated 28th March 1895 quoted 6ft.0in. as being the intended width of the platforms, they were, in fact, at both Rye and Camber stations, 8ft.6in. wide. The station building was sited centrally on the platform, flanked on either side by a lattice wooden fence with two primitive wooden benches, and a single nameboard to the right of the building which displayed the name "RYE" in capital letters.

The building itself was of a design that was to typify "Colonel Stephens'" stations on several of his railways in the future, being constructed, like the engine shed, of corrugated iron on a wooden framework. Similar, but larger versions had already appeared on the Cranbrook & Paddock Wood Railway across the border in Kent, and it was Messrs. Mancktelow Brothers of Horsmonden, Kent (a village served by the C & P. W. Railway) who had been the contractors for that line as well as the Rye & Camber Tramway. Apart from the centrally placed door which gave access to the waiting room that was reached by two concrete steps from the lower level of the station yard, the rear wall was plain. The waiting room, with simple, fixed bench seating provided around three walls, took up the greater part of the interior, the ticket office on the eastern side (which had its own exterior sash window added soon after the opening of the Tramway) being separated from it by a full width partition. As the office was rarely used, a large chalked notice on a blackboard by the ticket window in the waiting room advised passengers "TICKETS ON THE CAR".

The front wall had a sash window on either side of the central door, that to the ticket office having a clock facing the platform built into its upper right hand pane at a later date. Could this have been the time-piece that had adorned the partition of the First Class compartment of the Bagnall carriage prior to its re-building after the First World War? This window was a little shorter and narrower than the other, giving a lop-sided look to an otherwise symmetrical building. Between the right-hand window and the door a notice board was mounted whilst, in a similar position to the left, a solitary lamp was later fitted to provide the only illumination on the platform after dark. Originally the door had only two panels, the larger and upper one being of glass, but, probably after the second break-in on 26th October 1895, this door was re-built or replaced by one with four panels, this time all of wood. For those requiring refreshment as they waited for the tram, a

55. The subject of this photograph, taken at the end of the 19th century, may have been the 4 men posing in their small steam-powered craft, but it is the distant view of Rye Tram Station which is of more interest to us, for it shows how the 1896 carriage shed extends beyond the original engine shed at the rear alongside the elevated water tank on its crude diagonally-braced wooden framework. The built-up river bank gives the impression that the engine shed (now with 2 smoke ventilators and cowls of different heights) is longer than it really is. The Tramway Company has already started its unusual form of advertising with "RYE & CAMBER" painted in white on the red roof of the engine shed and "TRAM" and "STATION" on the station building and coal shed respectively. *(Richard Jones collection)*

56. A prospective passenger's view of Rye station from Monkbretton Bridge on 10th April 1931 with the Tramway heading away on its straight course between the iron fences across the Corporation fields towards Camber. The original engine shed and the later addition of 1896 have clearly seen better days with windows broken or boarded over and, as by this time the two steam locomotives were rarely used, the elevated water tank has been dismantled. Behind the station building the two open wagons stand at the end of the sand siding (which extended beyond the large shed) the lift-out end door of the one nearest the camera being missing. *(H. C. Casserley)*

57. CAMBER pretends to be in charge of the two immaculate carriages at Rye on 11th April 1931. The engine shed door is open in readiness for the petrol locomotive to return CAMBER safely home after her brief outing. As if to make up for the "RYE & CAMBER" that had faded from the engine shed roof, "TO CAMBER ON SEA" has been painted onto the later large shed. Note how the two large windows on this building behind CAMBER extend up to the roof. *(H. C. Casserley)*

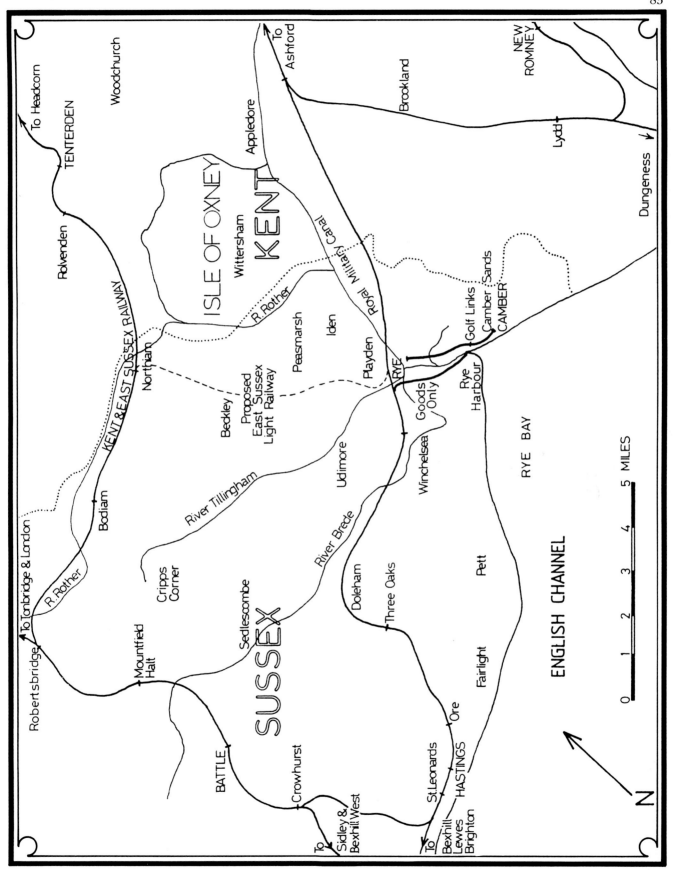

Nestles chocolate machine stood in the waiting room to the left of the ticket office door during the 1930's, by which time the interior colour scheme of the station was blue.

With the front of the building set back to the level of the lattice fence, the corrugated iron roof, carried by two wooden supports with "V" shaped joints at the top, was extended out over the platform to form an awning. Ornate bargeboards topped by simple, carved wooden finials added a nice finishing touch to the station. Adjoining the western wall was the roof-less corrugated iron gentlemen's convenience, comprising nothing more than a urinal, flushed solely by rain water; definitely a place to steer clear of in hot, dry weather, and rumour has it that even the flies kept away! Primitive as this was, the men-folk were so much more fortunate than the ladies for whom no facilities were provided whatsoever.

Perhaps as early as 1896, but certainly by the time VICTORIA arrived a year later, another corrugated iron shed was built over the locomotive spur alongside the original locomotive/carriage shed, the old northern wall (with the original windows blocked off with corrugated iron) being common to both structures. The double entrance doors opened inwards, whilst a single window was sited on the rear wall, and the outer wall boasted three further un-evenly spaced windows, the materials probably coming from the original shed. The new building was longer and extended rearwards beyond the original shed beside the previously mentioned elevated water tank, but as the new edifice was built over the platform ramp and the western point lever (which had to be moved some 4 ft. away from the building) the locomotive had to enter the shed each time it ran round its train. It was possibly at the same time that this shed was built, with the loss of the windows in the erstwhile eastern wall, that a long skylight was added on either side of the upper part of the front portion of the original shed roof, along with another matching roof ventilator which bisected the skylight into two un-equal sections. CAMBER, VICTORIA (when she arrived) and the open wagons would now share the original building, whilst the two carriages would be housed in the new shed next door.

By the early 1930's, two broken panes on the southern side of the skylight had been replaced with second-hand glass obtained from an unusual source, which proudly diplayed their ancestry with the easily deciphered legend "PUBLI" on one and "C BAR" on the other! Unlike the station building, the bargeboards on both sheds were plain, except that on the front of the later structure a curved wooden section was added that matched the roof outline of the passenger carriages. With the arrival of the Rother Ironworks carriage in the Spring of 1896, the platform was extended eastwards by about 10ft.0in., the new section being concrete-faced and brick-lined to match the original, but the ramp this time had three full width steps built into it, the risers being of wood held in place by wooden pegs. Later the

gravelled surface was given a coating of tarmac but, being so thin, much of it had worn away by the late 1920s.

The window added as an afterthought to the eastern wall of the ticket office was not to be effective for long (not that it mattered as the office had already fallen out of use) because around the turn of the century, with that part of the lattice fence removed, a shed for storing locomotive coal was constructed behind the platform to the right and in line with the station building. In later years this building was used for permanent way equipment. It was built of similar materials to its larger neighbour, but without the fancy bargeboards, and had but one door opening outwards onto the platform at its eastern end. The rear wall was a mirror image of that at the front, and in the absence of steps up to the door, coal was easily transferred from carts straight into the shed. Between the two buildings there was another water tank that had been provided shortly after the opening of the Tramway, and this was now hidden by a tall wall of horizontal planking which was often put to good use displaying large posters. The Rye & Camber Tramway now took a leaf out of the Corris Railway's book in mid-Wales [1] by advertising in large white painted capital letters on the red roofs of each of the buildings on the platform "TRAM" and "STATION" which could be clearly seen from across the River in the town itself. For a while "RYE & CAMBER" in similar large letters was added to the newly painted red engine shed roof as well!

The small triangle of land leased in December 1901 from Rye Council to the north of the station was used to add a siding for the developing sand traffic, and this left the main line east of the run-round loop and extended to a point close to and just to the rear of the station building. A sleeper-built enclosure completed the facilities, and from here local builders collected sand, though it can have been no easy task for horses to haul a loaded cart up the steep station aproach road! The new boundary was bordered by similar iron fencing to that which already lined the station approach road and graced the southern side of the premises, being of a type more commonly found on country estates.

When the entrance to the station was "improved" at the end of 1915, the lattice fence behind the platform to the west of the building was removed, together with the iron fence along the approach road, and the area between this and the engine and carriage sheds was built up with rubble and grit to the level of the platform. A short section of iron fencing was re-erected from the gentlemen's convenience at an angle towards the main road so that passengers gained immediate access to the platform rather than having to negotiate the steep steps via the waiting room. The western point lever of the run-round loop was now encased in a shallow pit beside the carriage shed and surrounded, firstly by a protective railing, and in later years by a simple wooden fence.

The station remained in this condition until just after the First World War when a large sign was fixed to the western side of the main station building above the

RYE TRAM STATION

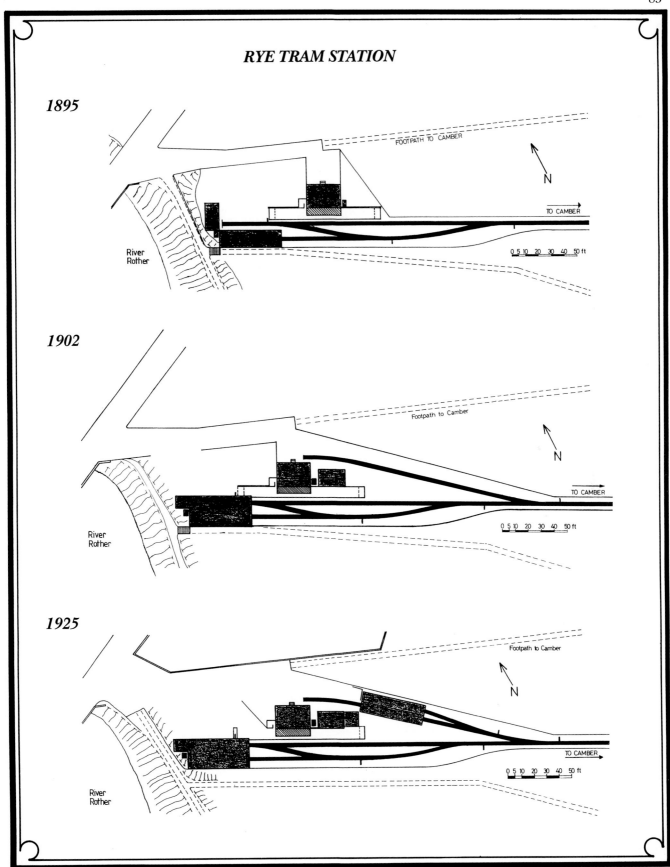

1895

FOOTPATH TO CAMBER

N

TO CAMBER

River Rother

0 5 10 20 30 40 50 ft

1902

Footpath to Camber

N

TO CAMBER

River Rother

0 5 10 20 30 40 50 ft

1925

Footpath to Camber

N

TO CAMBER

River Rother

0 5 10 20 30 40 50 ft

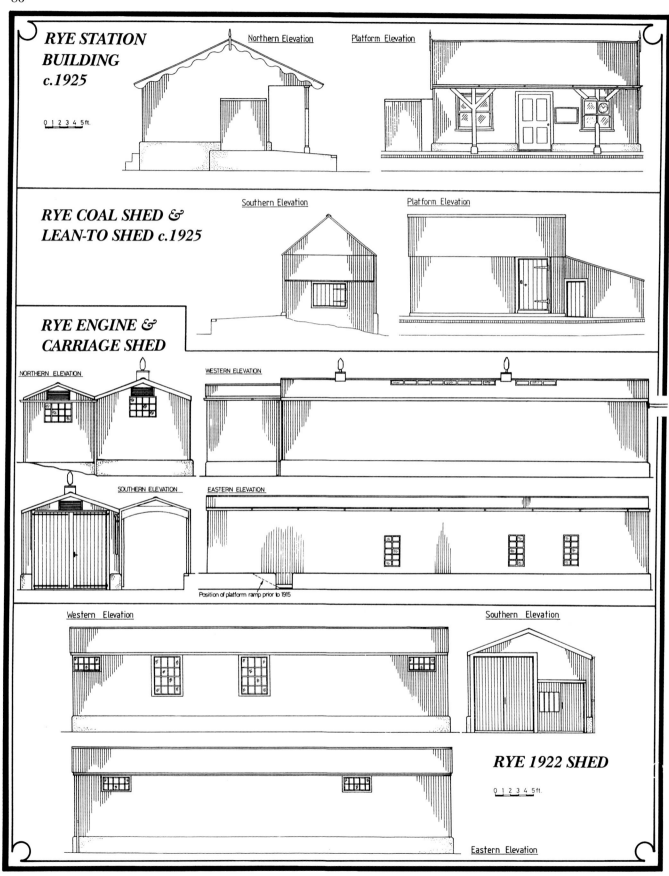

RYE STATION BUILDING c.1925

Northern Elevation

Platform Elevation

0 1 2 3 4 5 ft.

RYE COAL SHED & LEAN-TO SHED c.1925

Southern Elevation

Platform Elevation

RYE ENGINE & CARRIAGE SHED

NORTHERN ELEVATION

WESTERN ELEVATION

SOUTHERN ELEVATION

EASTERN ELEVATION

Position of platform ramp prior to 1915

Western Elevation

Southern Elevation

RYE 1922 SHED

0 1 2 3 4 5 ft.

Eastern Elevation

58. Taken on a warm summer's day in 1921 this photograph shows how the new lean-to shed takes up the remaining space along the back of the platform. Behind it is the sleeper-built sand dock, soon to be lost from sight behind a large shed that is about to be constructed over the sand siding.
(Colonel Stephens Railway Museum & Archives, Tenterden)

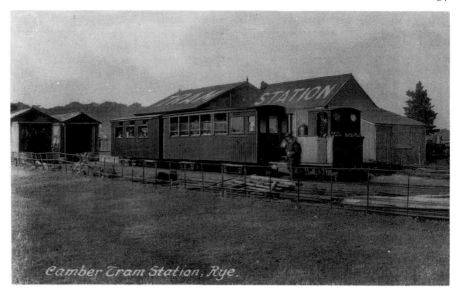

Camber Tram Station, Rye.

59. Looking almost model-like, all is spick and span at Rye Tram Station in August, 1937. Prior to its re-paint the previous year, the two large side windows of the double shed of 1922 have been inexplicably lowered to the level of the concrete base. Strangely, only the eastern side of this shed boasted guttering and a drain pipe!
(D. W. K. Jones)

60. Rye terminus from the south in the mid-1920s. When the large shed on the right was constructed over the sand siding, a second, shorter parallel siding was added which also entered the building and this was to become the home of the two open passenger wagons and the petrol locomotive when it arrived in 1924. Unusually, but in common with those on the 1896 carriage shed, the two sets of double doors opened inwards. Bellhouse garage (which formerly traded as The Petrol Engine Company) from where fuel was obtained in two gallon cans for the petrol locomotive, stands on the opposite (northern) side of the main Rye to Folkestone road to the left of the Monkbretton Bridge. *(Lens of Sutton)*

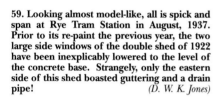

gentlemen's convenience advertising "TRAM TO CAMBER ON SEA" in large capital letters. A lean-to corrugated iron shed was also built onto the right-hand end of the coal shed to house permanent way tools and materials, thus taking up the remaining space at the eastern end of the platform as far as the top of the ramp. At the rear there was a door at yard level whilst a similar, but inward opening door gave access to the platform via a steep step, whilst a window on the eastern side of the shed was protected by a hinged wooden shutter. It was around this time that the solitary platform lamp was taken down from the station building.

By the Spring of 1922 another siding had been added alongside the northern boundary fence, which diverged to the right from and parallel to the 1901 siding. A large shed, again of corrugated iron, which abutted onto the rear corner of the latest lean-to shed on the platform (so blocking off access to that part of the yard alongside the main running line from the station approach road) was built over both sidings. The triangular area thus formed between the new shed and the main running line became a useful site for storing spare rails and sleepers. This latest building was a little taller than its predecessors, and had an odd arrangement of un-evenly spaced short and tall windows on its southern side. During the winter of 1936/7 the two taller windows that had extended to the roof were lowered so that their bottom edge was level with the top of the concrete base. Each siding had its own set of inward opening double doors, those to the left extending to the full height of the building, but the right hand ones were much shorter. The original siding continued beyond the building through a double door in the rear wall to serve the sleeper-built sand enclosure that was still in situ. A primitive workbench was provided at the rear of the northern side of this shed, and it was here that the maintenance of the Tramway's rolling stock was carried out each winter, the heavier work being done in the main by the staff of Rother Ironworks. When carriage wheels needed re-profiling, the bogies would be removed one at a time and pushed on their flanged wheels by hand over Monkbretton Bridge and along Fishmarket Road (much to the detriment of the road surface) for the work to be carried out at the Ironworks. Round about this time, the western finial of the station building disappeared, never to be replaced whilst, outside Company property, the nine steps beside the original engine shed were removed, probably in 1925, and that section of the footpath was diverted some 15 ft. into the field away from the southern boundary and fenced in.

With the arrival of the petrol tractor, the steam locomotives became little more than spares, so by early 1931 the water tank and its supporting framework behind the engine shed had been dismantled and removed. On a more positive note, in an attempt to attract more passengers in the mid-1930s, the words "TO CAMBER-ON-SEA" were painted in large white capital letters on the roof of the large double shed to add to the now rather faded "TRAM" and "STATION" on the roofs of the two buildings on the platform. The bench that had started life at the western end of the platform was now sited in front of the wooden wall between the station building and the coal shed, and a horizontal plank of wood had been added to the side of the latter shed to act as a primitive back rest for the other bench. Dining type chairs would often be brought out from the waiting room on hot, sunny days to supplement the meagre seating arrangements.

Until the mid-1920's the north eastern aspect had been of the vast expanse of Walland Marsh (which merges into Romney Marsh across the border in Kent) that stretches away as far as the eye can see with only occasional trees and bushes to add relief to an otherwise flat landscape, but from that time the view was lost behind four new semi-detached houses that extended away from the station along the tree-lined Guldeford Road. These properties were accompanied in 1933 by a new senior school which, although it had its entrance beyond the houses, was set back to occupy the land behind them, sharing a common boundary alongside the wide footpath that bordered the station premises.

On leaving the station the Tramway headed south-eastwards on level ground across Corporation owned meadows where sheep (and sometimes cows) regularly grazed. The straight, but narrow track formation was bordered by the now familiar iron fencing on either side, and telegraph poles were sited on the leased side of the fence to the right. Eleven and a half chains from Rye [2] the line passed between the fence that had divided the field into two before the arrival of the Tramway, and so helped Rye Council to increase its revenue! From the tram there was an excellent (considered by some to be the most attractive) view of Rye just across the River Rother to the west where, amongst the irregular mass of red-tiled cottages could be seen the 13th century Ypres Tower to the left, the Landgate of a hundred years later on the right, and above them all, the parish church of St. Mary the Virgin. Soon the view beyond the built-up river bank opened out to the south. The sleepy "new" town of Winchelsea hides amongst the trees on its hill, the straggling village of Pett nestles mainly out of sight in the undulating countryside of the middle distance whilst, forming the background, the land rises dramatically from the aptly named Cliff End to the lofty height of Fairlight church some 7 miles away and 540 ft. above sea level.

After just over quarter of a mile the line veered slightly, but suddenly, to the left, and on a low embankment with the iron fences nearer field level, crossed over a piped wide, but shallow drainage ditch (26 chains) that centuries before (when it was known as The Holm Bush) had formed part of the course of the River Rother. The only water that it carried now was that left by the rain. There were now distant views westwards along the broad Brede valley with its gentle hills rising to the villages of Icklesham on the northern side and Udimore to the south, but the former South Eastern

61. CAMBER (complete with headlamp) and her train are specially posed on the bridge across the Broadwater Stream c.1910. The aptly named "cradle bridge" on the footpath between Rye and Camber crosses the river a few yards upstream. Whereas iron fencing, peculiar to the Tramway, borders the embankment down to the level of the stream on this, the western side of the bridge, the eastern side is protected by iron railings.

(Colonel Stephens Railway Museum & Archives, Tenterden)

62. "Driving from the 17th tee" is the title on the back of the original of this photograph showing the Tramway breasting the top of the 1 in 160 gradient across Northpoint Beach to pass between "Camber Cottage" on the left and "Golf View". On the extreme right is the small weatherboarded cottage in which the harbourmaster, Charles Tunbridge, brought up his large family. *(Rye Golf Club)*

63. A high tide covers the saltings in the foreground as the tram, headed by VICTORIA, passes the impressive looking, but flimsy, "Golf View" on its way to Rye in this Whiteman postcard postmarked 10.7.1907. The house was later re-named "Beachlands" and finally "Squatter's Right". Although never advertised in the timetables, and lacking the luxury of a platform, trams would regularly stop here by request. Note the permanent way trolley that has been lifted from the track and parked beside the house.

(R. Clark collection)

GOLF VIEW. CAMBER

Railway heading away towards Hastings remains out of sight. With this part of the field on a lower level, the formation, still on a low embankment, bisected a wooden fence that marked the Rye Municipal Boundary (32 chains) and, after curving a little to the right, passed through the built-up northern bank of the Broadwater Stream by a short and shallow cutting, the only one on the Tramway. Through the cutting the fences came in closer on either side and were raised up above track level, that to the right being on a higher level than that to the east. The Broadwater had previously discharged its waters into the Holm Bush, and long before the arrival of the Tramway, the bank had been built up to ensure that the stream would follow the new course to the Rother.

The sharply curving stream was crossed at almost right-angles by a typical Holman Stephens' low cost bridge (36 chains) with the rails carried on longitudinal wooden sleepers fixed every 2 ft. onto two 12in. "I" section iron girders of 22ft.3in. span, that rested on concrete abutments. Each of the four angled side sections were decorated along their sloping tops with a row of 24 dark coloured engineering bricks similar to those that edged the station platforms, and the iron fences paralleled the formation down the river bank and curved inwards sharply to terminate close to the northern abutments on either side of the Tramway just above water level. Thirty yards upstream to the north-east, the public footpath that had accompanied the line since leaving Rye station, was carried over the stream on

a slightly lower level by a simple footbridge, known as the "Cradle Bridge".

Continuing on a low grass embankment the route, now un-fenced, became straight once more and passed over a short section of shingle, followed by a crossing of a branch of the just mentioned footpath on the level (40½ chains) that was to find its way to the River Rother via the eastern bank of the Broadwater Stream. There was now a complete change of scenery as the embankment gave way to level ground and the pebbles and coarse grass of Northpoint Beach surrounded the Tramway on either side (50 chains). The telegraph poles that had deserted the Tramway close to the Broadwater Stream to follow their own separate course, now once more accompanied the line to the right.

Passing a large pond in a dip to the south, another footpath was crossed (55 chains) whilst the line, laid directly on the shingle, developed a very slight tendency to curve to the right as it headed south-eastwards over the wasteland. The works of the Rye Chemical Manufacturing Company could now be seen opposite on the far bank of the River Rother, these being served by a siding off of the South Eastern Railway's Rye Harbour branch that became dual gauge when it joined the Company's own internal 2ft.2½in. gauge tramway that terminated at a landing stage on the River. A quarter of a mile further downstream the church and school on the outskirts of Rye Harbour village stood out above the low skyline. To the north the East Guldeford to Camber road had come within 150 yards of the Tramway as it

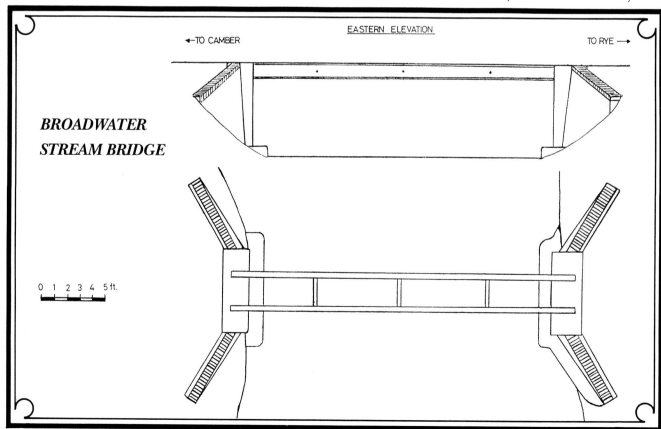

BROADWATER STREAM BRIDGE

EASTERN ELEVATION

←TO CAMBER

TO RYE →

0 1 2 3 4 5 ft.

twisted and turned on its uncertain course between the two places. whilst over on the horizon, the hills that formed behind Rye headed away north-eastwards towards Appledore in the neighbouring county of Kent.

Half way across Northpoint Beach the Tramway encountered its one and only gradient, a climb on a shingle embankment at 1 in 160 for 16 chains. To the right, between and behind the afore-mentioned chemical works and Rye Harbour church, the squat, circular central tower of Winchelsea Castle (later re-named Camber Castle) came into view, and as the tram gained height as it slogged up the gradient, the outer walls also became visible. Commencing in 1927, the whole area between the Tramway and the road to the left was excavated for shingle by Mr. G. T. Jennings, the works being served by their own 2ft.0in. gauge railway which, after 1939, passed under the Rye & Camber Tramway's embankment via a concrete culvert so as to provide access to the shingle to the south of the Tramway as well.

On level ground once more, the wheels of the tram sounded an eerie hollow note as it passed between two isolated houses. The first, "Gorse Cottage", (1 mile 13 chains) which stood just 35 ft. from the Tramway on the right hand side, was (and still is) a substantial building, tile-hung around its upper storey, that had been built in 1911. Access to the house from the East Guldeford to Camber road was provided by an 18 ft. wide track with an un-gated level crossing over the Tramway. With no water supply of its own for many years, the tram brought fresh water daily, and a newspaper, to the Miss Richardson who lived there. "Squatter's Right" (so named because it was built by a squatter on land owned by the Curteis Estate, but previously known as "Golf View" and later "Beachlands") to the left (1 mile 14 chains) was, in contrast, a flimsy structure of tile-hung lathe and plaster walls that had been built directly onto the shingle without proper foundations around an earlier black weatherboarded cottage in 1895. The large house was so frail that a night's lodging in a gale was described by Mr. John Symonds Vidler (who had purchased the property in 1907) as "an experience unlikely to be forgotten" and it was reported in later years that "even high tea there in a wind was precarious". [3]

From here there was a fine view of the many boats and barges tied up at the wooden stages on either side of the River Rother at Rye Harbour village with the English Channel beyond, before the line turned sharply to the right on a 20 chain radius curve to head almost due south on an embankment parallel to the River. Beside the curve, just 20 yards to the left, stood the small, black single storey weatherboarded cottage of Mr. Charles Tunbridge (1 mile 18 chains) who had been harbourmaster at Rye Harbour for 10 years until ill health forced him to resign in 1925. Here he brought up a large family, growing all his own vegetables in the far from ideal sandy soil of his adjoining enclosed garden, and it is said that he supplemented his income by beachcombing and selling lost golf balls back to members of Rye Golf Club for 3d. or 6d., according to their condition. [4]

Yet again the scenery changed as the Tramway, on a straight course once more, bordered the Golf Course with its low, well-kept grass-covered sand hills rising gently away to the east, with the Camber road becoming hidden behind them. The 12th fairway was bisected by the Tramway close to "Squatter's Right", that part to the west of the line, according to the Golf Club's Local Rule 4, being considered a "hazard". [5] A deeply rutted track, used by fish carts plying between the River and Camber, left the road close to the Club House and crossed the Tramway near Charles Tunbridge's cottage, a branch of which re-crossed the formation 8 chains to the south, to run behind the 13th fairway and head away from the line to the south-east. In the major alterations made to the Golf Course in 1932, the 13th green was moved eastwards, and the original site soon became overgrown with long grass, but the 12th fairway remained astride the Tramway. To the right the saltings would be regularly flooded at high tides when the errant waters would lap against the foot of the Tramway embankment that was protected by faggoting, and the telegraph poles had made another diversion, taking a short cut from "Gorse Cottage" across the saltings to re-join the formation a hundred yards to the south. With the village of Rye Harbour now directly opposite to the west, and the Golf Club House on the tallest sand hill overlooking the course some 400 yards away to the east, the straight section ended as the Tramway curved sharply to the left and arrived at Golf Links station (1 mile 38 chains).

This was the original southern terminus, and until the extension to Camber Sands opened it was named "Camber", but whereas the platform was of similar dimensions to that as built at Rye, the run-round loop was a little shorter. The station building at first sight looks identical, except that the gentlemen's convenience was sited at the opposite (southern) end, but further investigation reveals that the ticket office (that was rarely, if ever, used for its intended purpose) did not gain an extra side window, and the platform door would appear to have been constructed with four wooden panels from the start. Behind the gentlemen's convenience there was a water tank fed by rain water from the gutters of the main station building. Although the platform was straight for all of its short length, the curve, having eased considerably once beyond the loop points, did not actually straighten until it was level with the station building which was flanked on either side by a lattice wooden fence. Once again the platform was not positioned centrally alongside the loop, and it overlapped the points at the southern end.

In 1896 the platform was also extended here (this time northwards by 4ft.6in.) to accommodate the Rother Ironworks carriage. The new ramp was slightly longer and less steep than the original, with three full-width steps being built neatly into it, but unlike those at the other terminus, each step was built substantially using small stone blocks instead of wood for the risers.

64. A bird's eye view of Golf Links station in the late afternoon of 25th April 1929. Charles Tunbridge's small cottage with its separate enclosed vegetable garden stands beside the Tramway at the top of the picture, and below it the rough track onto the saltings crosses the line twice. With the tide out, quite a few vessels lie stranded at their moorings in the sticky mud on the eastern side of the River Rother. The harbourmaster's cottage stands between the hexagonal concrete light house and the shipping mast on its mound beside the station as the Tramway curves away off the bottom of the picture towards Camber Sands. *(Aerofilms)*

Centrally sited above the lattice fence to the left of the building was the single name board plus, set back behind the fence nearer the ramp, another sign of white capital letters on a dark background, complete with a painted pointing finger on a hand, directed passengers along the platform "TO THE SANDS". Two primitive wooden benches completed the facilities. The station was built on a natural mound, and for many years at the rear, a straight flight of rustic steps, with a neat wooden hand rail on either side, led down to the level of the Golf Course. These steps can have received very little use and most passengers would have gained access to the platform via its northern stepped ramp.

The iron fencing put in another appearance here, marking the western boundary of the premises, together with a short section near the northern platform ramp that curved round beside the public right of way that crossed the Tramway just inside the run-round loop, and connected the station to the Royal William Hotel on the Camber road and the ferry across the River to Rye Harbour village. As the ferryman's hut was on the western bank of the River, he would have to be hailed from the Camber side by shouting, or by striking a piece of iron hung from a wooden post with a stick or a stone. More often than not he would appear from the William the Conqueror public house, rather than his hut! Passengers would then have to negotiate some steep uneven stone steps and a slippery walkway at low tide when a flat-bottomed rowing boat would be in service, a second boat with a rounded keel being used when the tide was in.

A delightful account that illustrates just how primitive the facilities were accompanied a report of the Rye Harbour Commissioners' annual visit to the harbour on 5th July 1905: [6]

".... Some little difficulty was experienced by certain members of the party in effecting a landing on the harbour side. A narrow and wobbly plank led across a little lake of "juicy" mud and the passage across was productive of exciting interests galore. One Commissioner employed another to assist him. When near the other side he made a dash for it and let the oar drop. It fell with a splash into the mud and splashed numerous bystanders. However, all got safely on terra firma at last."

Close to the south end of the run-round loop a tall, white painted shipping mast, surrounded on all four sides by a black wooden picket fence, looked down on the station from its grass-covered mound. This was the Signal Station referred to in the 1895 Lease, and its purpose was to advise those on the River of the state of the daytime tides by the use of red flags and three 3ft.4in. diameter black circular discs known as "balls". A red flag on the yard denoted 7 ft. of water, one ball on yard: 8 ft., one ball on each arm of yard: 9 ft., one ball on masthead only: 10 ft., one ball on masthead and one ball on yard: 11 ft., and one ball on masthead with one ball on each arm of yard: 12 ft.. [7]

65. One solitary lady passenger waits for the tram at Golf Links station on 10th April 1909. The extension to Camber Sands has been open for nine months and curves sharply to the right behind the shipping mast's mound, and note how the main running line beside the platform does not straighten until it is level with the station building. Rustic steps with wooden handrails lead up to the rear of the premises from the lower level of the Golf Course, and the 1898 siding into the sand hills remains connected to the main line curving to the left in front of Councillor Longley's refreshment building which forms the background.
(Allan C. Baker collection)

66. This was the view from the shipping mast's mound on 12 July 1931 looking in the opposite direction with "Squatter's Right" prominent in the middle distance and "Camber Cottage" on the left. The less than sanitary gentlemen's convenience has been removed with the resulting gap being neatly filled by some matching lattice fencing, and the replacement iron fencing looks very smart occupying its original position beside the former run-round loop. The large bushes beyond the station on the embankment to the right are probably those that were cut down "by mistake" by "some Tramway employees" in July 1935!
(H. C. Casserley)

67. Two years later and Golf Links station is looking really dilapidated, but at least the platform ramp at the northern end has gained some replacement fencing, even if it doesn't match the original. Two gentlemen approach the station from the lower level of the Golf Course, whilst the Golf Club's notice board erected that Spring to their right advises Tramway passengers "THIS GROUND IS PRIVATE PROPERTY. THE PUBLIC ARE WARNED TO KEEP TO THE ROADS & FOOTPATHS. BY ORDER OF THE DIRECTORS".
(David J. Woodcock collection)

GOLF LINKS STATION

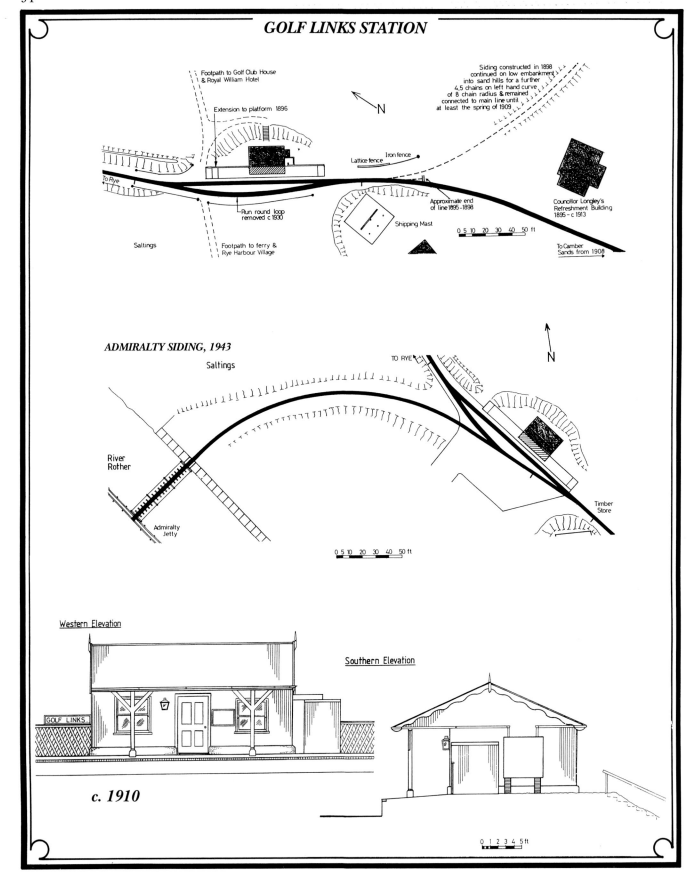

Footpath to Golf Club House
& Royal William Hotel

Extension to platform 1896

Siding constructed in 1898
continued on low embankment
into sand hills for a further
4,5 chains on left hand curve
of 8 chain radius & remained
connected to main line until
at least the spring of 1909

N

Lattice fence   Iron fence

To Rye

Run round loop
removed c 1930

Approximate end
of line 1895-1898

Councillor Longley's
Refreshment Building
1895 - c 1913

Saltings

Footpath to ferry &
Rye Harbour Village

Shipping Mast

0 5 10 20 30 40 50 ft

To Camber
Sands from 1908

ADMIRALTY SIDING, 1943

Saltings

TO RYE

N

River
Rother

Admiralty
Jetty

Timber
Store

0 5 10 20 30 40 50 ft

Western Elevation

GOLF LINKS

Southern Elevation

c. 1910

0 1 2 3 4 5 ft

When constructed in 1895 the main running line terminated in a locomotive spur (1 mile 43 chains), but this was extended in 1898 beyond the station to terminate amongst some large sand dunes (1 mile 46$^{1}/_{2}$ chains) from where sand was removed and transported by sea to Dover Harbour, and also sold to the local builders in Rye. The whole alignment was set on a left hand curve accompanied for a short distance by a length of lattice and then iron fencing to the north. Immediately to the south of this spur there was a large single storey weatherboarded property with a corrugated iron roof and a large, squat brick chimney breast prominent on the side facing the Tramway. This was Councillor I. Longley's refreshment building which he opened at the same time as the Tramway, and which was later to become known as "The Retreat" and finally the "Townpeople's Bungalow".

Just prior to the opening of the extension to Camber Sands in July 1908, the station was re-named "Golf Links" and the name board was moved in close to the station building. Until the early 1920s the run-round loop was regularly used for short workings in the summer and all services during the winter, but when the tram became seasonal only after 1925, it became rarely used and was taken out around 1930. The gentlemen's convenience was also removed, the resulting gap along the rear of the platform being filled by a section of lattice fencing to match the original. Up to now, and as was to be retained at Rye, the exterior walls of the building had been painted cream with the woodwork dark green, but now the main colour became a light sea green with the doors, window frames and barge-boards in cream. For some years the iron fence that bordered the loop had been replaced by a post and wire variety, but the familiar iron fencing was now re-instated, still occupying its original position.

Commencing immediately beyond the southern loop points the extension to Camber Sands curved quite sharply to the right, close to the shipping mast's mound, and for the first 9 months, at least, the original spur into the sand dunes was connected to the new formation. The locomotive and carriages would call up for one second another eerie echo as they passed the single storey harbourmaster's house to the right, behind which, beside the river, stood a concrete hexagonal lighthouse which advised shipping the depth of the River at night by showing red, white and green tide signals. Guarding the far side of the Rother stands "The Enchantress", the 28th of 86 Martello Towers that had been built to protect the Kent and Sussex coast against possible invasion by the French in the early 19th century.

The land dipped a little to the east as the line negotiated a left hand curve that sharpened suddenly for a short distance before the route, on a low embankment once more, headed south-eastwards on to what had been the foreshore from when the extension opened until the late 1920s. The post and wire fence to the left was added in 1910 when the Tramway Company leased the reclaimed land to the Golf Club, but the land to the south remained un-fenced. The Rother, making its straight course towards the English Channel, was now left behind and the sea, which had receded steadily over the years, now came into full view beyond the low sand and shingle bank away to the right. Sometimes, high tides would rise over this insignificant obstacle to leave, on their retreat, shallow waters right up to the edge of the Tramway embankment, reminiscent of those earlier days. To the north the row of sandhills that began behind Golf Links station, gradually gained height so that only the top of the Club House was visible, along with the tall chimneys of "the Billy" and the Professional's house on the opposite side of the Camber road behind.

The formation continued in an almost straight line, but with a tendency to curve slightly to the left until, after another left hand curve, the line entered a last straight section to head eastwards, at the end of which was situated Camber Sands station (2 miles 4$^{1}/_{2}$ chains). It was certainly in an isolated situation amongst the sand dunes, and as one railway historian [8] suggested, it appeared that the position of the terminus was dictated by there being only a certain amount of rails available, and construction stopped at the point where the supply ran out! Its position was always difficult to find as it was not served by a road, or even a footpath, and it was still almost half a mile west of the village and the best part of the sands. So much for Mr. Cuthbert Hayles' suggestion of February 1902 that the extension would be of benefit to the residents of Camber!

This station was completely different to those at Rye and Golf Links, and was built to an even simpler design. The embankment had widened sufficiently to allow space for the run-round loop on the right with the platform to the left. The loop was the longest on the Tramway, but the straight platform, constructed of second-hand standard gauge railway sleepers and backed by a simple wooden fence that carried the single nameboard, was shorter. This time, it was sited centrally alongside the loop but strangely, the main running line curved slightly to the right away from it half way along its length. Another unusual touch was the addition of a full stop after the station name on the 1908 name board both here and at Golf Links.

When the station was opened there was but a primitive wooden bench beneath the nameboard, but sometime prior to the First World War a window-less weatherboarded wooden shelter with a corrugated iron roof was added to the rear of the platform on a concrete plinth two-thirds of the way along towards its eastern end. It had an open doorway onto the platform with fitted wooden seats around the other three sides, and over the years the inside acquired a covering of people's names with the dates of their visits scratched into the woodwork. During the early 1930s a second wooden bench joined the original at the western end of the platform.

In an unsuccessful attempt to discourage passengers from wandering over the running lines a short lattice

96

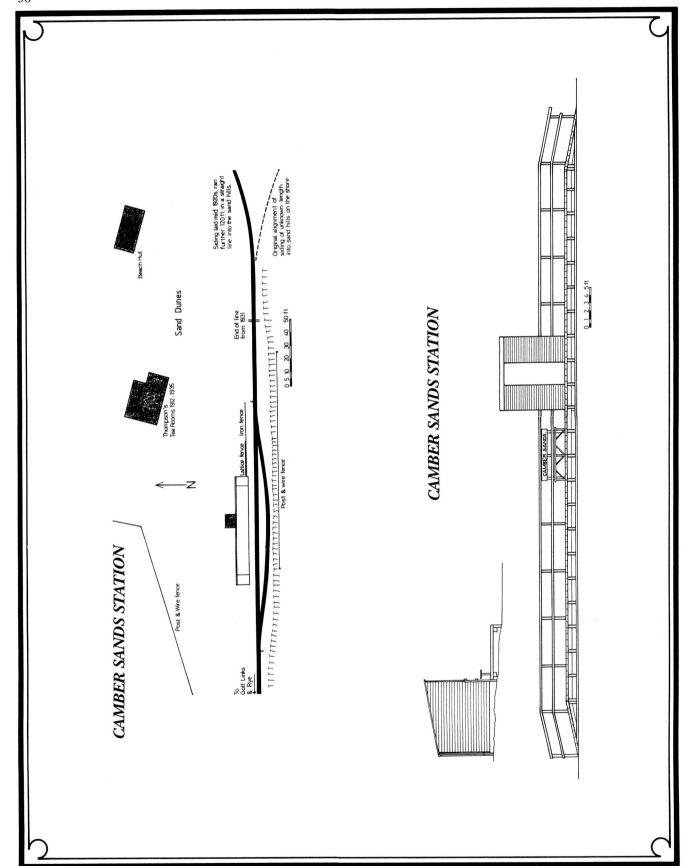

CAMBER SANDS STATION

Beach Hut

Sand Dunes

Thompson's
Tea Rooms 1912-1935

N

Lattice fence   Iron fence

Post & wire fence

Siding laid mid 1920s, ran
further 120 ft. in a straight
line into the sand hills.

End of line
from 1931

Original alignment of
siding of unknown length
into sand hills on the shore

0 5 10 20 30 40 50 ft

Post & Wire fence

To
Golf Links
& Rye

CAMBER SANDS STATION

CAMBER SANDS

0 1 2 3 4 5 ft

68. Camber Sands station, with Thompson's Tea Rooms, built in 1912, in the background, from where welcome cups of tea and sticky buns could be purchased, together with buckets and spades for the children. With no water laid on, it was brought out daily from Rye on the tram throughout the summer season. By the mid-1920s the sand siding had been re-aligned to curve to the left into the larger sand hills to the north. The notice board leaning against the wooden shelter on the platform has a copy of the Company's timetable attached to it. *(Lens of Sutton)*

69. A group of young lads listen intently as George Wratten chats to them at Camber Sands station on 11.4.1931. The siding into the sandhills has been lifted, leaving just a locomotive spur with nothing more than a spare sleeper held in place by three redundant pieces of rail to act as a simple stop block. *(H. C. Casserley)*

fence followed by a slightly longer length of the now familiar iron fencing, extended from the foot of the platform ramp beside the Tramway to just beyond the eastern point lever, and an isolated section of post and wire fencing ran alongside the run-round loop, almost hidden by the long grass in later years. As at the original Camber station, the Tramway continued beyond the run-round loop, still on a low embankment, to curve to the right and head towards and behind the low sand hills on the sea shore. In the mid-1920's this siding was re-laid to curve in the opposite direction and terminate, after a short, straight section, in the much taller sand dunes to the north (2 miles 10½ chains). It was agreed in the 1908 Lease that the end of the siding "is not to be nearer to the present site of Coastguard Lookout hut than nine chains". By 1931 the Company's sand trade seems to have ceased altogether and the siding had been lifted to leave a short locomotive spur. To prevent any an-wanted progress eastwards, a sleeper was laid across the end of the line, held in place by the simple expedience of one redundant piece of rail in front and two behind, being hammered into the sandy soil. A little to the south-east of the station was a large shingle bank, and it was here that the people of Rye would congregate in their thousands on hot, sunny days, whilst courting couples would seek the privacy of the sand dunes. The tide washed over the beach bank twice a day and would leave warm water in a large natural pool at the western end which was popular with those who did not wish to walk the half mile to the sea when the tide was out.

During the summer months, for many years, Messrs. Thompsons, who had a bakery and tea rooms next to the Landgate in Rye, sold cups of tea and sticky buns, along with buckets and spades for the children, from a large green-painted wooden shack complete with a verandah, that was situated 75 ft. north-east of Camber Sands station on the narrow strip of land between there and the sand hills. As there was no water laid on, the tram also brought fresh water here daily from Rye in the summer season. By the mid-1930s, however, it had closed down, and after remaining derelict for several years (becoming an exciting adventure playground for young local lads) it was eventually dismantled.

When the Tramway was diverted in conjunction with the alterations to the Golf Course during the winter of 1938/9, a new 3 ft. high embankment was built commencing 21 chains short of the original Camber Sands station part way along the curve that led onto the erstwhile last straight section. The new formation headed south-eastwards in a straight line for a quarter of a mile and then curved to the left on a 47 chain radius curve on the sea side of some sand hills to travel eastwards before arriving at the new terminus (2 miles 14 chains from Rye) and some 275 yards closer to the Coastguard Cottages and the better part of the sands than before. The simple track layout remained as

before, with a similar sleeper-built platform to the north of the runing line and the run-round loop to the south. If anything, the new terminus was even more difficult to find than the original Camber Sands station of 1908, there still being no footpath to serve it, access being gained from beside the coastguard cottages a quarter of a mile to the east.

The Tramway was worked throughout its life on the "one engine in steam" principle so that no signals were required, but Mr. Arthur B. Withers, who was employed as engine driver and fitter until 1914, remembered that ".... the only times two locos were run was at Bank Holiday...." [9] This suggests that each engine must have taken it in turns to run down the line whilst the other remained at Rye to couple onto the Camber end of the train as soon as it arrived back, thus reducing the turn-round time!

The permanent way between Rye and Golf Links consisted of 24 lb./yd. flat-bottomed steel rails 24 ft. long, spiked direct to creosoted pine sleepers 5ft.0in. x 9in. x 4in. spaced at 2ft.7in. centres, and the 1908 extension to Camber Sands was probably constructed with similar materials. However, several lengths of rail recovered from the 1938 deviation in July 1993 were only 15 ft. long. Rail joints were staggered, but whereas it may have been more economical to lay the track in this manner, it required more maintenance to keep it in good order. The original spikes were 3½in. x ½in., but some of these have been replaced at random over the years by larger ones 4in. x ⅝in. and 4½in. x ⅝in.. At the stations the points were sprung to the normal direction of running, so that regular manoeuvres such as running round the rolling stock, or gaining access to the engine shed at Rye, could be accomplished without the driver having to leave his cab. Percy Sheppard recalled [10] that in the 1930's pranksters would sometimes change the points as the tram approached Rye station, so "a sort of box" was rigged up over the levers to prevent them from being interfered with. Unlike many narrow gauge and light railways, the permanent way was always kept in first class condition, hardly difficult on such a short line, particularly after 1925, with the whole of the winter available for maintenance.

1. From the 1880s the Corris Railway in Wales had advertised its horse bus service to Talyllyn by painting on the roof of its station at Machynlleth "CORRIS RAILWAY STATION - CADER IDRIS & TALYLLYN LAKE".
2. Distances have been measured from the map appended to the 1908 Tramway Extension Lease.
3. The Rye Gazette No. 105, 31.10.1984.
4. "A Maritime History of Rye" - John Collard, 1978.
5. An obstruction in playing a shot.
6. South Eastern Advertiser, Saturday, 9.7.1910.
7. Day Tide Signals taken from Deacon's Almanac 1935.
8. Alan A. Jackson in an article entitled "The Rye & Camber Tramway" which appeared in "Trains Illustrated" in February 1957.
9. "Rye's Own", Volume 3, No. 1, November 1967.
10. John Miller interview with Percy Sheppard, September 1975, published in the "Tenterden Terrier" No.10, Summer 1976, House Journal of the Kent & East Sussex Railway.

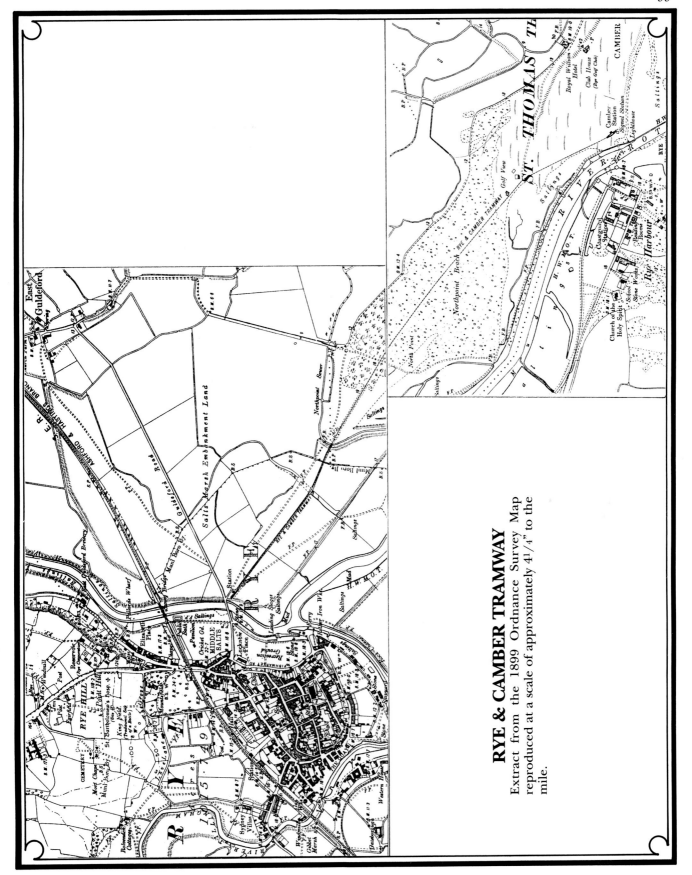

RYE & CAMBER TRAMWAY

Extract from the 1899 Ordnance Survey Map reproduced at a scale of approximately 4¼" to the mile.

70. Messrs. Bagnall's "official" view of CAMBER shows the locomotive loaded onto a standard gauge wagon awaiting despatch from outside their works at Stafford on 10.7.1895, complete with lamps front and rear.
(Allan C. Baker collection)

71. One of the many photographs depicting a young boy standing on the footplate of CAMBER at Rye. The locomotive is in its original livery with her name in gold serifed letters on her side tanks, and if the collision with a yearling heifer in May 1901 was the cause of the dent in her left hand cylinder casing, the picture can be dated to have been taken between then and 1907. A pair of 6-spoked front wheels have already replaced the earlier disc type. The driver is Albert Edward "Jokey" Rhodes and the conductor on the platform is Frederick Sheppard.
(Richard Jones collection)

Chapter Eleven

MOTIVE POWER

As late as 11th March 1895 a decision had not been made as to what motive power would be the most suitable for the Tramway, for at the Rye Trade Association's Meeting that evening, Councillor Cuthbert Hayles (on behalf of the Tramway Company) advised that "they were in treaty as to the motive power" and that "they would say nothing on that subject until the actual figures were before them, and then the prospectus would be issued". He then informed the meeting

"We found petroleum the cheapest, but it had not been successfully used in England, but if we could obtain a guarantee that it would work satisfactorily, the order would be given. If the scheme did not work we would be compelled to fall back on steam as we hear that the initial cost of electricity is too expensive. From what we had heard on Saturday, petroleum was the best workable force, but we did not want to, or intend to make any experiments ourselves."

Yet back on 16th February, "a correspondent" was convinced that the line was to be worked by steam and bitterly wrote in the Sussex Express & County Herald that day:

"And so we are to have a steam tramway to Camber, after all, and the hopes of those who were wishing to see electricity employed are dashed to the ground. At least, I presume that the letter addressed to Mr. Sharpey by the secretary pro tem, on behalf of the self-elected directorate is final, and has not to be endorsed by the shareholders, a great many - if not the majority - of whom, are in favour of electricity.... For my part, I believe the whole thing was, I won't say a pre-arranged job, but a foregone conclusion, and I don't believe that Mr. Sharpey's carefully prepared papers and estimates ever were "thoroughly considered", and if they were, they weren't understood; what for instance is meant by saying that "the initial cost of working by electricity would greatly exceed that of steam?" What is the "initial cost of working?" If by this obscure expression is meant the initial cost of the concern, electricity may possibly be a trifle more expensive; but in an absolutely incommensurate degree with the ulterior advantage. It is a well known fact that the usual working expenses of a steam tramway exceed that of an electric tram by something like 30 per cent, the working expenses of steam averaging 78 per cent of the takings, those of electricity 50 per cent, witness Volk's electric tramway at Brighton, and many others. There are other advantages of electricity over steam, much too numerous to name. I don't suppose for a minute that this is a piece of jobbery, but it looks un-commonly like it. I should like to see an expression of opinion from some of those

easy-going gentlemen who so readily put their money down for the benefit of the town, and who never asked how it was going to be expended, nor, in fact, have ever had any voice whatever in the matter."

His reference to Magnus Volk's electric railway is somewhat misplaced. It had opened in August 1883, and ran along the beach at Brighton on its own right of way, picking up current from a third rail, hardly a method suitable for an un-fenced tramway running across pastureland! [1] Two years, later the first true electric street tramway commenced working in Blackpool using the conduit system of current collection, but because of problems caused mainly by sand, this line was converted to overhead trolley wire operation in 1898-9. Even by 1895, electric propulsion was still in its infancy, and the "initial cost of working", obviously refers to the installation of the overhead traction poles and a small power station.

The newly appointed engineer of the Tramway, Holman Fred Stephens, had his own ideas regarding motive power, and in his letter to the Board of Trade dated 28th March 1895 wrote ".... The power will be an oil motor on a passenger bogie car, with a load of not more than one ton per wheel or two tons per axle, with a wheelbase of 20ft.0in.. There will be but one motor on the line, and speed restricted to 10 m.p.h., or 4 m.p.h. though points."

He then added ".... The company are anxious to run temporarily a small engine and car whilst the oil motor is being constructed, or should the oil motor not prove a success, then to work the line by steam."

According to a note in "The Locomotive" dated 15th September 1922, Holman Stephens had motorised "a tramcar bogie" in 1890 using a Priestman oil engine, so he possibly holds the distinction of having built the first internal combustion engined railway locomotive in Britain. His design for the Rye & Camber Tramways vehicle would more than likely have used a Hornsby-Akroyd engine, which would be considerably smaller than a Preistman of comparable power. A $9^1/_2$ b.h.p. 0-4-0 locomotive, built by Messrs. Richard Hornsby & Son, Ltd. of Spittlegate Ironworks, Grantham (works number 1805) with 20in. diameter wheels on a 3ft.6in. wheelbase and with a single cylinder engine (11in. bore by 15in. stroke) was subsequently despatched to the 1ft.6in. gauge Woolwich Arsenal railway some 16 months later on 23rd July 1896, where it operated successfully for several years. It was reported as being able to haul 70 tons on the level at 3 m.p.h., or 40 tons at 5 m.p.h. [2] so there is every reason to suppose that a similar power

72. An excellent side view of CAMBER on the run-round loop at Rye on 10.4.1909 showing the replacement lettering on her side tanks (complete with full stop!) that she received after her major overhaul in 1907.
(H. L. Hopwood, L.C.G.B. Ken Nunn collection)

73. A fine portrait of the now un-named CAMBER at Rye in the early 1920s with "Jokey" Rhodes in charge and Frederick Sheppard's younger brother Percy the conductor in the background. CAMBER received a new boiler in 1921, her chimney being shortened at the same time, and the spoked leading wheels have now been replaced themselves by either the original disc variety, or some very similar.
(H. Sheppard collection)

bogie could have been used to support one end of a 3ft.0in. gauge rail motor. Either design of engine would have suffered a great deal from vibration and noise, the Woolwich Arsenal locomotive and her later sisters could be heard functioning over a mile away! The Rye and Camber project possibly progressed as far as the drawing board sketch stage, but absence of reports in the technical press must surely indicate that the vehicle was never built.

CAMBER

In the event, the directors did opt for steam traction, and for the opening, Mr. E. P. S. Jones of the Rother Ironworks, Fishmarket Road, Rye ordered, on behalf of the Rye & Camber Tramways Company, "one $5^1/_2$" cylinder locomotive, 3ft.0in. gauge to be painted dark blue", from Messrs. W. G. Bagnall, Ltd. of Castle Engine Works, Stafford. Although Bagnall quote the order as having been made on 28th May 1895, construction of the locomotive had actually commenced thirteen days earlier on 15th May. It is not known why Messrs. Bagnall were chosen to construct the engine or, if indeed, any other builders were invited to tender. They did regard themselves as "railway", not just locomotive engineers, and they also supplied the Tramway's first carriage and possible part, if not all, of the permanent way.

The locomotive was despatched from Stafford on board a standard gauge railway wagon on 10th July 1895. Described by the South Eastern Advertiser on 20th July as "of pretty construction and pattern", she was a diminutive 2-4-0T with inside frames and she carried the works number 1461 on brass oval plates mounted one on each side of the small flared 16 cu.ft. capacity coal bunker. Her name CAMBER was painted in large serifed gold letters, shaded in red, on the side tanks. For some un-explained reason, instead of the dark blue colour scheme ordered, she arrived in a standard Bagnall livery of bright olive green, lined in black edged with red on the outside and white inside, with the interior of the cab painted cream. The coupling rods were red, as were the buffer beams, which were fitted with "Patent" link and pin couplings, together with safety chains.

She was 11ft.3in. long, 4ft.10in. wide and 8ft.0in. from rail level to the top of the cab that boasted large round brass-rimmed spectacle glasses front and rear. Possibly because the engine was so small, a single hand rail was fitted high up on each cab side sheet, rather than the normal position of one on either side of the doorway. With a coupled wheelbase of 3ft.0in. the six-spoked 1ft.8in. diameter driving wheels had their laminated springs positioned above the straight footplate, the rear ones protruding into the cab, and both steam and hand brakes were provided, operating on the driving wheels only. The leading disc wheels, mounted on a radial pony truck, were 1ft.0in. in diameter, and placed behind the slide bars of the $5^1/_2$in. x 9in. cylinders which were angled slightly, thus aligning them with the front driving axle centres. The valve gear was operated by Stephenson's Link Motion, and to

protect the piston rods and crossheads from the sand that blows on all but the calmest days from the surrounding sand hills, they were hidden behind fully-lined out metal covers that, for maintenance purposes, were hinged to the footplate.

CAMBER's 1ft.10in. boiler (internal diameter), constructed of $^5/_{16}$in. plates, was 4ft.3in. long and contained 26 brass tubes of 1.75in. external diameter, being fed by two Gresham & Craven No. 3mm injectors. Working pressure was 140 lbs. per square inch. [3] A large dome was positioned slightly ahead of the short 100 gallon capacity side tanks, and Duplex Ramsbottom safety valves were mounted over the conventional round top copper firebox. Behind the tall, graceful, tapered chimney, on top of the smokebox was a brass displacement lubricator, and a high-pitched whistle (also of brass) was fitted to the front of the cab. Normal average speed was 10 m.p.h., but one early report ("Railway World", March 1896) quotes CAMBER as having travelled the $1^1/_2$ miles between Rye and Camber in just four minutes. In working order she weighed just 6 tons and was capable of hauling 60 tons on the level, 31 tons up a grade of 1 in 100, or 15 tons on a gradient of 1 in 45. Her purchase price was £404.7s.6d..

The "Railway World" article did contain more than a few discrepancies in its description of CAMBER. The leading wheels were quoted as "solid wheels 10in. in diameter", the boiler pressure as 150 lbs. per square inch and that "the side tanks hold 140 gallons of water", so it is all the more curious that the article should be used, word for word, in several editions of Messrs. Bagnalls' own catalogue!

When delivered on Friday, 12th July 1895, CAMBER was arranged to work chimney first from Rye, but she was turned to face the other way very early on. One of Bagnalls' skilled engineers, Mr. T. Taylor, took charge of the locomotive for the first few weeks to check that it worked safely and that it accomplished all that was intended of it. On 8th November 1895, Mr. E. P. S. Jones ordered a "Gong for CAMBER" (Bagnalls' Order 797) but with no public roads to cross, and a more than adequate steam whistle, its use would have been very limited, and there is no evidence to suggest that it was ever fitted to the engine.

CAMBER was ideally suited to her work, exactly what W. G. Bagnall had intended of the design that dated back to 1882, and in February 1896, the chairman of the Tramway Company, Cuthbert Hayles, proudly called the engine "an un-commonly good one". Yet only two years later, with profits down and repair expenses more than double those of the previous year, one of the directors, Mr. T.G. Sharpe, described her as "not up to the work" and that she "had to be kept going much harder than it was capable of running", which suggests that with her small boiler and heating surface, she may have soon got winded. Even with both carriages and a full complement of 57 passengers, her train would only weigh around 10 tons, and with just the one gradient of 1 in 160, and that on straight track, surely she was working well within her

74. When Mr. H. C. Casserley visited the Rye & Camber Tramway on 11.4.1931, he was disappointed to find that neither of the steam locomotives were in service that day. With the aid of the petrol locomotive, the friendly George Wratten kindly brought CAMBER out of her shed for this picture to be taken.

(H. C. Casserley)

75. CAMBER poses for another picture whilst, in the background, George Wratten tends to his trusty petrol locomotive. 11.4.1931.

(H. C. Casserley)

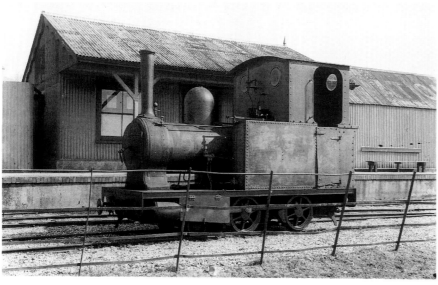

76. CAMBER had not been in service for many a long year when she was brought out into the sunshine for this photograph to be taken in July 1937. *(J. M. Jarvis)*

capabilities, so perhaps it was the lack of proper maintenance that was causing her problems.

During the summer of 1897, CAMBER at last received her long overdue overhaul during which a pair of 6-spoked leading wheels replaced the original disc type, and two circular holes were cut into the front buffer beam to provide easier access to the cylinder covers and pistons. As the platform at both stations was on the "down" side, a crude metal door, held in place by four sprung hinges, was added to the opposite cab opening which would provide the driver with a little protection from the prevailing south-westerly winds. After this overhaul she was described as being "in very good condition", but there were still to be regular complaints that she was "small and needed constant repairs and labour".

For the next ten years CAMBER served her Company well until, in 1907, she received another major overhaul, after which her name in serifed letters on the side tanks gave way to ordinary gold-painted capital letters, again shaded in red, complete this time with a full stop! With the work completed, Cuthbert Hayles was able to report that the engine "is now in first class condition, and capable of doing the work properly for some time to come".

On 5th January 1921, a new boiler was ordered from Bagnall (Order 9513) and it was probably when this was fitted that her tall, graceful chimney was cut down by some 4in., and her livery was simplified to overall black, without lining or name, and the little locomotive lost a little of her original character. At this time her maker's plate disappeared from her bunker on the near side, but that on the platform side remained, at least for a few years. The front lamp iron above the smokebox door was removed, but though it could have received very little use, if any, that on the rear cab sheet remained, whilst the spoked leading wheels that had replaced the earlier disc type were replaced themselves by either the originals, or some very similar.

Surely the original directors could not have been so naive as to imagine that they could run their Tramway efficiently with just the one locomotive, or perhaps they were genuinely awaiting the arrival of Holman Stephens' rail motor. Whatever the reason, it became apparent all too soon that CAMBER could not be expected to run the services by herself indefinitely, and Messrs. Bagnall were approached regarding the supply of a second engine, confirming that the Tramway Company must have been reasonably satisfied with the original locomotive's performance, or they would have surely gone elsewhere. Bagnall prepared two sketches numbered 4158 and 4158A, dated 17th March 1896, for a 5½in. x 9in. and 6in.x 9in. cylinder engine respectively, which were basically identical except that the smaller of the two had a more basic open cab and a spark arresting chimney! The latter adornment was not such a ridiculous suggestion as CAMBER regularly managed to set the lineside grass alight with red hot cinders blown from her traditional chimney. Both designs incorporated Baguley

patent valve gear, and the larger locomotive had RYE added to the side tank on the diagram.

With funds of only £180 available, no further action was taken, and the search for a second-hand engine began. Nothing more was heard on the subject until almost a year later when at the Annual General Meeting on 5th March 1897 Cuthbert Hayles explained "I might say that we have not yet succeeded in getting a second-hand engine - we have been trying for a considerable time, but cannot find one in a satisfactory condition at a suitable price. We do not want to increase the capital of the Company by expending £400 or £500 in the purchase of a new engine, and second hand ones are not things that grow on every bush. We are now enquiring into one or two offers, and I hope we might be successful in purchasing on moderate terms an engine which will meet our requirements."

He then added that had the directors cared to have purchased a second-hand engine which could not be relied upon, it would have been done twelve months ago, but that the utmost care was being exercised in its selection.

77. Time is running out for CAMBER as she waits at the front of the engine shed at Rye in August 1937. The wooden framework on the left suggests that there were windows along the southern wall prior to the carriage shed being built alongside in 1896. The large set of wheels on the right must surely belong to VICTORIA which was reported as being scrapped that year. Might the Rye & Camber Tramway have had more luck if the horseshoe on the door had been fitted the other way up?
(D. W. K. Jones)

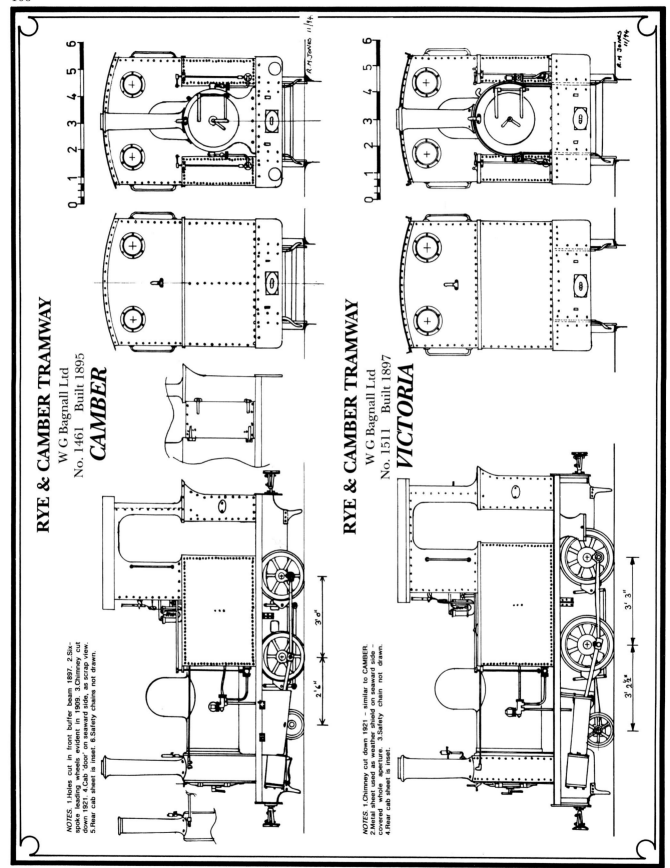

RYE & CAMBER TRAMWAY

W G Bagnall Ltd
No. 1461 Built 1895

CAMBER

NOTES. 1.Holes cut in front buffer beam 1897. 2.Six-spoke leading wheels evident in 1909. 3.Chimney cut down 1921. 4.Cab 'door' on seaward side, as scrap view. 5.Rear cab sheet is inset. 6.Safety chains not drawn.

RYE & CAMBER TRAMWAY

W G Bagnall Ltd
No. 1511 Built 1897

VICTORIA

NOTES. 1.Chimney cut down 1921 - similar to CAMBER. 2.Metal sheet used as weather shield on seaward side - covered whole aperture. 3.Safety chain not drawn. 4.Rear cab sheet is inset.

78. Following the Tramway's enquiry regarding the proposed purchase of a second locomotive, two sketches were prepared by Messrs. Bagnall dated 17.3.1896. Sketch 4158 shows their design for a locomotive with 5¹/₂" x 9" cylinders, Baguley valve gear, a basic open cab and, a little surprisingly, a spark arresting chimney!

(Allan C. Baker collection)

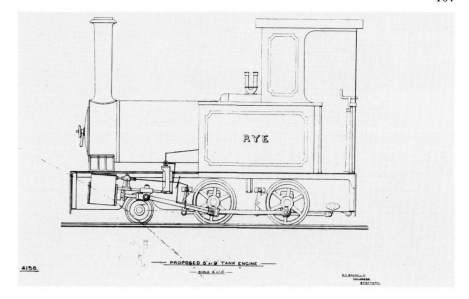

79. Sketch 4158A was for an almost identical locomotive, but with larger 6" x 9" cylinders, a traditional chimney and a more enclosed cab. Was it Bagnall's idea to add the name RYE to the side tank?

(Allan C. Baker collection)

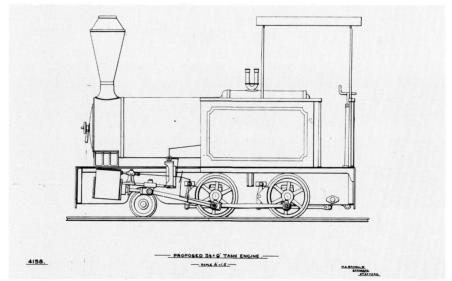

80. Messrs. Bagnall's diagram of VICTORIA as built.

(Allan C. Baker collection)

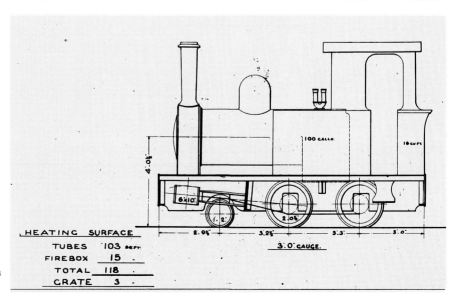

81. With the background blanked out on the original glass plate negative, which sadly, is not longer in existence, this is Bagnall's rather blotched "official" view of VICTORIA, May 1897. *(Allan C. Baker collection)*

82. One of the few known photographs of VICTORIA in service with her name in gold serifed letters clearly visible on her side tank, so her arrival in Rye with the Bagnall carriage in tow can be dated at the latest to around the turn of the century. *(Lens of Sutton)*

83. Frederick Sheppard, with head bowed, stands nonchalantly with both feet on the running line in front of VICTORIA as she waits with her train for Rye at Golf Links station on 10.4.1909. Her name has long since disappeared and her yellow lining is heading the same way. The locomotive stands astride the right of way between the Royal William Hotel on the Camber road and the ferry to Rye Harbour village, hence the gap in the iron fencing.

(H. L. Hopwood, L.C.G.B. Ken Nunn collection)

84. As the Tramway was worked on the "one engine in steam principle", photographs of both locomotives together are understandably rare. On 10th April 1909, VICTORIA has pulled CAMBER cold from her shed to provide this excellent opportunity to compare the differences between the two locomotives. The two 4-plank open wagons of 1897 lurk in the background on the sand siding.

(H. L. Hopwood, L.C.G.B. Ken Nunn collection)

85. "Locomotive Eats Man!" Soon after her overhaul in 1922 VICTORIA, looking very smart in her all over livery of un-lined black, receives some attention between services on the run-round loop at Rye. Ever safety conscious, the side chains are connected between the two carriages standing at the platform. The Company's wheelbarrow lies out of use beside the loop with its spoked wheel amidst the clutter a few yards beyond. *(Lens of Sutton)*

86. VICTORIA did not look so smart on the day that the petrol locomotive arrived in 1924.

(Lens of Sutton)

VICTORIA

Unfortunately, the hoped-for bargain did not materialise, and on 8th April 1897, the Rye & Camber Tramways Company Ltd. ordered from Bagnall "one locomotive to their specification to be in Rye by 31st May 1897". The cost of the new engine was £425, and it was purchased by the issue of new debentures and shares. It is not clear if it was the original intention to name the locomotive RYE as per Bagnall's sketch No. 4158 of March 1896 but, presumably in honour of Queen Victoria's Diamond Jubilee, a later instruction, dated 19th May, was sent to Bagnall to "name the locomotive VICTORIA".

The new engine (works no. 1511) left Stafford on 1st June 1897, and although built to the same basic design as CAMBER, now that there were two carriages to haul, and taking into account some of the lessons learned, she was a little larger and more powerful than her older sister. Her livery was dark blue with yellow lining, and her name VICTORIA was painted in un-shaded serifed gold letters on the side tanks. By the early 1900s, however, the lining had rather faded and the name, which had possibly been allowed to fade away after the Queen's death in 1901, had disappeared altogether, never to be replaced. One departure from the original sketch was the fitting of Stephenson's Link Motion instead of the Baguley patent valve gear illustrated. Her boiler was considerably larger than CAMBER's, being 4ft.9in. long, with an internal diameter of 2ft1³/₈in. and it contained 45 x 1.75in. brass tubes. The firebox was again of copper and the tubes brass. To list all of the leading dimensions of VICTORIA would be tedious, so for a comparison between the two engines, reference should be made to the following table.

Apart from size, there were several distinguishing features that helped to tell the locomotives apart. VICTORIA's buffer beams were deeper and less rounded at the bottom edge, the sides of the smokebox saddle were straight and not waisted in, her chimney was less tapered and of a larger diameter, and there was a displacement lubricator of a different pattern mounted towards the bottom at the rear of it. Whereas CAMBER had small crescent-shaped driving wheel balance weights, those on VICTORIA took up the whole area between 3 of the 8 spokes, and the piston rods and crossheads were protected by a much smaller metal cover. A crude sheet of metal was soon added to block off the lower section of VICTORIA's nearside doorway and this was often joined by a sheet of similar material so that the opening was filled in completely.

Mr. E. P. S. Jones ordered some spares for VICTORIA on 12th August 1913, but what these were is not recorded, and then in the early 1920s, the locomotive also received a major overhaul. Being the more powerful of the two steam locomotives VICTORIA had been worked far more than CAMBER with the result that many of her parts were virtually worn out, but although not lucky enough to receive a new boiler, she did re-appear in an un-lined all over black livery, including the buffer beams. A single footstep beneath each cab doorway had been fitted from new, the support of which curved sharply under the footplate to keep within the limited loading gauge, but the left hand step (at least) was removed during the overhaul, and her chimney was cut down at the same time. Not long afterwards, the front of the smokebox had to be patched up, a metal plate being bolted on immediately below the smokebox door.

THE PETROL LOCOMOTIVE

It was probably inevitable, especially after his original proposal of 1895 to run "an oil motor on a passenger bogie car" that Lt. Col. H. F. Stephens should suggest to the Tramway Company that they purchase a petrol locomotive. His first experiment with petrol propulsion occurred around 1919 when he mounted a lorry body onto a Wolseley Siddeley car chassis that had been fitted with flanged wheels and tested at Rolvenden on the Kent & East Sussex Railway. Within a year the chassis had acquired a bus type body, and after further trials it was moved to another of the Colonel's lines, the Selsey Tramway in West Sussex where it must have proved successful as two new railcars based on Ford components were ordered for the Kent & East Sussex Railway in 1923, followed by another pair in 1924.

The type of machine ordered for the Rye & Camber Tramways Company Ltd. had been the brain-child of Mr. T. Dixon-Abbot, the Managing Director of the Motor Rail and Tramcar Co. Ltd. of Lewes, Sussex, who had designed it as a cheap and simple petrol locomotive for use by the British Army behind the Front Line in the 1914-18 War. Known as the "Simplex" design, it

	CAMBER	VICTORIA
Length over buffer beams:	11'3"	12'3"
Height to top of cab:	8'0"	8'4"
Overall width over footplate:	4'10"	4'10"
Height of footplate from rail level:	2'0"	2'3"
Internal diameter of boiler:	1'10"	2'1³/₈"
Centre line of boiler from rail level:	3'9"	4'0¹/₂"
Cylinders (bore x stroke):	5¹/₂" x 9"	6" x 10"
Driving wheel diameter:	1'8"	2'0¹/₂"
Leading wheel diameter:	1'0"	1'2"
Fixed wheelbase:	3'0"	3'3"
Total wheelbase:	5'6"	6'5¹/₂"
Water capacity:	100 gals.	150 gals.
Coal capacity:	16 cu.ft.	16 cu.ft.
Heating surface		
Tubes:	55 cu.ft.	103 sq.ft.
Firebox:	12¹/₂ sq.ft.	15 sq.ft.
Total:	67¹/₂ sq.ft.	118 sq.ft.
Working pressure:	140 p.s.i.	140 p.s.i.
Grate area:	2¹/₂ sq.ft.	3 sq.ft.
Weight in working order:	6 tons	6 tons 12 cwt.

87. The shape of things to come! On the day of its arrival at Rye in 1924, the Kent Construction Company petrol locomotive is thoroughly inspected whilst the man in the white suit (believed to be none other Lt. Colonel Holman Fred Stephens) looks on. The number 1364 on the side of the engine cover may be its works number, but it is highly un-likely that the Kent Construction Company built that many locomotives. They could, of course, have started their order numbers from a much higher figure that "1", or numbered orders for other products in the one series. *(Lens of Sutton)*

88. This picture may also have been taken on the day that the petrol locomotive was delivered to Rye, the gentleman at the controls being recognisable from the previous photograph. Perhaps the little engine is about to make its trial trip along the line to Camber. The half cab gave very little protection to the driver, his legs and feet being fully exposed to the elements.
(Lens of Sutton)

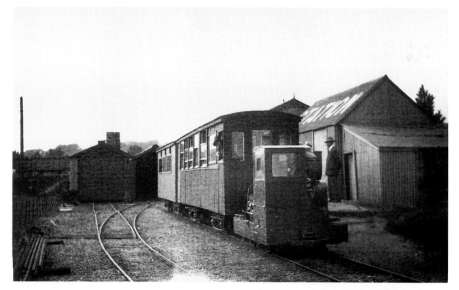

89. An early view of the petrol locomotive with its bonnet open to reveal the Dorman 2JO engine. Already the original exhaust pipe has been replaced by one which curves downwards through 90 degrees to discharge its gases below the footplate.

(Colonel Stephens Railway Museum & Archives, Tenterden)

RYE & CAMBER TRAMWAYS Co. Ltd.

Kent Construction Co. Petrol Locomotive

1925 Soon after delivery, but with modified exhaust pipe

0 1 2 3 4 5 ft.

1930

1931

1936

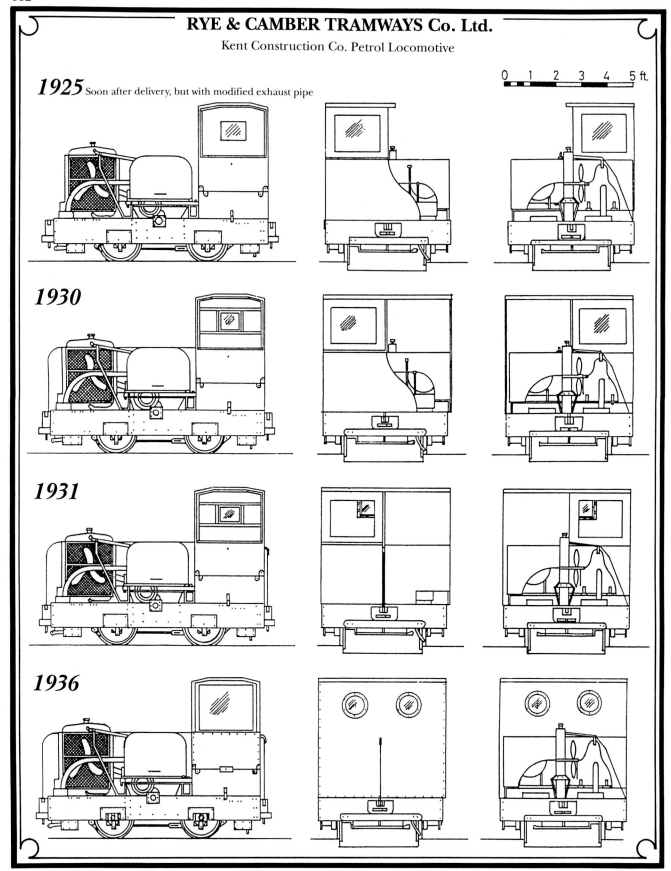

90. After running round and re-joining her train at Camber Sands, the petrol locomotive ticks over quietly in readiness for her next trip back to Rye. Perhaps the window behind the driver had suffered from too much vibration for it has now been strengthened with the addition of some neat wooden framing. George Wratten has rigged up a wire across the bonnet which can be seen curving downwards through 90 degrees in front and to the left of the Reliance pressed steel radiator, to enable him to lift the pin from the front coupling without having to leave his cab. 11.4.1931.

(H. C. Casserley)

91. This view of the other side of the petrol locomotive and her train taken at Rye the same day shows the simple controls, the horizontal brake wheel being the most prominent. "Automatic" coupling has yet to be fitted to the rear of the machine.

(H. C. Casserley)

92. During the next few months the petrol locomotive received some further modifications when metal sheeting was crudely added to the full width of the cab. This angle shows how it reached down only as far as the bonnet at the front, and fell short of the footplate by some 12" at the rear.

(L. Bearman collection)

114

93. Shortly afterwards, the larger part of each of the windows front and rear was blocked off leaving an even smaller hinged glazed section than that behind the driver's head. 29.8.1931.
(L.C.G.B. Ken Nunn collection)

94. By 1933 the looks of the locomotive were greatly enhanced by the acquisition of some fine brass-rimmed spectacle glasses that George Wratten had removed from the out of service VICTORIA. Small squares have also been cut into the side frames to reveal and provide better access to the axle boxes.
(H. Sheppard collection)

95. In its final form the petrol locomotive looked very smart sporting, since 1936, a brighter shade of apple green paint with the smaller details picked out in gloss black. The tiny window behind the driver's head has been replaced by a large full-drop window, shown here in the open position, and the rear panel has, at long last, been finished off neatly. August 1937.
(Author's collection)

consisted of a water-cooled 2 cylinder 20 h.p. Dorman 2JO petrol engine mounted transversely amidships on a 4-wheeled underframe, with the drive taken to all 4 wheels by chains via his patent gearbox that gave 2 speeds in each direction. The radiator was sited lengthways just behind the centre line at the front end of the chassis, whilst at the other end the driver sat sideways so that he could see clearly in either direction.

To trace the brief history of the Kent Construction Company, who supplied the locomotive, we must go back to 13th October 1921, when the Honeywill Brothers, with their office at 79 Mark Lane, London, E.C.3, ordered some spares from the Motor Rail & Tramcar Co. Ltd. (who had moved to larger premises in Bedford in 1918) and started dealing in second-hand locomotives, advertising the sale of "a 20 h.p. Simplex locomotive, 2ft.0in. gauge, seen Ashford works" on 20th January 1922. On 15th February they announced that in future they would be trading as "The Kent Construction & Engineering Co. Ltd., a new concern which takes over the business of the British Saw Sharpening Machines, Ltd. of Ashford", but only one week later they had decided to trade under their own name and act as agents for "The Kent Construction Co. Ltd.". Their last order for parts from Motor Rail was made on 5th April 1922, and on 10th May 1922 they offered for sale in the "Contracts Journal" 20 h.p. re-conditioned locomotives at £300 each. Second-hand 20 h.p. and 40 h.p. Simplex locomotives were easily obtained (around 820 had been built for War service) and many of these were subsequently offered for sale, being regularly advertised in the Ministry of Munitions' own publication "Surplus" that was published between 1919 and 1923.

It would appear that the Kent Construction Company were offering their re-conditioned "Simplex" locomotives for sale (much to the annoyance of Motor Rail) by just adding their own works plates, a practise that was continued by F. C. Hibberd & Co. Ltd., a Company that was formed on 18th August 1927 to purchase the stock of petrol locomotives and assets of the former Company who were by then in liquidation. Originally used by the Motor Rail & Tramcar Co. Ltd., and then by the Kent Construction Co. and F. C. Hibberd, "Simplex" has never been registered as a trade name by any of the 3 companies. Apart from supplying these reconditioned secondhand locomotives, the Kent Construction Co., and their successors also built some similar, but entirely new locomotives to the same "Simplex" design, and the Rye & Camber petrol tractor was evidently one of these.

Colonel Stephens had already had dealings with the Kent Construction Co. for, whilst occupying the post of Civil Engineer and Locomotive Superintendent for the 1ft.11½in. gauge Festiniog Railway in North Wales in 1923, he had purchased for that Company a 40 h.p. machine in an attempt to reduce running costs. It was undoubtedly the success of this locomotive that prompted the Colonel to suggest the purchase of a similar, but less powerful unit for the Rye & Camber

Tramway, which was delivered to Rye Tram station in 1924.[4] Page 10 of the Kent Construction Company's catalogue includes a drawing of a similar locomotive with the heading "20 H.P. Planet Light Locomotive 3 Ton Type" [5] listing the main dimensions as 8ft.11in. long over buffers, 4ft.10in. wide, with the height to the top of the cab as 6ft.0in. The Motor Rail bowed frame, that had been built up from channel steel, was replaced by a neat square version, [6] and with a wheelbase of 3ft.6in., the wheels were 17¾in. diameter on the tread and all four were braked. At an engine speed of 1,000 r.p.m., and at a travelling speed of 3½ m.p.h., the locomotive was advertised as being capable of hauling 50 tons on the level, or 25 tons at 8 m.p.h., although the engine could be run safely at 1,250 r.p.m., giving a speed of 10 m.p.h., with approximately the same tractive effort (700 lbs.) as at 8 m.p.h..

As delivered, the exhaust pipe and silencer emerged from the engine compartment in a horizontal straight line in front of a 3-bladed fan that cooled the Reliance pressed steel radiator. One of the first tasks was to replace the original pipe with another that curved downwards through 90 degrees so that the exhaust was discharged below the footplate. The Dorman 2JO engine, with both cylinders cast into one block and an integral cylinder head, was protected by a metal bonnet hinged down the middle, the opposite side providing access to the cylindrical 14 gallon petrol tank. Because there were no storage facilities on the Tramway, petrol was obtained in two gallon cans from the Petrol Engine Company's garage, conveniently situated a few yards away across the Monkbretton Bridge on the town side of the River Rother. Like CAMBER and VICTORIA, the petrol locomotive was arranged to work cab first from Rye, perhaps for no other reason than to prevent the starting handle from fouling the platforms!

The cab was a very basic affair stretching only half way across the vehicle so that the driver's legs and feet were exposed to the elements. There was a large window front and rear, with a smaller one behind the driver's head, whilst the rear panel was curved neatly down to practically conceal a toolbox fitted to the floor that would become a useful seat for specially privileged guests in future years. The space beneath the driver's seat was utilised to provide a small cupboard which housed, amongst other things, the starting handle, access to it being gained via a hinged flap on the outside of the cab.

It was not long before the roof of the cab was extended an inch or so beyond the full width of the locomotive, its outer end being held in position by two uprights and a cross member formed of one length of metal tubing bent to shape, with two horizontal rails of smaller diameter protecting the gap at the rear. The window behind the driver's head was partially covered over, leaving just a small glazed section in the centre which, to give it more strength, was bordered by some wooden framework. To save the driver leaving the comfort (?!) of his cab to un-couple the carriages at the termini, a wire was rigged up along the top of the bonnet

116

and then downwards through 90 degrees which, when pulled, would release the pin, to which it was attached, vertically from the coupling. This proved such a success that a similar, but shorter wire was later added to fulfil a similar purpose at the rear.

Canvas screens had been provided at the front and rear of the open section of the cab which could be rolled out of use and strapped to the roof in good weather, but during the summer of 1931, more permanent protection was afforded to the driver when they were replaced by some crude metal sheeting, that at the back finishing about 1ft.0in. short of the footplate, with the front section extending down only as far as the top of the bonnet. Held in place by wing nuts, the front section may still have been removable in hot weather, at least for the first few months. Around about this time, the greater part of the front and rear windows was also blocked off to leave tiny hinged square glazed look-outs, even smaller than the window behind the driver.

The little locomotive may have been a very basic machine, indeed, many people described her as "ugly", but she certainly had a charm all of her own, and to many locals who grew up in Rye in the 1930's, she WAS "The Camber Tram". Although a lot less powerful than CAMBER, she proved to be quite capable of hauling both carriages, but when the two open passenger wagons with a full complement of holidaymakers were added, two or three attempts would sometimes have to be made to get her train under way. [7] For this reason both steam locomotives had been kept, and prior to 1930, CAMBER would be steamed on summer weekends and Bank Holidays when traffic was expected to be the heaviest.

By 1933 the petrol tractor's appearance was greatly enhanced by the acquisition of two brass-rimmed spectacle glasses front and rear, that George Wratten had removed from the then out of service VICTORIA. Small squares had also been cut in the side of the frames to reveal and give better access to the axle boxes, and hinges and other small fittings were picked out in gloss black paint. Since delivery in 1924, her livery had been a plain dark green, but for the summer of 1936 she appeared in a lighter and brighter shade of apple green. The panel containing the small window behind the driver's head had now been completely removed and replaced with a large drop-light window, and a large tapered sand box had been fitted to the nearside of the front buffer beam. The little engine looked smarter than ever, and she was to remain in this condition until the Tramway closed to passengers in September 1939. VICTORIA, however, had been sold for scrap in 1936. [8]

It is doubtful if CAMBER turned a wheel after VICTORIA's demise, but by that time, William Henry Austen, who had succeeded Holman Stephens as Consulting Engineer to the Tramway following the latter's death in October 1931, had begun to realise the

tourist potential of running the line by steam again, and it is thought that it was he who suggested that the little locomotive (that he had driven on the opening day over 40 years previously) should be taken to the locomotive works at Rolvenden on the Kent & East Sussex Railway for a thorough overhaul. She left Rye in 1939 on the back of a lorry, Percy Sheppard remembering ".... She was an awkward thing though, and nearly overturned the lorry - perhaps she didn't want to go". [9]

Whether CAMBER received her overhaul or not is debatable, but when questioned many years ago, some of the old Kent & East Sussex Railway staff (regrettably now deceased) vaguely recalled a Rye & Camber locomotive arriving at Rolvenden, but by the summer of 1941 she was back on the Tramway. [10] In 1946 CAMBER was in the large shed, normally the resting place of the petrol locomotive and open passenger wagons, but minus her smokebox, right hand cylinder end and dome cover, so it looks as though work on her might have commenced, but with the outbreak of war, and the need for more space at Rolvenden, she had been returned to Rye for storage. By then, time for her was rapidly running out and a year later she was no more.

The petrol locomotive was much more fortunate and avoided the scrap man's torch when it was purchased by Mr. George W. Bungey, who had formerly been the Foreman at the Kent Construction Company's works in Ashford. He had left the Company when Messrs. F. C. Hibberd took over the business in 1927 and had subsequently formed his own company with works based at Hayes in West London, where he carried on in the same line, overhauling and re-selling petrol and diesel locomotives. Bungey advertised the locomotive for sale, together with a selection of 2ft.0in. gauge Simplexes, in the "Conract Journal" for 6th November 1946, but its subsequent fate is unknown, although it may well have been exported.

1. For full history of Volk's Electric Railway see "Volk's Railways Brighton", by Alan A. Jackson, - Plateway Press 1993.
2. "Industrial Railway Record", Volume 9, article on Hornsby Akroyd Locomotives by C. G. Down.
3. Boiler statistics for CAMBER and VICTORIA have been taken from "The Locomotive" 15.5.1909.
4. "The Railway Year Book" (with annual statistics provided by the Rye & Camber Tramway) for the year ending 31.12.1923 quotes 3 locomotives in stock for the first time, suggesting that the petrol locomotive was ordered during that year, with delivery in 1924, and not 1925 as is so often quoted.
5. "Planet" was another trade name used by the Kent Construction Co., and later F. C. Hibberd.
6. It has been suggested that the bowed frame remained in situ behind the new square frame on the Rye & Camber locomotive.
7. "Meccano Magazine" March 1935, short article by John F. Burke.
8. Railway Year Book, 1937.
9. "The Tenterden Terrier" No. 10, Summer 1976, House Journal of the Kent & East Sussex Railway.
10. "Railway Observer" July 1941.

Chapter Twelve

ROLLING STOCK

THE BAGNALL CARRIAGE

Along with the locomotive CAMBER, Messrs. W. G. Bagnall Ltd. supplied just the one passenger carriage for the opening of the Tramway, and as if to bear out the Company's title, it more resembled a tramcar than it did a railway carriage. Rumour has it that the design was adapted from some metre gauge carriages that were under construction for French Railways at the time. The South Eastern Advertiser dated 20th July 1895 described the vehicle as being "of lengthy proportions, divided into two compartments capable of accommodating 32 passengers, 12 First Class and 20 Second Class. The First Class is protected with permanent windows and is fitted with cushioned seats, whilst the Second is more open to the elements, but, nevertheless, in fine weather is the more preferable".

The car was 25ft.10in. long, 5ft.10in. wide and 9ft.3in. from rail level to the top of the roof, and was carried on two bogies spaced 12ft.6in. apart with a wheelbase of 3ft.6in. and wheels of 1ft.2^1/$_2$in. diameter, each with 7 curved spokes. Bagnall's original drawing (W80 dated 17th May 1895) shows entrances on either side of the 2ft.0in. wide balconies fitted to each end of the carriage, but when delivered, access was from the platform side only, with the metal dashes being carried round to block off the opposite side. [1] Hand brakes operated on all 4 wheels of both bogies and the brake handles, horse tramcar style, were situated just off-centre on the outside of the dashes on each balcony. Completely open above the 3ft.6in. high tongue and groove planked sides, the Second Class portion had inward facing wooden slatted seats fitted along each side and across the horizontally planked partition that

separated it from the First Class compartment, whilst the roof of wooden boards, covered with oiled canvas, was supported by eight 2^1/$_2$in. square wooden pillars, four to each side. There was no bulkhead or door to this section, but the seat ends on either side were finished off with straight planking resembling the ends of a church pew. In comparison, the 8ft.6in. long First Class compartment was quite luxurious with curtains at the windows and cushioned seats along the sides and across the partition which boasted a clock on this side - an unusual touch. This section was completely enclosed, access from the balcony being via an externally-hung sliding door, with fresh air being provided by 4 louvred ventilators fitted centrally above the 2 fixed windows on either side.

On hot, summer days the Second Class compartment may have been all very well, but although the makers' drawings do not show any provisions for blocking off the open sides, the "Railway World" dated March 1896 advised "....The second class portion is provided with glass windows during the winter months....". The article would be referring to the two fixed windows mounted on a single wooden panel that could be bolted to the roof supports between the waist and cant rails of the centre section on each side and, because these windows were of similar dimensions to those in the First Class section, they must surely have been provided by Bagnall. The northern end of the carriage still remained open and it seems likely that the Tramway Company had to make its own arrangements and similarly sized sections of planked panelling (that matched the sides) were used to block off the remainder of the carriage, complete with similar sections to add to the ends of the seats at the northern end so that, viewed from the side, the vehicle took on the appearance of a brake composite carriage.

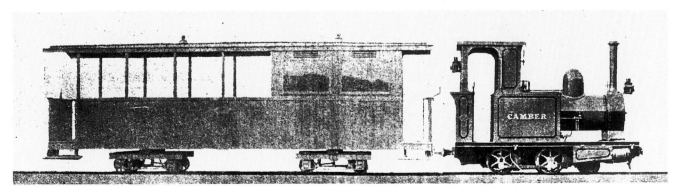

96. This interesting photograph was published in the 1.10.1895 edition of "Machinery Market". CAMBER has been made to look larger than she really is; the photograph of her on the wagon outside their works on 10th July 1895 being reproduced at a different scale to the carriage. Note that on the carriage (that looks very model-like) it is possible for passengers to enter the balconies from either side and that the roof boasts two oil lamps, a luxury that the Rye & Camber Tramway's vehicle was not to receive for several years.
(Allan C. Baker collection)

RYE & CAMBER TRAMWAYS Co. Ltd.
W G Bagnall Ltd.
Composite Tramcar

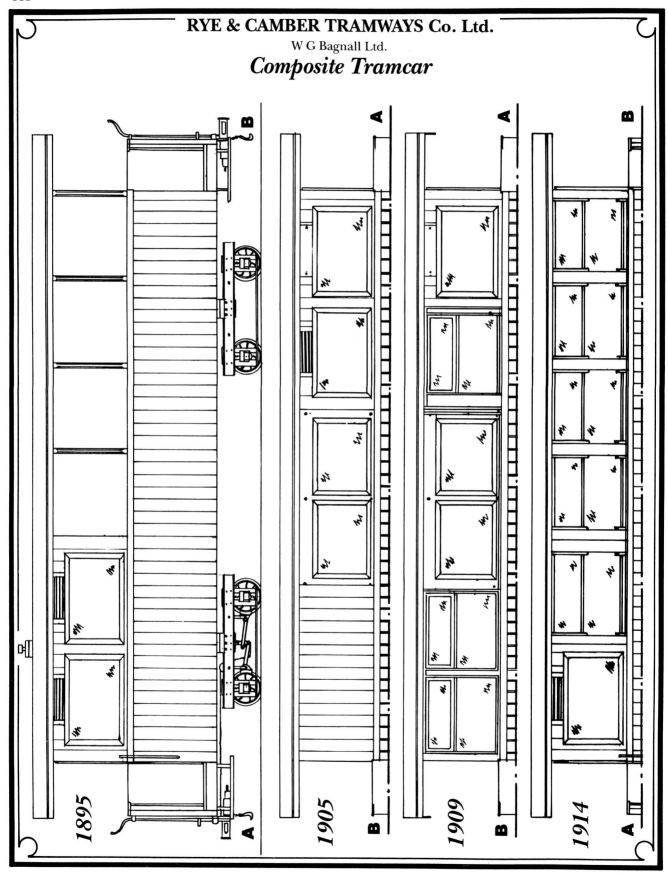

1895

1905

1909

1914

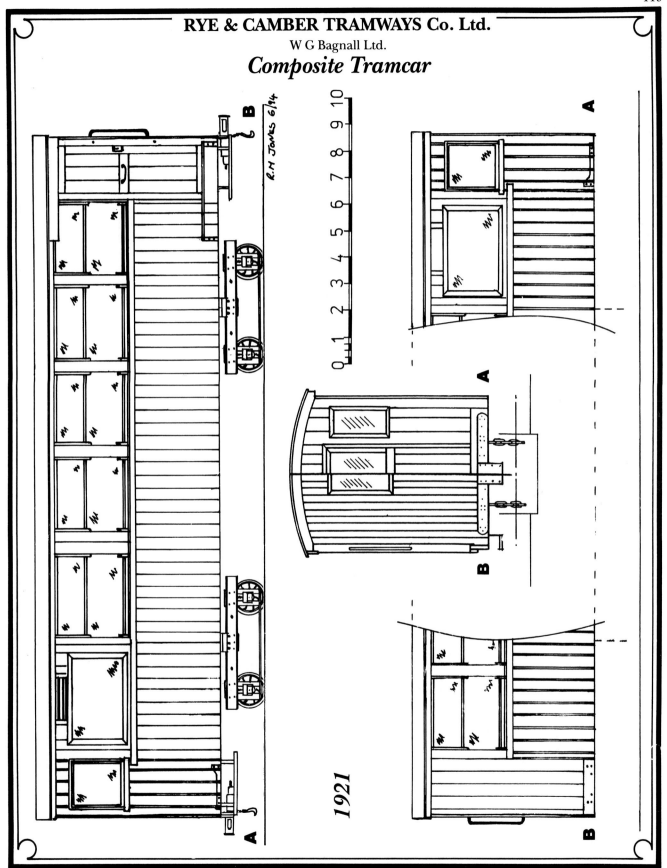

RYE & CAMBER TRAMWAYS Co. Ltd.

W G Bagnall Ltd.

Composite Tramcar

R.H Jones 6/94

0 1 2 3 4 5 6 7 8 9 10

1921

Each of the four side sections (2 per side) were held in place by 6 bolts so that they were easily and quickly removed in good weather. The wooden panels must have made the interior very dark and a second oil lamp, mounted centrally above the Second Class portion, later joined the one that had been provided in the First Class compartment from new. On fine, but windy days, a white canvas screen would be attached to the open western side of the carriage, this being held in place by 3 hooks on the cant rail, with the lower edge tied to a rail provided specifically for the purpose that was fixed two-thirds of the way up the side and ran the length of the Second Class compartment. The eastern side, away from the prevailing south-westerly winds, would remain open. It was not only the passengers that suffered at the expense of the wind, and in an effort to stop sand being blown into the gaps in the planked western side, they were filled with beading but, surprisingly, the opposite side was not altered and it remained in its original condition to the end.

When the Rother Ironworks carriage was delivered in April 1896, a continuous wooden footboard was added to the platform side of that and the Bagnall carriage so that the conductor was able to collect fares and issue tickets whilst the tram was in motion. To help him keep his footing on this precarious perch a brass hand rail was fitted above the windows to the cant rail of each carriage.

Ventilation in the First Class saloon must have proved inadequate because c.1905 a new window replaced the fixed original on both sides adjoining the partition that separated this compartment from the Second Class. The new windows were taller, reaching up to the cant rail, and were in two sections, the smaller upper portion being hinged along its bottom edge so that it dropped through 180 degrees inside the carriage when opened. No adjustment appears to have been available so that the windows were either opened or closed! While this work was being carried out, the rail attached to the western side of the body was moved along the carriage, so that the canvas screen provided some shelter from the elements for the First Class passengers as well. The wooden "windows" in the Second Class compartment cannot have been very popular, and within the next two years they had been replaced with opening windows similar, but with a lighter framework, to those in the First Class section. With the addition of a matching externally-hung window-less sliding door, the planked removable bulkhead panels at the northern end were fixed permanently in place, as were the two remaining non-opening windows on their panel on the centre of each side, which also received the luxury of their own curtains! By now the brakes had been removed from the southern end of the carriage, together with the brake handle on the First Class balcony, but the braking arrangements at the opposite end remained.

The hinged opening windows could not have been too successful and by the First World War they, and those on their removable central panel had been replaced, unusually for a railway carriage, by the sash variety more commonly found in houses. Each was fitted permanently in place and the upper section opened downwards on the outside of the lower fixed portion. Of the original windows, only those adjacent to the First Class balcony on either side remained. Once the new windows were in place the canvas screen was made redundant and the side-mounted rail was removed, though its 3 fixing lugs were to remain in situ for several years.

To date the many alterations to the carriage had been quite straight-forward, and would have been put into effect as and when finance and time permitted. The major re-build carried out after the First World War was a different matter altogether, and in view of the complexity of the work involved, it was almost certainly undertaken by the staff of Rother Ironworks. The remaining brake gear was removed, together with both balconies so that the ends of the underframe became visible for the first time, and the sides were extended the full length of the vehicle in similar planking (complete with beading in the gaps) at the southern end, but plain, vertical planking at the other. A crude, window-less wooden sliding door (without doubt that added latterly to the Second Class bulkhead) was fitted externally at this end to become the only access into the re-built carriage, and the new Rye end was constructed using smaller width planking and had a small fixed window added in the centre. The full length footboard on the platform side with its associated handrail was discarded, and the remaining foot step beneath the door was extended by 9in. beyond the end of the carriage to almost the length of the link and pin central coupling.

The Camber end consisted of an odd, but balanced mixture of wide and narrow planking with a smaller window on either side of a similar sized window to that at the other end, which was built into a beaded panelled central section that resembled (though it was not) a door. With the clock removed, the partition that had separated the two compartments had a doorless doorway cut into it and the slatted seats were extended along the sides and across the end where the First Class balcony had been. A small drop-light window was added on either side. The metal plate that had been bolted temporarily over the remaining louvred ventilator above the window on the west side of the First Class section around 1905 now re-appeared, and the two oil lamps were removed from the roof, being replaced by electric lighting powered by dry batteries which were charged weekly at a local shop.

When the Tramway's fares were increased on 8th June 1919 following the re-building of the carriage, First Class was still available, and it is likely that the cushions remained in the old First Class section, at least until all of the rolling stock became one class only in 1925. From that date no further alterations were carried out, and the carriage was to remain in this condition for the rest of its working life. By the late 1930's the sash windows rattled so much that it was almost impossible to hold a normal conversation whilst the tram was in motion!

97. (*Top*) VICTORIA at Rye with both carriages on
10.4.1909. The First Class compartment has
gained a hinged opening window on either side and
the two windows mounted on one panel in the
Second Class section are now fixed permanently in
place, but the rail above the windows and the lugs
that held the rod to which the white canvas screen
would be attached to this side on windy days are
still in position on the Bagnall carriage. Although
rated as Third Class, the Rother Ironworks carriage
bringing up the rear still boasts curtains at its
windows.   (*Allan C. Baker collection*)

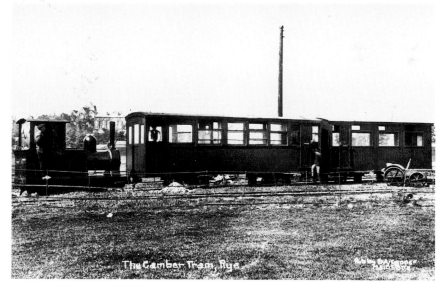

98. (*Middle*) Immediately after her 1921 overhaul
CAMBER, in her new overall un-lined black livery,
poses with both immaculate carriages at Rye. The
plain wooden door of the Bagnall carriage and that
on the Rother Ironworks carriage came from the
erstwhile Second and Third Class balconies
respectively. Once again the row-boat permanent
way trolley has managed to get in on the act and is,
this time, standing in the "V" between the main
running line and the two sidings that serve the
large shed.   (*L. Bearman collection*)

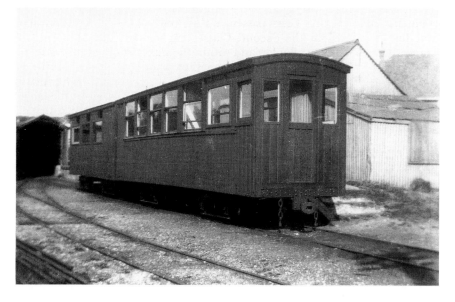

99. (*Bottom*) Soon after their re-building, both
carriages await their locomotive in the afternoon
sun at Rye in the early 1920s. The ends of the
underframe, previously hidden behind the metal
dashes of the balconies on the Bagnall carriage are
now visible. At the far end of the Rother Ironworks
carriage, one window on either side had been
converted in the winter of 1901/2 to slide up and
down, their position being adjustable by a leather
strap of the type found on main line railway
carriages at the time.   (*Lens of Sutton*)

100. (*Top Left*) This and the following two photographs were taken in 1962, and although some attempt has been made to reinstate some of the missing panelling, the Bagnall carriage has deteriorated in her field at East Guldeford.

(Richard Jones collection)

101. (*Top Right*) The remains of the wooden sliding door lean against the side and some planking has been added to what was the Rye end where part of the link and pin coupling and one safety chain are still in place. Unlikely as it may seem, but both bogies are still in position underneath the carriage.

(Richard Jones collection)

102. (*Middle*) A look inside the carriage provides details of the sash windows, a part of the wooden partition that separated this the Second Class section from the First, and the position of the oil lamp that was added in the late 1890s to the roof.

(Richard Jones collection)

103. (*Bottom*) The bogies and frame of the Bagnall carriage await restoration at Amberley, 1982.

(Colonel Stephens Railway Museum & Archives, Tenterden)

Apart from the Kent Construction Company petrol locomotive, the Bagnall carriage was the only other item of rolling stock to escape the scrap man, being purchased for the sum of 10 shillings and moved to a farm half a mile away at East Guldeford within sight of the Hastings to Ashford railway line. She was hauled to her new home by two tractors on her own wheels with the rear bogie tied with ropes, and the 3ft.0in. gauge grooves cut by the wheels in the road surface remained there for several years. Here the carriage was to remain in use as a shed until 1962 when it came to the notice of some railway enthusiasts at Brockham Museum, near Dorking, Surrey, which had been founded by a group of members of the Narrow Gauge Railway Society that year. Their somewhat optimistic hope was that after laying temporary rails across two fields, they would be able to "simply push" the carriage to the main A259 road, from where the Territorial Army might be willing to transport the unusual load to the museum, but with winter setting in, plans had to be put on hold. Various dates in August and October 1963 had to be cancelled, but comprehensive drawings were made and photographs taken in preparation for the proposed re-building. After an attempt to lift the coach bodily onto a lorry failed when the scaffolding gantry collapsed under the weight, it seemed that the carriage was destined to finish its days at East Guldeford after all, although, on this occasion, both bogies were removed and taken to Brockham for safe keeping.

With no finance available, 1964 came and went and by early 1965, much of the panelling had been removed. After more than 18 years of neglect at the mercy of the elements and the children that used to play in her, there was no way that the whole of the remaining body would survive the trip to Surrey (a 100% re-build would be necessary anyway) and it was reluctantly decided to salvage just the wrought-iron frame and the extremely sound roof. On Saturday, 7th August 1965 a party from Brockham successfully accomplished the removal of the roof in one section without damage by removing all the bolts securing it to the rest of the body and then giving "a calculated push"! The following Saturday an even larger party of members lifted the two tons of underframe onto a low-back lorry, and with the centre of the frame filled with sleepers and sections of framing, a dozen members bodily lifted the roof section onto the frame, luckily without breaking its back or roof arches. The whole operation took only an hour and the lorry pulled out of the field at 11.45 a.m. to start its journey to Brockham. Unloading later that day was much easier, and with the frame re-united with its bogies, it was pushed into a siding with the roof placed on top. Good sections of the body's wooden frame were stored, but the rest was, regrettably, only fit for firewood. [2] In 1981 Brockham Museum merged with the Amberley Chalk Pits Museum, near Arundel, West Sussex, where the main frame and bogies remain to this day. It is still hoped that a replica body will be constructed as and when time and finance permit.

THE ROTHER IRONWORKS CARRIAGE

A second carriage was ordered, this time from Messrs. Rother Ironworks of Fishmarket Road, Rye by February 1896, when it had become clear that the one carriage and the two open wagons with their "unsafe seats upon which they (the public) had ridden on occasionally, but had no business to ride" would be insufficient to handle all of the passenger traffic by themselves. It was delivered on Tuesday, 31st March 1896, and was shorter (20'3") and taller (9'5") than its predecessor, but the width remained the same at 5'10". The bogies, with coil springs, spaced at 11'0" centres, were identical to those on the Bagnall carriage, and were almost certainly supplied by that Company, but unusually, the overhang at the balcony end was 5'3" compared with 4'6" at the Camber end.

The body was again of tongue and groove planked construction, but of a slightly wider section, and each side had 3 large windows, complete with curtains, even though the carriage was only rated as Third Class. Just one balcony with a metal dash was fitted at the Rye end, from which an externally-hung sliding door gave access to the saloon with its wooden slatted seats to accommodate 25 passengers arranged along the sides and across the bulkhead at the southern end. Braking arrangements were similar to those on the Bagnall carriage, but were fitted at the Rye end and worked on that bogie only. During the winter of 1901/2 the carriage was taken out of service and "done up and re-decorated" and it may have been at this time that the windows on each side at the Camber end were converted to slide up and down, their position being adjustable by a leather strap of the type found on standard gauge railway carriages at the time. No lighting was provided until about 1907 when a solitary oil lamp was added centrally to the carriage roof, but it did not last long, and by 1914 the louvred ventilators above each window had been superseded by glazed, sliding replacements sited, not centrally as the originals, but to one side.

After the 1914-18 War this carriage was also re-built with the main body being extended similarly over the end balcony, but the new end panel, complete with a small fixed window, was of a smaller section planking than the sides. Whilst the work was being carried out the whole carriage was turned to face the opposite way and the entrance, with its externally-hung sliding door (taken from the old balcony bulkhead) was accordingly built onto the opposite side of the vehicle. By marshalling the two carriages with their entrances adjacent it was thus still possible for the conductor to move between them via the extended foot-boards beneath the doorways whilst the tram was between stations. As built, the cant rail on either side the length of the balcony was cut away slightly to allow a little extra headroom, and this feature remained, looking rather odd with the doorway having been removed from its position at what was now the Camber end. A final modification was made prior to 1935 when the maker's

RYE & CAMBER TRAMWAYS Co. Ltd.

Rother Ironworks

Third Class Carriage

1896

1921

Dotted lines mark
position of windows
cut into end B
c. 1936

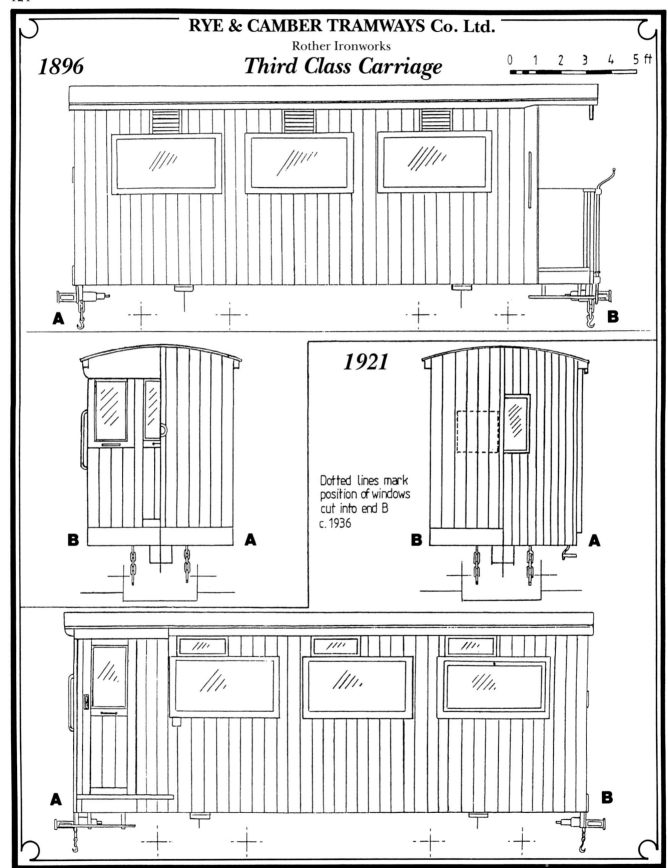

plate that had been proudly displayed on the now northern end of the carriage was removed, and two square fixed windows were built side by side into the previously plain bulkhead so that the driver of the petrol locomotive could see into the saloon from his cab.

Throughout the Tramway's history both carriages had been painted in an all over dark reddish-brown livery, but the white roofs would soon discolour to grey due to the effects of smoke, steam and the elements. Around the turn of the century the metal dashes on the balconies were painted a darker colour (possibly black) with a contrasting lighter coloured panel (cream lined gold?) on the ends, but by 1905 the dashes appear to have been painted a reddish-brown to match the rest of the bodywork and the decorative panels were painted black. The interiors were finished in gloss white with the wooden fittings and trimmings varnished dark brown, whilst small pictures and posters would adorn the bulkheads of both vehicles and, after its re-building, the partition in the Bagnall carriage. The staff may have been few, but they took a great pride in their Tramway, and the rolling stock was always kept in immaculate condition.

THE OPEN PASSENGER WAGONS

In 1918, two small 4-wheel open wagons were acquired which, with leather padding, were reported to have been used to carry ammunition on a trench railway during the conflict. They were 9ft.6in. long, 5ft.10in. wide, and the 2ft.0in. high sides were extended downwards to mask the tops of the wheels on either side. Each chassis was extended at either end beyond the body to form a buffing bar onto which side chains were fitted, these being the only means of attaching the trucks to the rest of the train. With a wheelbase of 5ft.6in., the 1ft.9in.diameter 4-spoke wheels were mounted on inside bearings, but their long protruding axles clearly showed evidence of their having at some time in the past been mounted in outside bearings.

The bodies were re-built to resemble those found on miniature pleasure railways of the time with an odd arrangement of 2 sets of wooden slatted seats facing each other and an extra row behind, giving a cramped seating capacity of 20 passengers per wagon. The 9in. high seat backs were level with the top of the western side that had a cut-out section with curved bottom ends that ran almost the length of each vehicle. Other than short arm rests to the seats that, at least for a while, were lined in leather held in place by copper rivets, the platform side was completely open. No brakes were fitted.

Sometimes the passenger wagons would be marshalled at the Rye end of the train throughout the day, or else they would bring up the rear in each direction, involving a considerable amount of shunting at each of the termini. Most of the time the trucks worked together, but occasionally they would be operated singularly when, with no fleet numbers or other distinguishing features, there would be no means

of telling them apart. Both wagons were painted inside and out the same dark reddish-brown livery to match the carriages, and they proved to be very popular with the locals and holidaymakers alike. As Mr. John F. Burke later wrote ".... on really fine days when a rush was to be expected, (the) open trucks were coupled on behind the larger coaches, and to ride in these was the greatest treat of all. One could never tell when those wooden trucks without springs (how one was jarred!) would appear; sometimes they were not brought out until a crowd came over the (Monkbretton) bridge, sometimes they were all ready and waiting, according to some whim of the driver...." [3]

GOODS ROLLING STOCK

For the opening of the Tramway, two small open wagons were supplied, definitely not by Messrs. W. G. Bagnall Ltd. of Stafford, but bearing in mind Mr. E. P. S. Jones' close involvement with the Tramway, they may have been built by his Rother Ironworks in Fishmarket Road, Rye. Recalling Mr. H. G. Henbrey's letter to the Board of Trade dated 6th July 1895, in which he stated ".... the tramway is being used for luggage etc....." the two wagons must have been delivered prior to that date. At this early stage there had been no suggestion of developing a traffic in sand, so apart from luggage, their purpose would have been to carry parcels and fish to and from Rye Harbour, together with permanent way duties. Commencing with the first August Bank Holiday Monday, they would be pressed into service at busy times as passenger vehicles with temporary wooden plank seats added.

The wagons looked extremely flimsy, and might be considered by some to be the prototype for the kind of toy that a small child might pull along loaded with different coloured wooden building blocks! They were carried on four tiny 4-curved-spoked wheels mounted on inside bearings, and there is a slight possibility that this running gear could have been supplied by Bagnalls. Their chassis was extended at each end to form a buffing bar that was so low as to only just align with CAMBER and the carriage. No brakes were fitted, and in the absence of link and pin couplings, side chains were fitted to either side of the buffing bars. Each end was externally diagonally braced upwards in wood from a position half way up the sides to the centre, whilst the smooth 4-plank sides were carried down to hide the tops of the wheels. There was nothing to suggest that the sides or ends could be lowered, so that all goods would have had to be bodily lifted into and out of the trucks.

The usefulness of these two small vehicles would have been very limited, and early in 1897 three more robust (but still crude by most railways' standards) open wagons entered service. Once more the maker is unknown, Rother Ironworks again being the most likely candidate, but the wheels and running gear this time were almost certainly supplied by Bagnall. With a wheelbase of 5ft.6in., each wagon was carried on four 4-spoked wheels

104. Quite what is going on here is un-clear, but "LOT 242" is almost certainly the body of what will become one of the pair of passenger wagons which were acquired in 1918, and it is balanced precariously one one of the 1897 open sand wagons. Percy Sheppard looks concerned at having torn the sleeve of his jacket and could it be the body of the other passenger wagon standing on its side on the platform?

(Richard Jones collection)

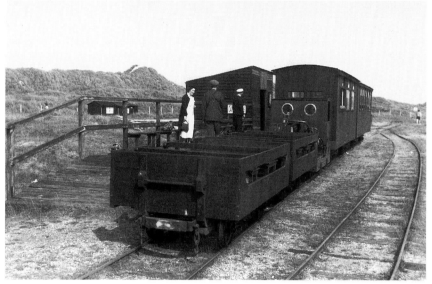

105. How the petrol locomotive (with her bonnet completely removed) managed to get herself in between the open passenger wagons and the two closed carriages at Camber Sands station on 16.8.1936 is difficult to explain; surely the tram had not run out from Rye in this fashion! The open passenger trucks are shown off to good advantage, and close inspection reveals how each of the axles were once located in outside bearings. While Messrs. Thompson's refreshment hut has been demolished, 2 beach huts remain, but not for much longer. In the background is the concrete post and wire fence that the Tramway Company accused the Golf Club of erecting on land leased to them in March 1933.

(Author's collection)

106. It is possible to count no less than 22 people who have managed to squeeze into one of the open passenger wagons in this rare view of the platform side of these little vehicles photographed at Rye station c.1930. The odd arrangement of two sets of slatted seats facing each other with another row behind can be clearly seen. These two wagons were immensely popular with old and young alike, being preferred to the closed carriages on sunny days, but without springing and no seat backs to speak of, they must have given a really rough ride!

(Mrs. E. Lamb (nee Sewett) collection)

27

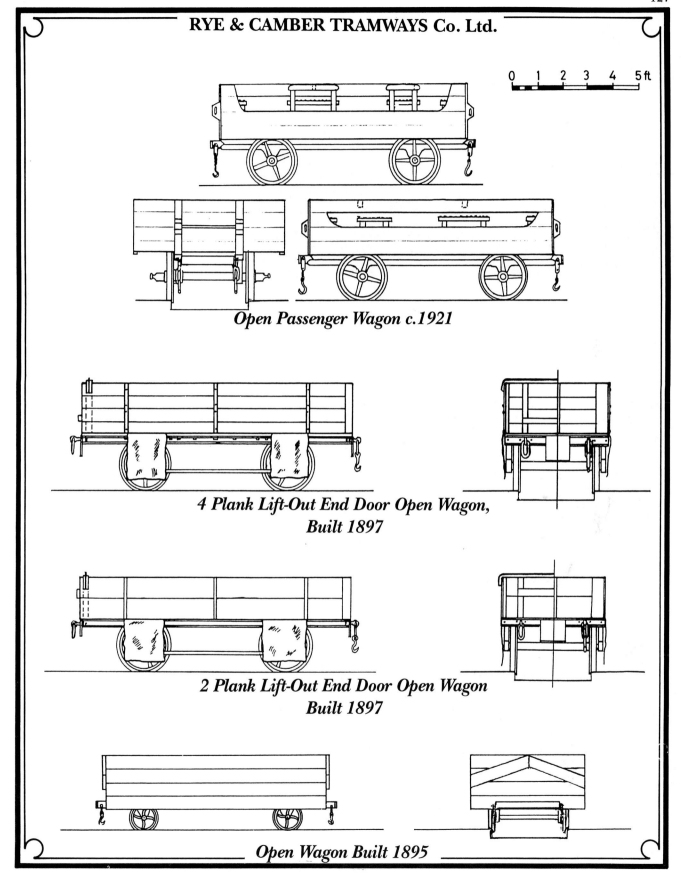

RYE & CAMBER TRAMWAYS Co. Ltd.

0 1 2 3 4 5 ft

Open Passenger Wagon c.1921

4 Plank Lift-Out End Door Open Wagon,
Built 1897

2 Plank Lift-Out End Door Open Wagon
Built 1897

Open Wagon Built 1895

128

107. The two 4-plank open wagons of 1897 await their next turn of duty on the sand siding at Rye on 10th April 1909. Each had a wooden-braced lift-out door at one end only that slid between two vertical wooden uprights fitted to each side. Note the canvas covers to protect the axle boxes from blown sand, the crude coupling arrangements and that the wagons are arranged to work as a mirror image of each other.

(H. L. Hopwood, Ken Nunn collection, courtesy of L.C.G.B.)

108. This portrait of VICTORIA busily shunting at Rye on 18th July 1914 is the only known picture to include the elusive two-plank open goods wagon of 1897, albeit only a small part of it. Like its two 4-plank sisters, its sides at the opening end are held in place by a simple shaped piece of angled iron.

(Ken Nunn collection, courtesy of L.C.G.B.)

109. A close-up of the row-boat permanent way trolley standing beside the run-round loop at Rye c.1905.

(Colonel Stephens Railway Museum & Archives, Tenterden)

of 1ft.9in. diameter, the outside bearings of which were hidden behind fabric covers to protect them from blown sand. No brakes were fitted, and for coupling the hooks on one truck would be engaged in a large diameter shackle on another, or to the safety chains fitted to the locomotives and passenger rolling stock. They had a wooden-braced lift-out door at one end only that slid between two vertical wooden uprights fitted to each side, and a crude shaped piece of angle iron that curved downwards through 90 degrees at its outer ends would be wedged over the un-supported sides at the door end to hold them firmly in place. Two of the wagons were of 4-plank constuction, and they were arranged to work as a mirror image of each other with their doors at the outer ends, their main purpose being to carry sand from the Camber sand hills for transhipment into barges at Rye Harbour in connection with the building of the Admiralty Pier at Dover, and to the local builders at Rye. The third wagon was a 2-plank version of the above that would have been employed on permanent way duties. Their estimated dimensions are 10ft.6in. long, 4ft.0in. wide, with sides 2ft.0in. and 1ft.6in. from rail level respectively.

Whether or not the two original small open trucks were disposed of when the three new wagons arrived in 1897 is not clear; they may have been kept for occasional passenger use on busy days, but the Company's returns for 1901 [4] showed just 3 goods wagons in stock, so it is reasonable to assume that they were out of service by then. The later trucks would then be used as reserve passenger vehicles, their wooden plank seats being fitted with the added luxury of strips of carpet! By the end of 1909 only the 2-plank and one of the 4-plank trucks were listed, and they remained on the books until 1918 when the number of wagons recorded suddenly rose to six. Two of these would have been the open passenger wagons, and it is possible, though not confirmed, that 2 new goods trucks were delivered during that year. The last statistics provided by the Tramway Company for the Railway Year Book published in 1940 (referring to 1939) still quoted 6 wagons. When the Tramway was visited early in 1947, just the two passenger wagons and two open goods trucks remained, and these must have been scrapped on site at Rye station by Messrs. M. E.

Engineering during the Spring of that year. The livery of the 1895 and 1897 wagons was more than likely a reddish-brown to match the passenger rolling stock, but by the 1920s open wagons were painted light grey with the ironwork picked out in black.

There was one other item of rolling stock - a ganger's trolley that was probably in service from the opening of the line. It was approximately 5ft.6in. long, 3ft.6in. wide and with a wheelbase of 2ft.9in., the pair of 6-spoke driving wheels were 2ft.6in. in diameter, whilst the leading wheels, also with 6 spindly spokes, were 1ft.9in. in diameter. To propel the vehicle the operator, in a seated position on the flat platform with his feet resting below, had to pull backwards and forwards on a pair of parallel wooden handles (resembling those fitted to a porter's sack truck) as though he was rowing a boat. The handles, pivoted to the main wooden frame below, protruded 1ft.6in. above the platform and were connected to the rear wheels by a system of cranks and rods. As the driving wheels were slightly higher than the metal platform, the latter had to be raised up on either side over and beside them to form a curved mudguard. Short wooden stretcher-like handles were placed at each end so that the trolley could be easily lifted onto and off of the track, but neither brakes or springs were fitted. The vehicle would regularly be used in conjunction with permanent way maintenance, and Percy Sheppard remembered that if, during the winter when there was a passenger service prior to 1926 and they were at the Camber end of the line, rather than work it back to Rye they would attach it to the last tram of the day and travel back in style! [5] The fate of the row-boat trolley is not known or, indeed, whether it was still on the Tramway when it was dismantled in 1947.

1. There are several inconsistancies between Bagnall's drawing W80 and the carriage as delivered (i.e. 36 planks per side compared with the 47) suggesting that the drawing is a modification of the metre gauge French Railway carriages.
2. The Narrow Gauge News No. 37, October 1965.
3. The Sussex County Magazine, September 1952.
4. Although the Railway Year Book was first published in 1898, returns were not provided by the Rye & Camber Tramway until 1902, the statistics referring to the year 1901.
5. "The Tenterden Terrier" No. 10, Summer 1976, House Journal of the Kent & East Sussex Railway.

110. This and the pictures on pages 133 and 134 feature VICTORIA and both carriages in service on Saturday, 18th July 1914, less than 3 weeks prior to the start of the First World War. Conductor Frederick Sheppard looks down at the photographer as the 1.45p.m. short-working from Golf Links arrives at Rye.

(H. L. Hopwood, Ken Nunn collection, courtesy of L.C.G.B.)

Chapter Thirteen

TIMETABLES, FARES & TICKETS

As detailed in Chapter Three, the first weekly timetable of July 1895 advertised 11 return trams between Rye and Camber spread over a 12 hour day commencing at 8.20 a.m., with 8 return trams on Sundays starting at 2.00 p.m., but in practise the times were slightly altered. From 1st October, the service was reduced as follows:

WEEKDAYS

	a.m.		a.m.
Leave Rye	9. 0	Leave Camber	9.15
"	10. 0	"	10.45
"	11.30	"	12. 0
	p.m.		p.m.
"	1.20	"	1.40
"	2. 0	"	2.30
"	3. 0	"	3.30
"	4.20	"	4.30
"	5. 0	"	5.15
"	6. 0	"	6.15
"	7.45 Saturdays only	"	8. 0

SUNDAYS

	p.m.		p.m.
Leave Rye	2. 0	Leave Camber	2.15
"	2.30	"	2.45
"	3. 0	"	3.30
"	4. 0	"	4.15
"	4.30	"	4.45
"	5.15	"	5.30

No tram on Friday till 2.0 p.m.

The 8.20 a.m. departure from Rye and the corresponding return service from Camber had already disappeared from the timetable, and were never to be re-instated. In November the intending passenger was advised that "the 6 p.m. tram from Rye and the 6.15 p.m. from Camber will not run during the months of December and January next, with the exception of a Saturday tram at this time", [1] but this reduction in the service could not have been popular as from 1st January 1896 "the 6 p.m. from Rye and 6.15 p.m. from Camber will be continued on and after today". [2]

It was not until Good Friday, 3rd April 1896, that a service was provided on Friday mornings, the time having previously been used "to allow the engine being cleaned out". The weekday afternoon timetable was also altered from that date "so as to leave Rye at 4. 0 p.m. instead of 4.20 p.m., and 4.30 p.m. instead of 5. 0 p.m., and to leave Camber at 4.15 p.m. instead of 4.30 p.m.,

and 5. 0 p.m. instead of 5.15 p.m., thus enabling passengers to catch the 5.25 p.m. train to Hastings". [3] On Saturday, 2nd May a new summer timetable came into effect:

WEEKDAYS

	a.m.		a.m.
Leave Rye	9. 0	Leave Camber	9.15
"	10. 0	"	10.15
"	10.30	"	10.45
"	11.30	"	12. 0
	p.m.		p.m.
"	1.20	"	1.40
"	2. 0	"	2.45
"	3. 0	"	3.30
"	4. 0	"	4.15
"	4.30	"	5. 0
"	6. 0	"	6.15
"	7. 0	"	7.30
"	*8. 0	"	*8.30

* This tram will run on Saturdays only until 1st June.

SUNDAYS

	p.m.		p.m.
Leave Rye	2. 0	Leave Camber	2.15
"	2.30	"	2.45
"	3. 0	"	3.30
"	4. 0	"	4.15
"	4.30	"	4.45
"	5.15	"	5.30
"	6. 0	"	6.15
"	7. 0	"	7.30
"	a8. 0	"	a8.30

a Commencing 1st June

A belated notice appeared in the Saturday, 13th June edition of the South Eastern Advertiser stating that "The tram will not run on Thursday, 11th June". No explanation for the stoppage was given, but it was probably so that CAMBER could receive a further inspection and overhaul similar to that which she had received on 19th and 20th December the previous year. The Friday morning trams were short-lived and were withdrawn from 19th June. The summer timetable continued un-altered until Tuesday, 1st September when the 8. 0 p.m. from Rye and the 8.15 p.m. from Camber [4] were cancelled on weekdays, but the additional note "the tram will not run on Fridays until 1.20 p.m." suggests that a complete daily service may have been operated during the peak holiday period.

From 1st October the weekday trams from Rye at 10.30 a.m. and 7.00 p.m. were withdrawn, along with return workings from Camber at 10.15 a.m. and 7.30 p.m., and on Sundays the 5.30 p.m. from Rye with the corresponding return tram from Camber were brought forward by 15 minutes. The last tram from Rye was re-timed to leave at 8.15 p.m., and the return journey from Camber reverted to 8.30 p.m.. The daily 6. 0 p.m. from Rye and 6.15 p.m. from Camber ran during October only, becoming Saturdays only after that date. Coming into operation at the beginning of December, the winter timetable was reduced still further:

WEEKDAYS		SUNDAYS	
Rye	Camber	Rye	Camber
10.00	10.40	2. 0	2.15
11.30	12.00	2.30	2.45
1.20	1.40	3. 0	3.30
2.30	2.45	4. 0	4.15
4. 0	4.15	4.30	4.45
6. 0 S.O.	6.15		
8. 0 S.O.	8.30		

After the arrival of the second locomotive, VICTORIA, the tram ran again on Friday mornings from the beginning of July 1897 at the same times as on other weekdays. By now the pattern was set with plenty of trams for the holidaymakers and golfers during the summer with a lesser, but quite adequate service, mainly for the latter, during the winter.

From the opening of the Tramway the First Class fare had been 4d. single and 6d. return, with a Second Class ticket costing 3d. single and 5d. return. At the end of November 1895 the Tramway Company announced that they had decided to reduce the Second Class single fare to and from Camber to 2d. The South Eastern Advertiser commented: "As there has been a demand for a reduced fare for some time past, we think that this concession on the part of the Tramway Company is well timed, and we are also pleased to think that they find themselves in a position to afford the reduction. We feel sure that they will increase the traffic in consequence."

Once the Rother Ironworks carriage had entered service in the Spring of 1896, Third Class fares were available for the first time at 1d. single and 2d. return. Children under the age of 12 travelled at half fare. An Annual First Class season ticket (used mainly by golfers) was available for one guinea and for £1 10s.0d. the whole crew of a fishing boat could travel on the Tramway for one year!

In an effort to counteract the losses that had been incurred during the first two winters, the fares were increased from 1st November 1897, so that First Class became 6d. single and 9d. return, Second Class 3d. single and 6d. return, and although the third Class single fare was advertised as 2d. single, a return fare was not quoted. A note added to the announcement advised that no alterations would be made to the fares in the case

of "bona fide mechanics, fishermen or labourers". [5] It should be noted that only First Class passengers benefitted by purchasing return tickets! Commencing in June 1898, adult Second Class return tickets were advertised as being available on Tuesday afternoons (early closing day for the majority of shops in Rye) by any tram after 2. 0 p.m. for 3d. [6], children travelling by any service for 2d. return. [7]

Early in 1899, what can best be described as the most extraordinary system of fare collection ever devised, came into operation. Rather than pay the relevant fare according to the compartment in which the passenger travelled, the conductor had the unenviable task of having to decide whether a person was of the working class or not, and charge a higher or lower fare as he thought applicable. Needless to say, this evoked much criticism, and resulted in a series of letters being published in the South Eastern Advertiser, the first of which appeared on Saturday, 12th August:

"Sir,

"On my arrival in Rye, I am an artist, I would not but be impressed with its antiquity - but after having been a resident for a couple of weeks the feeling has deepened, and I am full of wonder why, with the object lesson of other coastal towns around you, you try to drive visitors away.

"My vocation takes me to Camber by the steam tramway once or twice daily, and I ask you, why should my party be asked to pay 4d. for the journey, while the other passengers pay 2d.? It is not a matter of the 2d., but one does not care to be treated so in this manner.

"Yours truly, An Admirer of Rye, 9.8.99."

One week later the following letter was printed:

"Sir,

"The letter published in your last issue from "An Admirer of Rye" will find an echo in the bosom of every "Uitlander" visitor who is disallowed the rate of proper treatment at the hands of a civilised community, namely that of paying his "Scot and lot".

"It is well known that residents only pay 2d. for a ride to Camber, while the visitor is muleted in double that sum.

"By the way, if the tram is a public convenience, are the directors not, by law, compelled to exhibit publicly a list of fares?

"Yours truly, A. Visitor, Rye 17.8.99.

"P.S. May I add that we do not use the Tramway on account of the difference in the charges."

On 26th August, "Once Bitten" added his complaint when he wrote:

"Sir,

"I was very pleased to see the correspondence in your last two issues, also the wise words of "Diogenes" [8] respecting the absurd custom of the Camber Tram Company in charging passengers, not according to the compartment they occupy, but according to their dress and general appearance. Your correspondent of last week, however, seems to think that it is only strangers that are overcharged. But this is not so. I and my

111. A little less than half a mile short of Rye VICTORIA drifts over the Broadwater Stream on the simple bridge consisting of two iron girders resting on concrete abutments, with the rails carried on longitudinal wooden sleepers. VICTORIA has not been idle since the last picture was taken, having made a return trip to Camber Sands before working this tram, the 3.25p.m. short-working from Golf Links. Her day will not end until she safely returns the Saturdays only 8.15 p.m. tram from Golf Links back to Rye. *(H. L. Hopwood, Ken Nunn collection, courtesy of L.C.G.B.)*

112. Before VICTORIA runs round her train, Frederick Sheppard appears to be organising a group of young ladies on the platform who will be travelling on the next service to Golf Links and Camber Sands that is timetabled to depart at 2.10 p.m. *(Ken Nunn collection, courtesy of L.C.G.B.)*

113. VICTORIA has now run round her train and, having propelled the two carriages well down the platform, waits patiently with the 2.10p.m. service to Camber Sands. The party of young ladies have taken their seats in the Third Class Rother Ironworks carriage, and a few passengers will get more than just a little fresh air (judging by the way that VICTORIA's western cab opening has been completely blocked off!) by travelling on the open balconies. Look for the row-boat permanent way trolley and the wheel set from one of the 1897 open wagons that lies next to the engine shed road point lever beside the run-round loop.

(Ken Nunn collection, courtesy of L.C.G.B.)

family, who are residents, have on several occasions used the tram and only paid 2d.. Last week this amount was refused and 4d. demanded on the pleas that we were not working people. Now I have not the slightest objection to sitting next to a labouring man, but I do object to having to pay twice as much as he for the same accommodation. If there is to be a special charge for the working-man, there should be a working-man's tram, or passengers should be accommodated according to the amount charged. And why should it not be possible to secure tickets before starting, as on the railway, so that one might know what he was doing. In what is called "the station" there is a ticket box, but I don't think that it is ever used. I, for one, shall boycott it till the change is made, and am glad to know that many more are of my mind."

"A. Visitor" contradicted the postscript of his letter of 17th August when a second letter from him was published on 26th August:

"Sir,

"As a visitor to Rye, I should like to add my protest against the eccentric ways of the Tramway Company. If visitors have to pay fares double, and sometimes treble, those of an inhabitant of the town, which is bad policy, and by no means a way of inducing strangers to use the trams, at least, as one of your correspondents writes, there should be some settled scale of charges, and

passengers should not be called upon to pay 9d. first class return one day, as happened to myself and party one day last week, and two or three days later 6d. first class return, both journies (sic) being by the 4.30 tram from Rye, and the only alternative compartment being a smoking one. It is also extraordinary indeed, not to say ridiculous, that with two engines passengers should be exposed to the risk of being stranded on the Camber platform from seven until half-past eight-o'clock in the evening, waiting for the tramcar to take them back to Rye, there being for old and invalid persons no other possible means of returning.

"I enclose my card, and remain,

Yours truly,

A. VISITOR."

Whereas the writer may have been justified in condemning the way in which the fares were charged, he had no cause to complain of the running of the evening tramway services as a timetable was displayed at Rye station, and probably at Camber as well. Even with so much ill feeling being generated, it was not until Easter, 1900 that the (possibly unique) system of fare collection was replaced by the fairer (no pun intended!) standard First, Second and Third Class structure depending in which compartment the passenger travelled.

A notice in the South Eastern Advertiser dated 9th March, 1901 advised "Additional trams leave Rye at

9.0 a.m. and 6. 0 p.m.; Camber 9.15 a.m. and 6.15 p.m. have been put on. The summer timetable will shortly be published; upon 1st April third class tickets will be issued. Batches of tickets of twenty and upwards may be purchased at Mr. J. Adams, 7 High Street at a discount of 10 per cent." From 1st December 1901 the cheap return tickets at single fares on Tuesday afternoons were extended to include Sunday afternoons as well, but this only lasted until the end of May 1902, and by September that year the facility had been withdrawn altogether.

Up to the turn of the century the Tramway operated just two timetables, one in winter and the other in the busy summer season, but from that time, as Spring evenings lengthened into Summer, so the service was extended with the addition of extra trams, with the reverse taking place in the Autumn. Just to complicate matters, daytime services would be regularly adjusted resulting in as many as ten timetables being issued in the course of a year. No one year was the same, but as a typical example, the timetables for 1904 are reproduced here in full. The winter timetable had come into effect in November 1903, and was the first to have the name of the Secretary, Mr. G. W. Strick, appended. Headed "TIMETABLE FOR NOVEMBER" it was to remain in use until the end of February 1904, with the addition of an extra weekday tram from Rye at 3.20 p.m., returning from Camber at 3.35 p.m. commencing on 9th January.

Weekdays:
Leave Rye   10.00 12.00 1.30 2.30 4.30 & Sats. only
                 6. 0 & 8. 0
Leave Camber 10.30 12.15 1.50 2.45 4.50 & Sats. only
                 6.15 & 8.15

Sundays:
Leave Rye   10. 0 2. 0   3. 0   4. 0
Leave Camber 10.15 2.20   3.30   4.30
        GEO. W. STRICK, Secretary.

A subsidy was paid by the Golf Club to guarantee the operation of the 10. 0 a.m. Sunday tram from Rye from November, 1900, but the service was not limited to JUST golfers. The First Class fare charged was a successful ploy to put off most other people who might have wished to travel on it, but of course, only the first 12 passengers would have the choice of the cushioned luxury of the First Class compartment!

MARCH TIMETABLE
Weekdays:
Leave Rye   10. 0 11.45 1.30 2.30 3.30   4.30 &
                 Sats. only 6. 0 & 8.15
Leave Camber 10.30 12. 0 1.40 2.45 3.45   5. 0 &
                 Sats. only 6.15 & 8.30
Sundays:
Leave Rye   *10. 0 2. 0   3. 0   4. 0   4.30   5.30
Leave Camber 10.15 2.20   3.30   4.15   4.45   5.45
        * First Class Fares

The first timetable signed by Mr. W. Jeffery was published on Saturday, 26th March:

Weekdays:
Leave Rye   9.30 (Saturdays only) 10. 0 11.45 1.30
                 2.30 3.20 4.30 6. 0 & Sats. only 8.15
Leave Camber 10.30 12. 0 1.40 2.45 3.35 5.0 6.15
                 & Sats. only 8.30

Leave Rye   4.30   6. 0 & Sats. only 8.15
Leave Camber 5. 0   6.15 & Sats. only 8.30

Sundays:
Leave Rye   10. 0 2. 0 3. 0 4. 0 4.30 5.30
Leave Camber 10.15 2.20 3.30 4.15 4.35 5.45
        W. Jeffery, Secretary.

It is interesting to note that there is no return working advertised in connection with the Saturdays only 9.30 a.m. departure from Rye, but it is difficult to imagine that the staff would turn away any prospective passengers who might wish to travel into Rye on it.

TIMETABLE FOR APRIL & UNTIL FURTHER NOTICE

Weekdays:
Leave Rye   9. 0 10. 0 11. 0 12. 0 1.30 2.30 3.20
                 4.30 5.15   6.0 8.15*
Leave Camber 9.15 10.20 11.20 12.15 1.50 2.45 3.35 5. 0
                 5.30   6.15 8.30*   * Saturdays only
Good Friday and Sundays:
Leave Rye   10. 0+ 2. 0 2.30 3. 0 4. 0 4.30 5.30 6. 0
Leave Camber 10.15+ 2.15 2.45 3.30 4.15 4.45 5.45 6.15
        + Special Fares   W. Jeffery, Secretary.

JUNE - AUGUST
Weekdays:
Leave Rye   9. 0 10. 0 10.40 11.40 12.30 1.30 2. 0
                 2.30 3.20   4.30 5.15 6.00 6.45 8.15
Leave Camber 9.15 10.20 11. 0 12. 0 12.45 1.40 2.15
                 2.45 3.35   5. 0 5.30 6.15 7.0 8.30
Sundays: (Special Fares by 10. 0 a.m. Tram from Rye)
Leave Rye   10. 0 2. 0 2.30 3. 0 4. 0 4.30 5.30 6. 0
                 6.45 8.15
Leave Camber 10.15 2.15 2.45 3.30 4.15 4.45 5.45 6.15
                 7. 0 8.30

SEPTEMBER
Weekdays:
Leave Rye   9. 0 10. 0 10.40 11.40 12.30 1.30 2. 0
                 3. 0 4. 0   4.30 6.0 6.45 8.15*
Leave Camber 9.15 10.20 11. 0 12. 0 12.45 1.40 2.33
                 3.30 4.15   5. 0 6.15 7.0 8.30*
                 * Saturdays only
Sundays: (Special Fares by 10. 0 a.m. Tram from Rye)
Leave Rye   10. 0 2. 0 2.30 3. 0 4. 0 4.30 5.30 6. 0
                 6.45
Leave Camber 10.15 2.15 2.45 3.30 4.15 4.45 5.45 6.15
                 7. 0

The timetable for October was similar except that the weekday and Sunday departures from Rye at 6.45 p.m. and Camber at 7. 0 p.m. had been withdrawn.

NOVEMBER 1904 to MARCH 1905
Weekdays:
Leave Rye   10. 0 12. 0 1.30 2.30 3.20 4.30 & Sats. only 6. 0 8. 0
Leave Camber 10.15 12.15 1.50 2.45 3.35 5. 0 & Sats. only 6.15 8.15

Sundays:
Leave Rye   *10. 0 2. 0 3. 0 4. 0
Leave Camber *10.15 2.20 3.30 4.30

All Trams on Sunday afternoons will be 1st, 2nd, & 3rd Class
 * First Class Fares only   Season Tickets not available.

Every Easter extra trams were added over the holiday weekend, the most ambitious service being that operated in 1902:

ADDITIONAL TRAMS EASTER 1902
Good Friday (28th March 1902)
Rye 9.30 & 10.30 & 6 p.m. (Special Fares)
Camber 9.45 & 10.15 & 6.15.

Afternoon trams as on Sundays.

Saturday (29th March 1902)
Rye 9. 0, 9.30 a.m. & 2. 0 p.m.
Camber 9.15, 9.45 a.m. & 2.45 p.m.

Sunday (30th March 1902)
Rye 9.30 & 10. 0 (Special Fares) & 6 p.m
Camber 9.45 & 10.15, 2.45 6.15 p.m.

Monday (31st March 1902)
Rye 9. 0 9.30 & 6. 0 p.m.
Camber 9.15 9.45 & 6.15 p.m.
If fine additional trams will also be run.

It will be seen that on Easter Sunday an extra 2.45 p.m. service from Camber was operated, although there was no corresponding outward departure. The Easter arrangements for 1908 were more typical, the following notice being printed in the South Eastern Advertiser on Saturday, 11th April:
"On Good Friday and Easter Sunday trams leave Rye at 9.30 and 10 a.m. [9] (The notice actually showed "p.m." in error!), also Camber at 6.30 p.m.; on 18th, 20th, and 21st April extra trams will leave Rye at 9. 0 and 9.30 a.m., and Camber at 6.45 p.m.."
The ultimate timetable to the original terminus was issued in June 1908 and advised "The extension to Camber Sands will shortly be opened when a Supplementary Timetable with Fares will be issued". Camber station had already been more realistically re-named "Golf Links". (*See reproduction opposite*).

On Tuesday, 14th July 1908 the extension to Camber Sands opened to the public:

JULY SERVICE
Weekdays:

Rye:	9.30	10.00	11.00	12.00	1.30	2.00	2.30
Golf Links:	9.38	10.09	11.09	12.09	1.38	2.10	2.39
Camber Sands:	–	10.14	11.14	12.14	–	–	2.44

Camber Sands:	–	10.18	11.18	12.25	–	–	2.48
Golf Links:	9.40	10.23	11.23	12.30	1.40	2.15	2.53
Rye:	9.50	10.32	11.32	12.40	1.50	2.24	3.02

Rye:	3.15	4.00	4.30	5.30	6.30	7.20
Golf Links:	3.23	4.08	4.39	5.38	6.38	7.28
Camber Sands:	3.30	–	4.44	–	6.43	–

Camber Sands:	3.34	–	4.50	–	6.50	–
Golf Links:	3.40	4.10	4.55	6.00	7.00	7.40
Rye:	3.48	4.18	5.03	6.08	7.08	7.48

Extra Saturday tram - Leave Rye 8 p.m. Leave Golf Links 8.15 p.m.

Sundays:

Rye:	10. 0	2. 0	2.30	3.15	4. 0	4.30	5.30	6. 0	6.40
Golf Links:	10.08	2.08	2.38	3.23	4.08	4.39	5.38	6.08	6.48
Camber Sands:			2.43	3.30		4.44		6.13	6.53

Camber Sands:			2.47	3.34	4.48			6.15	7. 0
Golf Links:	10.15	2.15	2.52	3.40	4.15	4.53	5.40	6.20	7.05
Rye:	10.23	2.23	3. 0	3.48	4.23	5.02	5.48	6.28	7.14

Although there was no note regarding special fares by the Sunday morning departure from Rye (possibly a printer's error), this tram, together with that at 2.00 p.m. were clearly run primarily for golfers, both services running only as far as Golf Links. The timings on this timetable (and many others) for each of the journeys between Rye and Golf Links and vice versa are fascinating, varying between 8 and 10 minutes for the $1^1/_2$ miles for no apparent reason.

With the opening of the extension the fares between Rye and Golf Links remained as before, and because most First Class tickets were issued to golfers (who would rarely wish to travel beyond Golf Links) the First Class fares to Camber Sands were identical at 6d. single and 9d. return. From now on everyone benefitted with a reduction on purchasing a return ticket, the Second Class fares being 4d. single and 7d. return, and 3d. single and 5d. return for Third Class passengers. The price of a First Class season ticket was increased to £1 10s.0d., but a large reduction was offered for "Two Persons from one household" where a Second Class season ticket would cost 2 guineas. Apart from saving money by purchasing season tickets, regular travellers could buy books of forty 6d. tickets at a reduction of 10% from Messrs. Adams &

RYE & CAMBER TRAM SERVICE (Subject to Alterations.

Week-Days   JUNE.   Sundays.

LEAVE RYE. A.M.		LEAVE GOLF LINKS. A.M.
10 0		10 20
11 0		11 20
12 0		P.M.
P.M.		12 30
1 30		1 50
2 0		2 15
2 30		2 50
3 30		3 40
4 40		5 0
5 50		6 0
6 30		7 0

Parcels are conveyed between Rye and Camber and Rye Harbour at very low Charges.

Extra Saturday Trams.

a.m.	a.m.
9 30	9 40
p.m.	p.m.
8 0	8 15

Picnic, School, and Pleasure Parties carried at Reduced Fares for Parties of not less than 12 Adults.

Sundays.

LEAVE RYE. A.M.	LEAVE GOLF LINKS. A.M
10 0	10 15

Special Fares by 10 a.m. from Rye.

P.M.	P.M.
2 0	2 15
2 30	2 45
3 0	3 30
4 0	4 15
4 30	4 45
5 30	5 40
6 0	6 15
6 30	6 45

Camber as a Health Resort is very Invigorating. No one should miss the opportunity of a Visit to the Sands.

Cheap Return Tickets can be obtained at Messrs. Adams & Son's, 7, High Street, Rye.

The Extension to Camber Sands will shortly be opened, when a Supplementary Time Table with Fares will be issued.

Sons of 7 High Street, Rye. [9] A parcel service was also offered by the Company, the rates being 2d.per small parcel, 4d. for large ones and 1/- for the sole use of a truck. Small parcels could be conveyed from Rye to Rye Harbour village, via the ferry, for 4d. including delivery, and builders' sand was advertised as being available, prices on application to the Tram station at Rye. [10]

On 27th July 1908 the South Eastern Advertiser advised under the heading "LATE TRAM FROM CAMBER" - "An addition to the Rye and Camber train (sic) service that will be much appreciated has been made. On Tuesday evenings a special late tram will leave Camber Sands at 7.30, calling at the Golf Links Station at 7.35 and arriving at Rye at 7.45. This tram will leave Rye on the down journey at 7.10, arriving at the Golf Links at 7.20, and the Sands at 7.25"

This amendment was destined to last only through August. During September, 12 weekday trams were operated, of which 7 still ran through to Camber Sands, but these were reduced to 10 and 4 trams respectively in October. On Sundays, 4 out of 8 trams ran through to Camber Sands, but only 2 out of 7 trams ran down to the southern terminus during October. From the beginning of November all services terminated at Golf Links, and throughout the winter the extension was used only for the cartage of sand.

NOVEMBER SERVICE

Weekdays:
Leave Rye   10. 0 11. 0 12. 0 1.30 2.30 3.30
     4.40 (SO) 6. 0 8. 0
Leave Golf Links 10.10 11.20 12.30 1.50 2.50 3.50
     4.50 (SO) 6.15 8.15

Sundays:
Leave Rye   10. 0 2. 0 3. 0 4. 0
Leave Golf Links 10.15 2.20 3.30 4.30

The confused passenger, hoping that with the opening of the extension to Camber Sands the timetables might become simpler, was to be disappointed. There was a little uniformity appearing, however, the winter timings matching those of the previous year, but the Company still found it necessary to issue between 7 and 10 different timetables every 12 months between 1909 and 1914. Emphasising just how important the Golf Club was to the Tramway Company, commencing in the Spring of 1909, the tram that left Camber Sands at 3.20 p.m. on Sundays was held-over at Golf Links for 5 minutes (increased to 10 minutes from 1911, the 4.20 p.m. departure being similarly timed from that date) to enable the conductor to walk across to the Golf Club House to advise the "well-to-do" golfers that their tram was waiting! This unusual procedure was to remain in force until the commencement of the summer timetable in June 1919.

At the request of the Golf Club, a second Sunday morning tram was introduced at the beginning of March 1910, leaving Rye at 9.30, and this, too, was First Class only. A 9.30 a.m. departure on Saturdays and Mondays also commenced at the same time, but this had become daily by April when, commencing with the 11.00 a.m. from Rye, 4 trams ran through to Camber Sands. Starting in the summer of 1911 a 10.30 a.m. tram was added to the Sunday timetable (also for First Class passengers only) which ran through to Camber Sands, arriving at 10.45 a.m.. No return working was advertised, as was the case with the 9.30 a.m. departure from September onwards, and the same arrangements applied to the shortened service to Golf Links only throughout the winter.

The November 1912 timetable was unusual in that the trams were advertised as running through to Camber Sands on Sundays only:

NOVEMBER TIMETABLE
Weekdays:

Rye	9.30 10. 0 11. 0 12. 0 1.15 1.45 3.15 4.25 (SO) 6. 0 8. 0
Golf Links	9.39 10.09 11.09 12.09 1.24 1.54 3.24 4.34 (SO) 6.09 8.09

Golf Links	9.40 10.20 11.20 12.15 1.30 2. 0 3.40 4.35 (SO) 6.15 8.15
Rye	9.49 10.29 11.29 12.24 1.39 2.09 3.49 4.44 (SO) 6.24 8.24

Sundays:

Rye	9.30 10. 0 10.30 2. 0 3. 0 4. 0 4.30 5.30
Golf Links	9.39 10.09 10.40 2.09 3.09 4.08 4.39 5.40
Camber Sands	10.45 2.14 3.14 4.45

Camber Sands		2.20 3.20 4.50
Golf Links	10.20	2.25 3.35 4.15 4.55 5.50
Rye	10.29	2.34 3.45 4.23 5.03 6. 0

Special Fares by 9.30, 10. 0 and 10.30 a.m. trams from Rye

This may have been a misprint, of course, but by the middle of the month the Sunday timetable had fallen into line with that of weekdays and trams operated as far as Golf Links at 9.30 a.m., 10.00 a.m., 10.30 a.m., 1.30p.m., 2.30 p.m. and 4.15 p.m., returning at 10.15a.m., 2. 0 p.m., 3.30 p.m. and 4.30 p.m.. Possibly because of the War, the 9.30 a.m. Sunday service from Rye was withdrawn in November 1914, and the 10.30 a.m. had followed suit by the following February when the timetable was confusingly printed as follows:

Weekdays:
Leave Rye 10. 0; 10.20; 12. 0; 12.20; 1.30; 1.45; 4.20; 4.35
Sundays:
Leave Rye 10. 0; 10.20; 2. 0; 2.25; 3. 0; 3.35; 4.30; 4.45

The late Saturday tram was temporarily suspended from January 1915, but it was re-instated in April leaving Rye at the customary time of 8. 0 p.m. and Golf Links at 8.15 p.m., only to disappear from the timetables once and for all in October that year. During the War the timetables continued to contain the odd little idiosyncrasies, for instance, there was no outward service advertised to connect with the daily (including Sunday) departure leaving Golf Links at 5.30 p.m. commencing in November 1915, the same arrangements applying to the re-timed 5.35 p.m. departure on Sundays only throughout the following main summer timetable. From the beginning of January through to the end of May 1915, and between mid-October 1916 and the end of May 1917, the "Special Fares" announcement for the Sunday morning trams was omitted, so perhaps, during those lean months, season tickets and second/ third class fares were accepted on that service. Another short-lived experiment was the running of a tram outward from Rye at 7.30 p.m. that returned from Camber Sands at 8.00 p.m. on Tuesdays only between June and early September 1916. With fewer people travelling the service became very sparce, yet even with so few trams running the Company found it necessary to alter the schedules every month or so!

RYE TRAM SERVICE

JANUARY, 1917

	Weekdays:	Sundays:
Leave Rye:	10. 0 1.30 4.15	10. 0 2. 0 3. 0 4. 0
Leave Golf Links:	10.20 1.45 4.30	10.20 2.25 3.25 4.30

Subject to Alterations

REVISED TIMETABLE
COMMENCING 15TH MARCH 1917

	Weekdays:	Sundays:
From Rye:	10. 0 1.30 4.30	2. 0 4.30
From Golf Links:	10.20 1.45 4.45	2.15 4.45

SERVICE OF TRAMS FOR MAY
Weekdays:

From Rye:	10. 0 11.30 1.30 4. 0 5.30
From Golf Links:	10.20 11.50 1.45 4.20 5.45

Sundays:

From Rye:	10. 0 2. 0 3.30 5.30
From Golf Links:	10.20 2.25 3.50 5.45

C. A. Gafford, Secretary

March and early April 1917 was to be the leanest time in all of the Company's history, and had it not been for the intervention of the Rye Trade Association, it is likely that the Tramway would have closed down completely until the holidaymakers and day trippers returned in July. The timetable for weekdays and Sundays during August and September 1917 was unique in that, following a short working from Rye at 5.00 p.m. (that returned from Golf Links at 5.20 p.m.) a non-stop tram operated from Rye at 5.40 p.m., returning from Camber Sands at 6.00 p.m., again omitting the stop at Golf Links, with just 10 minutes being allowed for the two mile homeward journey! This attempt by the Tramway Company to segregate golfers from the day-trippers cannot have been too successful as the experiment was never repeated. What was to become a standard summer timetable over the next few years came into effect in June 1918, with 7 return trams in operation on weekdays, of which 5 ran through to Camber Sands, and 6 on Sundays (the 11.30 a.m. departure from Rye to Golf Links being ommitted) with 4 of them terminating at Golf Links. For the first time the winter service commencing in October 1918 showed identical timings for weekdays and Sundays with trams departing Rye at 10.0 a.m., 1.30 p.m. and 4.10 p.m, returning from Golf Links at 10.20 a.m., 1.45 p.m. and 4.30 p.m.. On Friday, 6th June 1919, the following notice appeared in the Sussex Express & County Herald:

RYE & CAMBER TRAMWAYS CO. LTD.

"Notice is herby given that on and after Sunday the 8th day of June 1919, Passenger Fares will be as follows:

| | To & from Rye & Golf Links: | | Camber Sands | |
	Single	Return	Single	Return
Ist. Class	4d.	7d.	6d.	9d.
3rd. Class	3d.	-	4d.	7d.

Children under 12 half price, Dogs 3d. each journey.
By order of the Directors
4th June 1919.   C. A. Gafford, Secretary."

From April 1925 First Class was abolished and the tram became one class only, fares being charged at the previous Third Class rate which was identical to the second Class tariff of July 1908. Dogs were still charged 3d. per single journey, and primarily for the inhabitants of Rye Harbour village a single ticket was available between Golf Links and Camber Sands for 2d.. Sand was still an important part of the Company's income and was advertised at 2/6d. per ton from the Tramway station at Rye.

Now that the petrol locomotive was handling most of the traffic, the summer timetables settled down to a basic hourly service, typified by that for July 1925, *reproduced below.*

The Sunday service was identical (including the 8. 0 p.m. tram from Rye and the 8.15 p.m. from Camber Sands) save for the omission of the mid-day service from Rye and the corresponding return tram from Camber Sands at 12.15 p.m.. "Special Trams between for 12 or more passengers" were offered, but fitting these in without disrupting the main schedule would seem to be rather ambitious; as it was there was a turn-round time of only one minute on all services at Camber Sands! Other than the loss of the late evening service on Saturdays, Sundays and Wednesdays, the timetable for October was identical.

Parcels are conveyed between Rye and Camber and Rye Harbour at very Low Charges.

RYE & CAMBER TRAM SERVICE (Subject to Alterations

Summer Time			**Week-Days**						[JULY, 1925	
	a.m.	a.m.	p.m.	p.m.	p.m.	p.m.	p.m.	p.m.	p.m.	p.m.
Rye ..	10 0	11 0	12 0	2 0	3 0	4 0	5 0	6 0	8 0c	
Golf Links	10 9	11 9	12 9	2 9	3 9	4 9	5 9	6 9	8 9	
Camber Sands	1014	1114	1214	2 14	3 14	4 14	5 14	6 14	8 14	
Camber Sands	1015	1115	1215	2 15	3 15	4 15	5 15	6 15	8 15c	
Golf Links	1020	1120	1220	2 20	3 20	4 20	5 20	6 20	8 20c	
Rye	1030	1130	1230	2 30	3 30	4 30	5 30	6 30	8 30	

Special Trams between for 12 or more Passengers   Wednesdays and Saturdays

Sundays.

	.. a.m.	a.m.	p.m.	p.m.	p.m.	p.m.	p.m.	p.m.
Rye ..	.. 10 0	11 0	2 0	3 0	4 0	5 0	6 0	8 0
Golf Links	.. 10 9	11 9	2 9	3 9	4 9	5 9	6 9	8 9
Camber Sands	.. 1014	1114	2 14	3 14	4 14	5 14	6 14	8 14
		Special Fares by 10 a.m. Tram from Rye						
Camber Sands	.. 1015	1115	2 15	3 15	4 15	5 15	6 15	8 15
Golf Links	.. 1020	1120	2 20	3 20	4 20	5 20	6 20	8 20
Rye ..	.. 1030	1130	2 30	3 30	4 30	5 30	6 30	8 30

Picnic, School, and Pleasure Parties (not less than 12 Adults) carried at Reduced Fares.

Cheap Return Tickets can be obtained at Messrs. Adams & Son's, 7, High Street, Rye.

Camber as a Health Resort is very Invigorating.   *No one should miss the opportunity of a Visit to the Sands.*

114. Although looking very much like another photograph, CAMBER really is in steam here; note the smoke haze just visible above her chimney, and the driver can just be seen heading for the coal shed to fetch more fuel in an old bucket. As the points in the foreground are sprung to the engine shed road, it suggests that the photograph was taken prior to the arrival of the petrol locomotive in 1924. *(Lens of Sutton)*

115. According to the station clock there are 13 minutes to go before the 4.00p.m. departure for Camber Sands. The two windows cut into the end of the Rother Ironworks carriage can be clearly seen, as can the two white-painted bricks on the platform edge that indicate to the driver where to stop the train. The large shed of 1922 in the background has received a re-paint, losing the legend "TO CAMBER-ON-SEA" from the roof in the process. 16.8.1936.
(Author's collection)

116 & 117. Two views of the 4.25p.m. tram for Rye waiting at Camber Sands station with the petrol locomotive in charge on 29th August 1931, its hinged bonnet being open to reveal the cylindrical 14 gallon petrol tank.
(Ken Nunn collection, courtesy of L.C.G.B.)

Typical of the latter days of the line's existence was the timetable for 1935, opening after its winter break on 18th April (in time for Easter) to the following schedule which operated daily including Sundays:

Leave Rye	Leave Camber Sands	Leave Golf Links
10. 0	10.20	10.25
11.45	12. 0	12. 5
2. 0	2.20	2.25
3. 0	3.20	3.25
4. 0	4.20	4.25
5. 0	5.20	5.25

By Order,
C. A. GAFFORD, Secretary.

For the peak summer service in August, the timetable was amended to run hourly between 10.00 and 4.00 p.m. with a break between 12 noon and 2.00 p.m., the 5.00 p.m. tram was re-timed to run fifteen minutes later throughout, and there was the addition of an extra return service leaving Rye at 6.15 p.m.. Prior to closing down for the winter on 13th October the timetable was only slightly reduced with the loss of the last departure from Rye. Similar timetables were in operation in 1936 commencing on 9th April but the 1937 season did not start until 15th May, and in 1938, 4th June; the early season timetable being eliminated in each case.

Things changed for the better in 1939 when, with the opening of the new Camber Sands station in April, the Company put an advertisement in the "Rye & District Fixtures" (a monthly magazine that had been introduced by Messrs. Adams of Rye in 1935) as follows:

RYE & CAMBER TRAMWAYS CO.

TIME TABLE

From Thursday, 6th April to Sunday 16th April-

Leave Rye   10. 0 11. 0 12. 0 2. 0 3. 0 4. 0 5. 0

Leave Cam. Sands 10.20 11.20 12.20 2.20 3.20 4.20 5.20

Leave Golf Links   10.25 11.25 12.25 2.25 3.25 4.25 5.25

From Monday, 17th April and until further notice-

Leave Rye   10. 0 12. 0 2. 0 3.30 5. 0

Leave Camber Sands 10.20 12.20 2.20 3.50 5.20

Leave Golf Links   10.25 12.25 2.25 3.55 5.25

In June the Tramway Company was obviously feeling more its old self and the early season timetable was suitably altered and augmented with the addition of a 11.00 a.m. and a 2.45 p.m. return service from Rye, and the 5.00 p.m. tram was replaced by two new departures at 4.15 p.m. and 5.30 p.m.. What was to be the Tramway's last timetable, including yet again the inevitable slight alterations, commenced in July and operated as follows:

Leave Rye   10. 0 11. 0 12. 0 2. 0 2.45 3.30 4.15 5.15 6.15

Leave   10.20 11.20 12.20 2.20 3. 0 3.45 4.30 5.30 6.30
Camber Sands

Leave Golf 10.25 11.25 12.25 2.25 3.05 3.50 4.35 5.35 6.35
Links

As early as 1908 the Rye & Camber Tramways Company issued a monthly timetable booklet 3.9in. x 4.9in. which contained one full page and 14 half page advertisements for local businesses, plus separate full pages, one for each direction, of the South Eastern & Chatham Railway's timetable between Charing Cross and Hastings via Ashford and Rye, complete with the disclaimer "The Tramway Company do not hold themselves responsible for costs arising from inaccuracy". One page was devoted to a "Table of High Tides for Rye" underneath which it stated "CAMBER is celebrated for its Golf Links; the Keddle-nets, where Millions of Fish are caught during the Summer, and Miles of Sands for Picnics" and since at least 1905 the Company had amusingly boasted that Camber was "far from the madding crowd" and continued to do so for many years!

The outside front page gave details of the Company's fares, whilst the centre pages carried the Tramway timetable for the relevent month. Additional notes advised "Picnics, School & Pleasure Parties carried at Reduced Fares for Parties of not less than 12 adults" and "Cheap Return Tickets can be obtained at Messrs. Adams & Sons, 7 High Street, Rye". If this was not enough to whet the appetite of visitors they were further informed that "Camber as a health resort is very invigorating. No one should miss the opportunity of a visit to the Sands". The same format was still in use in 1925 (complete with identical additional notes) except that there were now two full page advertisements plus details of the Southern Railway train service between New Romney, Lydd and Rye. Out of the 15 businesses advertising in 1908, 8 were still buying space in the booklets 17 years later! Although the Tramway Company still issued regular timetables (by the 1930s they consisted of small, thin cards 1.8in. x 2.8in. showing the times printed in black on a light blue background with the back white and left blank) Messrs. Horrell's, the Chemist of Rye, issued their own leaflet advertising their many services with the Tramway's Timetable incorporated in it, *see reproduction opposite.*

Whereas the Tramway advertised the services of the South Eastern & Chatham Railway, and later the Southern Railway, her larger neighbour did not return the compliment, although they did allow a time card to

118. Keddle-net fishing at Camber. The nets were attached to stakes 11ft. tall arranged in straight lines between high- and low-water marks. When fish encountered the obstruction they would swim seawards to be caught in a circular pound, the catch then being loaded into high-wheeled carts.

(Alan Dickinson collection)

be hung in the booking hall at their station in Rye. However, a local S. E. & C. R. guide book of c.1920 did include the following advertisment which was, to say the least, vague as to the actual service provided:

RYE AND CAMBER TRAM SERVICE.

CAMBER AS A HEALTH RESORT IS VERY INVIGORATING.   NO ONE SHOULD MISS THE OPPORTUNITY OF A VISIT.

CAMBER SANDS ARE ABSOLUTELY UNIQUE.

There are about Six Services each way Daily

and Four Services on Sundays.

For Time Table please address :—

Mr. C. A. GAFFORD, Secretary, Rye and Camber Tramways Co., Ltd., Rye, enclosing stamped addressed envelope.

Parcels are conveyed between Rye and Camber and Rye Harbour at very low charges.

Picnic, School, and Pleasure Parties carried at Reduced Fares for Parties of not less than 20 Adults.   Special Fares by 10 a.m. on Sundays from Rye.

Cheap Return Tickets can be obtained at Messrs. Adams & Son's. 7, High Street, Rye.

The first Tramway tickets did not carry the name of the printer, but they would almost without a doubt have been supplied by Messrs. J. Adams of 7 High Street, Rye, especially when it is recalled that Mr. Joseph Adams resigned as a Tramway auditor at the First Annual General Meeting in February 1896 "as there is some question respecting my eligibilty to undertake work for the Company".   Two early surviving tickets are perforated at each end suggesting that they were issued from a roll, but all later specimens, with the exception of "DOG" or "CYCLE" tickets, have clean cut ends and would have been issued from a rack.   Throughout the Tramway's existence all tickets were of thin card and were cancelled by a bell punch, none of them being dated.   Each ticket was 58mm. x 31mm. and no destination was shown.   Even after the extension to Camber Sands was opened, the relevant destination was only recognisable by its price and colour.   The Class of travel appeared in capital letters beneath which the fare was displayed, i.e. "Single Fare 2d." and many of these early tickets carried an advertisement on the back for

Messrs. Horrell & Co., "Cash and Photographic Chemists" of Rye, the others remaining blank.

As a young boy, the Rev. J. E. Anderson lived in Gorse Cottage beside the Tramway and he remembered these tickets prior to the First World War, "... a tremendously thick clip of them carried by the conductor, with his bell punch machine on a strap over one shoulder. There were single tickets, returns at reduced rates, children's tickets, golfers' tickets, excursion tickets and party tickets - all in gloriously bright and varied colours. We used to pick them up in the carriages, at the stations and by the side of the track.....". [11]

Quite why Messrs. Williamson of Ashton took over the printing of tickets is not recorded, for Messrs. Adams and Sons continued to supply the Tramway's timetables and hand bills until the line's closure in 1939. For the first time, these tickets showed the destination, but whereas Golf Links received its full title, Camber Sands was always shown as "SANDS"! These later tickets were larger at 60mm. x 32mm., and the style of printing varied with different batches over the years. By this time other local businesses had got in on the act of advertising on the back of the tickets in place of Messrs. Horrells and these included two drapers, Messrs. Hide Brothers and Messrs. H. Lewes, Tom Golden "for Men's and Boys' Clothing" and Messrs. Ashbee & Son "Purveyors of High-Class Meat Only", though a few still remained blank. Messrs. Horrell & Co., the chemists, and Ashbee & Son, the butcher, are still in business to this day.

Early First Class Season Tickets had plain leatherette fawn covers and black printing inside on white paper with the serial numbers entered by hand when issued, whilst the Second Class equivalent was similar with a bright red cover. Later First Class Season Tickets were of the folded card type, red on the outside and black printed on blue inside, being 67mm. x 93mm. when opened up. A boldly printed note at the foot of the inside reminded the holder that "THIS TICKET must be returned to the Company at the expiration of Twelve Months", (*See reproduction below*).

1. South Eastern Advertiser, Saturday, 16.11.1895.
2. South Eastern Advertiser, Saturday, 1.1.1896.
3. South Eastern Advertiser, Saturday, 28.3.1896.
4. When the 8.30 p.m. service from Camber was re-timed to run at 8.15 p.m. is not recorded.
5. Sussex Express & County Herald, 30.10.1897.
6. South Eastern Advertiser, Saturday, 18.6.1898.
7. South Eastern Advertiser, Saturday, 9.4.1898.
8. "Diogenes" was the *nom de plume* of the South Eastern Advertiser's correspondent who compiled the "Rye Comments" in that newspaper. See Chapter 4 for the relevant article.
9. It was Mr. J. Adams, along with Mr. T. Bushby, who had originally agreed to sell tickets on behalf of the Tramway Company back in March, 1897.
10. "The Railway Magazine" August, 1912 - article by W. C. Gentry
11. "The Tenterden Terrier" No. 5, Winter 1974, House Journal of the Kent & East Sussex Railway.

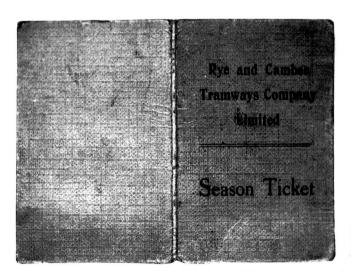 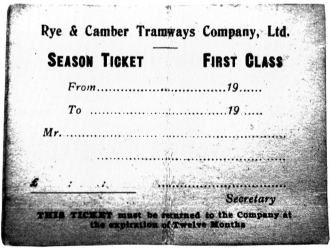

119 & 120. Front and Rear of First Class Season Ticket. The front is printed black on red textured card; the rear is printed black on white.
Author's Collection.

A selection of ordinary tickets is reproduced in Appendix 1.

Chapter Fourteen

PERSONALITIES

121. A Civic occasion in 1908 provides us with the opportunity to meet some of the Tramway Company's Directorate and Shareholders. They are left to right (standing) Cuthbert Hayles, Doctor E. W. Skinner, Walter Dawes and H. J. Gasson with (seated) Frank Jarrett, Kingsnorth Reeve and J. N. Masters.
(Alan Dickinson collection)

In their centre-stage position running the day to day affairs of the Rye & Camber Tramways Company Ltd., the characters of the likes of Cuthbert Hayles and John Symonds Vidler (although anonymous as far as most passengers were concerned) have shone through as the history of the Tramway has unfolded. The staff that were in daily contact with the passengers in the course of their duties never exceeded five at any one time, but they, too, were dedicated men and they all took a great pride in their work.

ALBERT EDWARD "JOKEY" RHODES was born in Rye to Alfred and Amelia Rhodes in 1877, being one of eight children and, owing to his cheerful demeanour, he soon became known to all of the community as "Jokey". It is believed that at the age of eighteen "Jokey" helped with the construction of the Tramway, and was taken on as a driver when the line opened in July 1895. In those early years his day would commence at 6.30 a.m., and after steam was raised, he would take his locomotive to Camber and back to check that the permanent way was in good order. By the time he had put his engine away at the end of the day it would be after 7 p.m. on weekdays and 9.00 p.m. on Saturdays, and he had to work one

weekend in two without any extra pay. It must also be remembered that apart from driving the locomotive, he had to fire as well! [1] In later years, with the first service not leaving Rye until 10.00 a.m., he was able to have something of a lay-in!

"Jokey" became quite a celebrity in Rye, not solely for being the driver of the Tram, but for his attacking performances as a player of Rye Football Club. Three years running from 1899 the Club reached the finals of the Junior Cup Competition, but three times they suffered defeat. Their most glorious hour came in 1904 when, with a capacity crowd to cheer them on, they won the Tunbridge Wells Charity Cup at Hastings. Special trains, as always, had been laid on for the faithful supporters, and on the team's return to Rye later that evening, "Jokey" and his colleagues were carried shoulder high as they and the Cup were paraded round the town.

These special match days posed no small problem for the young "Jokey" as he did not finish work until 11 o'clock on every other Saturday morning. This was fine for home fixtures played on the Salts as he had time to run home to Lucknow Place (and later Tower Street) to

122. A superb Whiteman photograph of Albert Edward "Jokey" Rhodes aged about 18 years – the time that he commenced working with the Tramway. *(Peter Ewart collection)*

123. "Jokey" Rhodes is photographed with his wife Bessie and daughters Blanche (standing rear) and Irene Mabel c.1916. *(Peter Ewart collection)*

124. The victorious Rye Football Club team pose with the Sussex Junior Cup that they won at the Central Ground, Hastings in 1904. "Jokey" Rhodes is seated in the middle row on the left.
(Peter Ewart collection)

get changed prior to the game, but for away matches he had to sprint straight from the Tram Station to the South Eastern Railway station to catch the special train on which the team travelled. Many a time he would be late, but the station master would hold the train until his arrival!

Somehow in his hectic work and football schedule, "Jokey" managed to find time for courting and in October 1901 he married Bessie Donovan Chapling, the third member of Rye Football Club to tie the knot in as many months! On the Tuesday prior to the wedding the Football Club arranged a special evening in "Jokey's" honour at the Cinque Ports Arms in Rye where they presented him with "a handsome mahogany chiffonier" to show "in a practical way the appreciation of his valuable services".

"Jokey" and Bessie had two daughters, Blanche in 1902, followed by Irene Mabel in 1914, and to help make ends meet "Jokey" grew all their own vegetables in the small garden behind their house and made and mended his daughters' shoes until they were old enough to go out to work and pay for them themselves. Even after a long day's work he and his father would often go out eeling, which would involve walking many miles, and he

also made and mended the nets. Like so many families in Rye, the Rhodes may have been poor, but owing to her good management Bessie was able to say, (and did so on many occasions) "Well, we haven't got a lot, but we have always managed to pay the Doctor's bill!" [2]

During the First World War "Jokey" served as a sapper with the Royal Engineers, and a metallic disc on a short chain embossed "A. E. Rhodes 201908 R.E.W. 268 RLY COY", now the proud possession of one of his relatives, suggests that he was employed on another railway somewhere in the hostilities. After the Armistice he resumed his duties on the Camber Tram until (it is said) he failed to receive an expected pay rise in the mid-1920s, and he joined the local building and joinery firm of G. Burnham & Sons of Landgate, Rye, where he stayed until he retired in 1952 at the age of 75.

"Jokey's" daughter Blanche was to work for the Tramway's competitor and successor, The East Kent Road Car Company. She joined that Company in 1925 at the age of 23 and served as a clerk in their Rye office for 42 years, deservedly receiving a clock in appreciation of her long service when she retired in 1967.

125. Shortly before his departure from the Tramway in the mid-1920s, "Jokey" Rhodes poses with Percy Sheppard on the platform at Rye. The solitary lamp has long since been removed from the side of the waiting room, but note the detail under the awning and the decorative carving of the "V"-shaped wooden supports. Perhaps the lawn mower was on its way to Rye Harbour village via the Tram and the ferry.

(H. Sheppard collection)

126. "Jokey" Rhodes' father Alfred also worked for the Tramway, being employed as a platelayer for 23 years before he retired in 1925.

(Peter Ewart collection)

"Jokey's" father, ALFRED RHODES (1852 - 1939) also worked for the Tramway Company, being employed as a platelayer for 23 years, probably between the years 1902 and 1925, before retiring aged 73. It is probably no coincidence that Alfred's retirement coincided with the winter closure of the Tramway.

It would seem that it was not only father and son Rhodes who worked on the Tramway, for it was mentioned in the South Eastern Advertiser on 23rd December 1911 that "…. Jerry Rhodes, living in Landgate Square, Rye, was returning from work at the Tram Station about 8 o'clock…." It is not clear whether WALTER GEORGE "JERRY" RHODES was officially employed by the Tramway Company, or whether he had a private arrangement to stand in for "Jokey" to save him getting up so early to prepare the chosen locomotive for its day's work!

Whilst "Jokey was serving his country in France during the First World War a MR. PARTLETON took over his driving duties on the Tram. He had moved to Cadborough on the western outskirts of Rye with his family from North Wales where he had been a driver on the Snowdon Mountain Railway. What a contrast from driving rack locomotives up gradients of 1 in $5^1/_2$ to a summit 3,493 ft. above sea level (and the highest railway station in Britain) to working on the almost level Rye & Camber Tramway with its stations barely above sea level!

It is possible that CHARLES THATCHER was employed as the Tramway's first conductor, assuming that this post existed when the line opened in 1895. As detailed in Chapter Three, the unfortunate Mr. Thatcher left the Company's employment after falling from the moving tram in October 1898, so at least he did not have to suffer the indignation of the passengers when the conductor was expected to charge them fares according to the way that they were dressed in the years 1899 and 1900.

There were probably several other conductors before the following advertisement appeared in the South Eastern Advertiser on 17th May 1902: "CONDUCTOR required for the Rye & Camber Tramway. Applications to be in writing stating age and wages required to be addressed to The Secretary, Faraday House, Rye." [3]

The successful candidate for this particular vacancy was more than likely the young lad FREDERICK SHEPPARD, but it will be Fred's younger brother PERCY CHARLES SHEPPARD (1896-1979) who will be the most fondly remembered by local people, not least of all for his longevity of service. On his 17th birthday, 4th August 1914 (the day that war was declared) he took over his brother's duties when he left the Company, having successfully passed an interview with the formidable Charles Gafford, (known "affectionately" by many as "Old Gafford"!) conducted at his office at Messrs. Ellis Brothers, the ironmongers in Rye High Street. Throughout the War, Frederick served in the Royal Navy, after which he was employed by the Canadian

127. (*Top Right*) **Percy Sheppard (2nd left) would have just joined the Tramway when this photograph was taken with his brothers Frederick (left) and Jack, and sisters Francis, Edith and Gladys (seated) c.1914.**
(H. Sheppard collection)

128. (*Bottom Right*) **Taken outside Playden church c.1930, where he was the sexton, Percy Sheppard stands proudly with his choirboy son Bert.**
(H. Sheppard collection).

Government as resident engineer at Canada House in London where he remained until he retired.

Percy was not actually a "Ryer", [4] having been born in Oxford, but his family moved to the village of Iden when he was a small child. It was when his father left the employment of the vicar of Iden (Rev. John Lockington Bates) to look after the horses of Messrs. Wright & Pankhurst, that the family moved to Rye. Percy's first job on leaving school was as a delivery boy for Thompson the Bakers of Landgate [5] and later he became a Telegraph Boy for the Post Office.

His first stint with the Tramway was short-lived as he joined the Sussex Regiment 5th Battalion (E. Company Rye) which took him to Belgium, France, Italy and Austria. By the greatest coincidence, whilst serving in France, he met up with none other than his Tramway colleague "Jokey" Rhodes. "Jokey" survived the war unscathed, but whilst engaged in the battle at O'Villiers, Percy sustained a shrapnel wound in the head. He recuperated for ten weeks at Rouen before re-joining his unit, but it was 1922 before the shrapnel was finally removed from his skull. For his service to his country he was awarded the General Service Medal and the War Medal.

With the return of peace, Percy resumed playing for Rye Town Football Club (not to be confused with the "other" team, "Jokey's" Rye Football Club) for whom he later became a linesman and served on the Committee. He loved sport and regularly enjoyed a game of golf on the links at Camber, fished in the River Rother, and boxed at the local Gymnasium Club.

Percy tried several other jobs before returning to his post as conductor on the Tram around 1920. On Monday, 20th September that year he married Gladys Grace Ashdown at St. Michael's Church, Playden and moved from his family's home at 9 Clifton Place, Rye to his bride's house at "New England", Playden where he was to spend the rest of his life. He was no stranger to Playden church for he was sexton there, the little money earned thus supplementing his low wages on the Tram.

By this time there were but three staff employed, the others being father and son Rhodes, and the only uniform that the Company provided was one hat each for the driver and conductor. Percy was usually the conductor, but they each took turns to do "a bit of everything". He had to clean the two carriages, polish the brass work on VICTORIA and CAMBER and, in between times, helped with the general maintenance of the rolling stock and track, even sometimes acting as relief driver. He was entitled to one day off every two weeks, but did not always get it; not that he minded too much as there was no rush working on the Tram and even at the height of the season he found life fairly lesiurely. During the 1920's he became very friendly with many of the famous golfing personalities during the course of his duties, and recalled that he and the driver would receive a half crown and sometimes even a half sovereign tip from some of them around Christmas time.

Percy stayed with the Tram until the line closed in

129. As they posed beside the petrol locomotive, George Wratten and Percy Sheppard could not have realised that within months the Tramway that they had served loyally for so many years would close suddenly with the outbreak of the Second World War in September 1939.
(Richard Jones collection)

1939 when Charles Gafford, who was still the Company's secretary, told him that he was sorry but he had to give him his cards. He was too old to fight in the war, but was offered two week's employment at Winchelsea station close by on the former Southern Eastern Railway. The fortnight was continually extended, and he carried on working as a lengthman for the Southern Railway until he retired 21 years later in 1961. He admitted that the work was similar, but a lot harder, than it had been on the Camber Tram, everything just being on a larger scale! From then until his death he was able to devote his full attention to his hobby of gardening in the acre of land attached to his house; his son Bert carries on the tradition to this day.

An amusing anecdote told by Percy Sheppard concerned a MR. HAMBROOK who came from the South Eastern & Chatham Railway and worked on the Tramway for a short while. One day, with some spare time between trams, he decided to have a bath in a bucket in the engineshed, the hot water being provided by the locomotive. Two girls, who had arrived too early for the next tram, decided to have a look around the station, and to their surprise, when they opened the engine shed doors, they were greeted by the sight of Mr. Hambrook in his birthday suit! The girls were more embarrassed than he was and ran off to hide their blushes while Mr. Hambrook continued with his bath undeterred! [6]

ARTHUR BENJAMIN WITHERS (1882-1972) was born in Great Yarmouth, and in the summers of 1909/10 he worked on the 1897-built steam driven "Revolving Tower" that lifted holidaymakers 125 ft. in a rotating cage from whence there were fine views along the seafront of his home town. Some time after this he came south looking for full time employment and was taken on by the Tramway Company as a fitter until he, too, had to leave for war service, becoming a War Munitions Volunteer in Rye on 9th July 1915. In a letter in Rye's Own Volume 3, No. 1, published in November 1967 he wrote "I controlled the two locos running from Rye to Camber Sands, with carriages and sand trucks.... Carrying golfers and passengers and fishermen, I worked under two managers, Mr. C. Gafford and Mr. Honeysett, keeping these engines on the track. I found the work interesting doing quite a good business with passengers, especially with golfers at the weekends. The tram carried people from many places, including Lords, Earls, Dukes and Judges....". Mr. Withers was able to proudly boast that he "never lost a day on the line" whilst in the Company's employment. Prior to the end of the First World War, with his wife and only son, he moved to Battersea, London, and from 1920 until his retirement in 1948 he drove a steam wagon for the Metropolitan Water Board.

130. After "Jokey" Rhodes left the Company in the early 1920s, Frederick Nelson took over as the Tramway's driver and is pictured here with CAMBER in steam on the engine shed road at Rye.

(P. Nelson collection)

131. An early picture of George Wratten with CAMBER at Rye, possibly before the arrival of the petrol locomotive in 1924.

(Rye's Own collection, courtesy of Rye Library)

"Jokey" Rhodes' replacement as engine driver was FREDERICK NELSON and he later worked alongside GEORGE AMOS WRATTEN (born 1902), who joined the Company around 1924. On 7th December 1925, at the age of 23, George married Dorothy Julia Goodsell (the daughter of a builder of South Undercliff, Rye) after which they lived at 40a Mermaid Street, a few houses above the famous and picturesque Mermaid Hotel, where they later brought up their only son Clive. Soon after George's arrival on the Tramway the Kent Construction Company petrol locomotive was delivered and with Frederick Nelson having left the Company, he held the distinction of being its one and only driver. Always dressed very smartly, he was to become a familiar sight on the tram wearing his own personal uniform of light flannel trousers, tennis shirt, dark jacket and a white yachting hat complete with the initials "R.C.T".

The little petrol locomotive was his pride and joy, and it certainly looked resplendent with its green paint and brasswork polished to perfection and gleaming in the summer sun. Even the locomotive's tools were painted gloss black to match its fittings, and it has been suggested that the Tramway Company might have been more profitable had George not spent so much on paint for his beloved machine! If addressed politely, a child's request for a ride on the footplate was rarely refused, the young guest occupying the toolbox fitted to the floor of the cab as a seat.

In later years, George, along with Percy Sheppard comprised the whole of the full-time Tramway staff, although casual labour would be employed to help out during the peak summer months. After the closure of the Tramway in 1939 George and his family moved away

132. George Wratten, dressed in his usual "uniform" of yachting hat and blazer, looks proudly down at "his" petrol locomotive, spotless as ever, as they wait at Camber Sands station with the Bagnall carriage in 1933. *(H. Sheppard collection)*

133. Towards the end of his life in the late 1920s, Mr. E. Percy S. Jones, the former proprietor of the Rother Ironworks, is pictured at Ivychurch in Kent with his son Michael who ran the Central Garage in Rye. *(Richard Jones collection)*

from Rye, although his wife did return to the town after his death for a short while in the 1960's.

1. "Tenterden Terrier" No. 12, Spring 1977, House Journal of the Kent & East Sussex Railway - letter from Blanche Rhodes.
2. "Rye Memories - Rye Childhoods", Thomas Peacocke School Local History Group, 1988.
3. "Faraday House" is situated at the lower end of The Mint, Rye.
4. A person having been born in Rye.
5. From 1912 Messrs. Thompsons ran the refreshment hut behind Camber Sands station.
6. "Tenterden Terrier" No. 10, Summer 1976, House Journal of the Kent & East Sussex Railway.

134. Rye Tramway station site taken from a similar view-point as the photograph on page 87. In recent years the river bank has been built up to obscure much of the Monkbretton Bridge, but a fix is provided by the petrol station to the left and the houses built in 1924 on the right. The pumping station occupies the site of the 1896 carriage shed and the spare ground to the north of the erstwhile station platform. 26.11.1992.   *(Author)*

135. This view of Rye, taken from the southern side of the Tramway bridge across the Broadwater Stream, is considered by many to be the best of the "Antient Town". 17.1.1992.   *(Author)*

Chapter Fifteen

THE SCENE TODAY

Standing on Monkbretton Bridge it does not take a great deal of imagination to conjure up how it must have been back in those far off days when the line was in operation. Beside a slight mound that marks the position of the Tram Station platform, a small brick-built pumping station now occupies the site of the engine shed, but strangely, some forty years after their removal, two parallel lines in the grass betray the position of the iron fences that had bordered the Tramway on either side as it headed on its straight course across the Corporation fields towards Camber and the sea. In the middle distance Gorse Cottage can be seen, alone now as, for safety's sake, the frail "Squatter's Right" had to be demolished in 1983. Behind, to the left, is the erstwhile Royal William Hotel and above everything, the white-painted Golf Club House continues to stand out boldly on the skyline.

A walk down the steep approach road from the bridge brings you to the gateway that led from the station yard onto the footpath that paralleled the Tramway across the fields where sheep and cows still graze. Known temporarily as Bretton Road until the demise of the nissen huts in the early 1960's, the wide tarmacked right of way suddenly deteriorates after a quarter of a mile into a rough grass track, this further part of the Corporation field having been used as an open rubbish tip back in the 1950's. Filling the greater portion of the course of the old Holm Bush, the tip later extended over the Tramway towards the River Rother, raising the land by a foot or so. Beyond the Borough boundary fence the Tramway's low embankment suddenly appears to the right from below the built-up field, but the track bed is soon lost from view again as it passes through the built up river bank to reveal on the far side that the bridge across the Broadwater Stream is still *in situ*. For many years it has carried a large water pipe rather than the 3ft.0in. gauge permanent way, but at least it is still there!

Beyond the bridge, the wartime concrete pill box stands ominously in the undergrowth beside the Tramway on the banks of the stream, but from here the route has been completely lost, first under a rough track that serves a further pumping station beside the Rother, and then by the large lake formed by excavating shingle from the former Northpoint Beach which, since May 1991, has become the home of Rye Windsurfers. The views to the left remain almost un-changed, but the flat featureless background to the south-west has been changed beyond all recognition with the Chemical Works on the west bank of the River Rother being joined in 1967 by Alsford's Timber Wharf, and more recently a sprawling light industrial development which is itself overshadowed by Messrs. A.R.C's new shingle processing

plant which replaced its smaller installation on Northpoint Beach.

After making a detour of approximately half a mile, the Tramway's right of way can be picked up once more as it emerges on the right from the garden of Gorse Cottage, to where some sleepers and a few lengths of rail are still embedded in the concrete. Over the years, concrete has been laid between the rails as well, but half way along the ensuing straight embankment (now in use as a "private" road to provide access to the harbourmaster's house and a car park beside the River Rother opposite Rye Harbour village) the concrete and remaining rotted sleepers were removed in the autumn of 1990 and the last 100 yards of the alignment received a coating of tar, complete with three "sleeping policemen". In an effort to prevent flooding, a built-up earth bank was added to the western side of the formation in July 1991.

Now in front of you stands the most pleasant surprise of all - Golf Links station is still extant. The "V" shaped supports that held up the awning at the front have been removed and the accommodation has been extended over the platform to the full width of the building, but although the original doorway inside is no longer there, the windows that replaced the originals some time during the Second World War on either side remain. A windowless extension in matching corrugated iron which, being a little longer, extends beyond the original building to the south, has been added to the rear, but none of the alterations hide the fact that this is a Colonel Stephens' station, the fancy bargeboards and finials, though rather rotted, still being an attractive feature. The lattice fence along the rear of the grass covered platform has long since disappeared, as have the neat row of bricks along its outer edge, but a concrete step from rail level has been added to provide easier access to the new front door. Here also the rails, but not the points (these were removed in 1947) are still in position, including a few yards of the short-lived Admiralty siding to the banks of the River Rother, but recent improvements to the car park have obliterated all further remains of the formation, and the old stone ferry steps have recently been replaced by new safer (though characterless) concrete ones.

The old station building managed to survive intact the hurricane of October 1987, but it did not fare so well in the heavy gales of January 1990 when more than half of its corrugated roof at the rear was torn off and hurled a hundred yards or so across the Golf Course. The Golf Club respect the importance of the building as a relic of the pioneering days of their Club, and by the Spring of that year they had replaced the damaged roof with

136. On the 20 chain radius curve north of Golf Links station some of the rails are still in place sandwiched between the concrete laid by the Admiralty during the Second World War. "Squatters Right" used to stand behind the white warning sign to the right of "Golf View" (formerly "Camber Cottage") and the town of Rye can be seen rising on its hill in the left background. 26.11.1992. *(Author)*

137. Golf Links station with the Golf Club House in the background. 26.11.1992. *(Author)*

138. Camber Sands station was situated on the levelled ground between, and a hundred yards or so beyond, the two bushes (centre left) whilst the 1938 deviation embankment heads away eastwards on its straight course across the Golf Club's "Jubilee Nine". 20.9.1992. (Author)

139. The site of the 1939 Camber Sands station looking towards the end of the line. The platform stood on the slightly raised ground to the left of the track that follows the course of the main running line. February 1993. (Author)

156

corrugated plastic which, now that it has been painted red, matches up to the remaining corrugated iron very well.

Standing on its mound, but minus the picket fence, the shipping mast still overlooks the station, its purpose now being to advise those on the River of expected shipping movements on tide. One Black Ball (disc) hoisted on the yard arm tells of a ship arriving from sea, two Balls side by side of a ship departing, and three Balls in a triangle that ships are arriving and sailing. [1] The old harbourmaster's house has been replaced by a modern and much larger weatherboarded structure closer to the Tramway on a slightly different site a few yards to the south, and there is no trace of the concrete hexagonal lighthouse that stood beside the Rother for it, too, has long since been demolished.

Back at the station, after passing through a five-bar metal gate situated at the foot of the southern platform ramp, the main track bed becomes a public footpath for a short distance as it curves sharply to the right (the eagle-eyed may find a few sleepers under foot) and the line passes the site of Councillor Longley's refreshment building before it veers away to the left through a post and wire fence on its overgrown embankment to cross that part of the Golf Course known as the Jubilee Nine, on which the first competition was played in 1979. It is difficult to imagine that the sea used to run right up to the foot of the Tramway embankment here, but since the late 1960's it has continued to recede and a new row of sand hills has sprung up several hundred yards away to the south, giving the area complete protection from flooding. The 1908 embankment is still in situ to just beyond the 1938 deviation, but the exact position of the original Camber Sands station has been lost under the re-developed Golf Course. Apart from the last curve leading towards the later station site which, following bomb damage in the Second World War, has been levelled to that of the surrounding area, the 1938 embankment remains intact. The raised position of the replacement Camber Sands station is quite easily found a short distance to the east where, hidden amongst the undergrowth, a fragment of one solitary upright support is still in position, showing where the platform had stood.

The 100 year old dreams of the likes of W. H. Delves and members of the erstwhile Rye & District Trade Association of Camber being developed into "a fashionable watering place" have still to be realised, the village having changed little over the years so that today it boasts three holiday camps, three pubs (including the replacement "Royal William") and two small housing estates. Otherwise development has been confined mainly to the main street where the shacks and converted tramcar bodies of the 1920,s have gradually given way to modern houses and bungalows. The resident population has increased from the steady 432 people of the 1950's/60's through 718 in 1981 to just over 1,000 in 1995.

Day trippers still flock to the sands at Camber by the thousand on summer weekends. Many make the trip down from East London and north Kent by car, but with the several car parks unable to cater for such large numbers, their vehicles will be parked on either side of the main street and along the narrow road from the village back to the Golf Club House and beyond - $1^1/_2$ miles away. It is not un-common for the police to have to close the road between East Guldeford and Camber at such times because of the congestion, leaving access only available via Lydd six miles to the east. When the homeward trek begins from 4.00 p.m. onwards, it will take anything up to three-quarters of an hour to travel the four miles into Rye!

Were it not for the Second World War, the Tram would surely have survived into the age of railway preservation, in which case it might have still been with us today, being a first class tourist attraction in its own right. But would today's day trippers be prepared to leave their cars in Rye to make the last stage of their journey to Camber by the tram? As it is, Rye has little in the way of car parking facilities for the all important sightseers who flock to the "ancient town" all the year round.

Now, in the Tramway's centenary year, there are plans to build a much-needed bypass to the south of Rye routed across the centre of the Council-owned fields and under the River Rother by a £20 million single carriageway tunnel. Subject to discussions with the local Highway Authority, there is an additional plan to demolish the two houses built in 1924 next to the Tram station and to construct a link road from immediately east of the Monkbretton Bridge to head due south beside the school to cross the proposed bypass via a roundabout and join onto the existing Camber road at Broadwater corner, thus completely obliterating the course of the Tramway. Owing to the cost of the scheme, it may not be implemented until after the year 2000, so there should be at least a few years left to be able to stand on Monkbretton Bridge and conjure up a vision of the tram, loaded with happy holidaymakers after a day on the sands, as it steamed slowly across the fields from Camber and into the station at Rye.

Oh that we could turn back the clock!

1. "Harbour of Rye" published by National Rivers Authority, Southern Region, January 1992.

Appendix 1
A SELECTION OF TICKETS

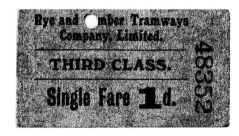  

Rye & Camber Tramways Company, Limited.

FIRST CLASS.

Single Fare 6d.

4630

Rye and Camber Tramways Company, Limited

A 2349

First Single

GOLF LINKS

6d.

Williamson, Ticket Printer, Ashton.

Rye and Camber Tramways Company, Limited

A 0799

First Single

Sands

Child

4d

Williamson, Ticket Printer, Ashton.

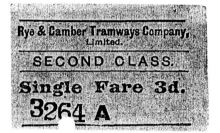

Rye & Camber Tramways Company, Limited.

SECOND CLASS.

Single Fare 3d.

3264 A

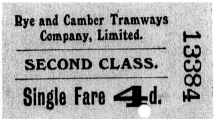

Rye and Camber Tramways Company, Limited.

SECOND CLASS.

Single Fare 4d.

13384

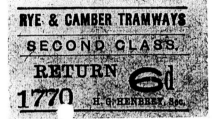

RYE & CAMBER TRAMWAYS

SECOND CLASS.

RETURN 6d

1770 H. G. HENBREY, Sec.

2031

RYE and CAMBER TRAMWAYS COMPANY, LIMITED

SECOND CLASS

Single Fare 3d.

Williamson, Ticket Printer, Ashton

1313

Rye & Camber Tramways Company, Limited

HALF-FARE

GOLF LINKS

1½d

Williamson, Ticket Printer, Ashton

1400

Rye & Camber Tramways Company, Limited.

SINGLE

GOLF LINKS

3d

Williamson, Ticket Printer, Ashton.

A 2879

Rye and Camber Tramways Company, Limited.

SANDS TO LINKS

2d

Williamson, Ticket Printer, Ashton

A 2383

Rye & Camber Tramways Company, Limited.

SINGLE

SANDS

4d

Williamson, Ticket Printer, Ashton.

B 2964

Rye & Camber Tramways Company, Limited.

RETURN

SANDS

7d

Williamson, Ticket Printer, Ashton.

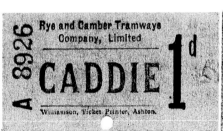

A 8926

Rye and Camber Tramways Company, Limited

CADDIE

1d

Williamson, Ticket Printer, Ashton.

A 9995

Rye and Camber Tramways Company, Limited

CADDIE

1d

Williamson, Ticket Printer, Ashton.

Rye and Camber Tramways Company, Limited.

Caddies' Single Ticket.

1d.

7824

A 4332

Rye and Camber Tramways Company, Limited

DOG or CYCLE

3d

Williamson, Ticket Printer, Ashton.

A 0749

Rye and Camber Tramways Company, Limited.

DOG

3d

Williamson, Ticket Printer, Ashton.

Appendix 2
DIRECTORS' REPORTS AND ACCOUNTS

THE RYE AND CAMBER TRAMWAYS COMPANY,
LIMITED.

Directors.

R. T. BLOMFIELD.	C. A. SELMES.
R. P. BURRA.	T. G. SHARPE.
C. HAYLES (Chairman).	E. W. SKINNER.
F. A. INDERWICK.	J. S. VIDLER.

Report of the Directors

For the period ending 31st December, 1895, to be presented at the Annual Meeting of Shareholders to be held at the Cinque Ports Hotel, Rye, on Friday, the 21st February instant, at 11 o'clock in the forenoon.

The Directors herewith submit the accounts from the formation of the Company to the 31st December last, and are pleased to be able to report that the line has been an unqualified success since its opening on the 13th July last, the receipts from daily takings alone having amounted to £269 10s. 5d.

The net profit for the six months amounts to £83 3s. 2d., and out of this the Directors recommend that a dividend at the rate of 7½ per cent. per annum (from the dates of payment for the respective shares), which will absorb £43 3s. 4d., be declared and paid, and that the balance, after payment thereof and of any sum which the Shareholders may vote to the Directors for their services, be carried to a reserve fund.

The question of extending the line along the sandbanks has been fully considered by the Directors, and they are of opinion that it would be unwise to attempt it (at all events for the present).

The total cost of construction and equipment of the Tramway has not yet been arrived at, as a further sum will be due to the Contractor for the line and buildings on the Engineer's final certificate, and the Directors have also arranged for the building of another car, in consequence of the extent of the traffic, which has considerably exceeded their expectations.

Three of the Directors, Messrs. C. Hayles, F. A. Inderwick, and J. S. Vidler, and also the Auditors, Messrs. J. Adams and G. W. Strick, retire at this meeting, but are eligible and offer themselves for re-election.

(By order of the Board),

H. G. HENBREY,
Secretary.

The Rye and Camber Tramways Company, Limited.

PROFIT AND LOSS ACCOUNT

For the 5½ months ended 31st December, 1895.

Dr.   Cr.

	£	s.	d.		£	s.	d.
To Wages	72	6	6	By Fares	269	10	5
,, Repairs and Stores	34	7	1	,, Season Tickets	45	9	0
,, Insurances	10	2	6				
,, Coal	31	15	11				
,, Rent, Rates, and Taxes	22	1	9				
,, Printing, &c.	9	3	4				
,, Sundries	10	16	3				
,, Secretary, Salary	10	0	0				
,, Balance, Gross Profit	114	6	1				
	£314	19	5		£314	19	5

	£	s.	d.		£	s.	d.
To Depreciation on Preliminary and Construction Expenses	19	8	10	By Balance, Gross Profit	114	6	1
,, Interest on Debentures	11	14	1				
,, Balance	83	3	2				
	£114	6	1		£114	6	1

BALANCE SHEET

From the 8th April, 1895, to the 31st December, 1895.

	£	s.	d.		£	s.	d.	£	s.	d.
To Share Capital, 372 Shares at £3 10s.	1302	0	0	By Cost of Permanent Way and Rolling Stock to date	1878	5	7			
,, Debenture Capital, 30 Debentures at £25	750	0	0	Less Amount paid by Rye Corporation for Fencing	50	0	0	1828	5	7
,, Amounts owing on Construction Expense Account	96	0	8	By Preliminary and Construction Expenses, Engineer's Fees,						
,, Amounts owing on General Expense Account	102	17	5	Law Costs, &c.	278	8	10			
,, Balance	94	17	3	Less Depreciation	19	8	10	259	0	0

	£	s.	d.
Less Interest on Debentures	11	14	1
Net Balance	83	3	2

	£	s.	d.
,, Account Owing	0	9	0
,, Balance at Bank	258	0	9

£2345	15	4

£2345	15	4

10th February, 1896.

Audited and found correct,

G. W. STRICK, } Auditors.
J. ADAMS,

THE RYE AND CAMBER TRAMWAYS COMPANY, Ltd.

PROFIT AND LOSS ACCOUNT for the Year ended 31st December, 1929.

Dr.   Cr.

	£	s.	d.		£	s.	d.
To Stock, 1st January, 1929	43	15	2	By Balance	36	15	1
,, Rent, Rates, Taxes and Insurance	68	7	9	,, Passenger Fares, Dogs and Parcels	633	6	0
,, Repairs, Stores and Trade Expenses	133	10	8	,, Sundry Receipts	10	14	3
Wages and Insurance	300	16	4	,, Stock	72	4	6
Petrol and Coal	84	5	10				
Secretary, Auditor and Petty Expenses	33	1	0				
,, Debenture Interest and Accrued	16	0	0				
,, Directors' Fees	10	0	0				
,, Law Charges	16	7	2				
,, Balance	46	15	11				
	£752	19	10		£752	19	10

BALANCE SHEET for the Year ended 31st December, 1929

	£	s.	d.	£	s.	d.		£	s.	d.
To Share Capital				2565	0	0	By Permanent Way and Rolling Stock	2950	0	0
,, Premium on Shares				50	0	0	,, Sundry Debtors	59	6	9
,, Debentures	400	0	0				,, Stock	72	4	6
,, Accrued Interest	5	6	8				,, Bank Balance	182	16	1
				405	6	8				
,, Reserve Fund				125	0	0				
,, Sundry Creditors				72	4	9				
Balance				46	15	11				
				£3,264	7	4		£3,264	7	4

CUTHBERT HAYLES, } Directors.
C. A. SELMES,

In accordance with the provisions of the Companies' (Consolidation) Act, 1908, I certify that all my requirements as Auditor have been complied with, and I hereby report to the Shareholders that I have compared the Balance Sheet with the Books and Vouchers of the Company, and that in my opinion the same is properly drawn up so as to exhibit a true and correct view of the state of the Company's affairs, as shown by the Books of the Company.

22nd July, 1930.   CHARLES J. SHOTTER, Auditor.